T5-AGT-405

Andrew Finlay

Nationalism and Multiculturalism

European Studies in Culture and Policy

edited by

Prof. Máiréad Nic Craith

(Academy for Irish Cultural Heritages, University of Ulster)

and Prof. Ullrich Kockel

(Ethnological Research Unit, University of the West of England)

Volume 4

LIT

Andrew Finlay

THE LIBRARY
ST. MARY'S COLLEGE OF MARYLAND
ST. MARY'S CITY, MARYLAND 20686

Nationalism and Multiculturalism

Irish Identity, Citizenship and the Peace Process

LIT

Bibliographic information published by Die Deutsche Bibliothek
Die Deutsche Bibliothek lists this publication in the Deutsche
Nationalbibliografie; detailed bibliographic data are available in the
Internet at http://dnb.ddb.de.

ISBN 3-8258-8161-x

© LIT VERLAG Münster 2004
Grevener Str./Fresnostr. 2   48159 Münster
Tel. 0251-62 03 20   Fax 0251-23 19 72
e-Mail: lit@lit-verlag.de   http://www.lit-verlag.de

Distributed in North America by:

Transaction Publishers
New Brunswick (U.S.A.) and London (U.K.)

Transaction Publishers   Tel.: (732) 445 - 2280
Rutgers University   Fax: (732) 445 - 3138
35 Berrue Circle   for orders (U. S. only):
Piscataway, NJ 08854   toll free (888) 999 - 6778

Contents

Preface   vii

List of Contributors   ix

Part One: Irish Pluralism Old and New

1. Introduction
ANDREW FINLAY   1

2. Pre-Political Groundwork and Cultural identity:
the Northern Ireland Experience
MAURNA CROZIER   33

3. Understanding One Another Better: Language,
Conflict and Cultural Diversity
LOUIS DE PAOR   43

Part Two: Critical Perspectives

4. Back to the Future? The Nice Referenda and the
Persistence of Irish Discourses of Autonomy
GERRY BOUCHER   60

5. Our Shelter and Ark? Immigrants and the
Republic
PIARAS MAC ÉINRÍ   85

6. Conceptions of Equality: the Case of Northern
Ireland
MÁIRÉAD NIC CRAITH   111

7. Me Too: Victimhood and the Proliferation of
Cultural Claims in Ireland
ANDREW FINLAY   131

8. Where Difference Lies: Democracy and the
Ethnographic Imagination in Northern Ireland
ROBIN WHITAKER   157

Part Three: Looking to the Future

9. From Nationality to Citizenship: Cultural Identity
and Cosmopolitan Challenges in Ireland
GERARD DELANTY   183

10. The Unbidden Ireland: Materialism, Knowledge
and Inter-Culturality
MICHAEL CRONIN   207

11. Conclusion
ANDREW FINLAY   223

Index   239

Preface

This book originated in a conference, 'Cultural Identity and Political Transformation', held in October 2002 under the auspices of The Irish Association for Cultural, Economic and Social Relations. The Irish Association was founded in 1938 to promote communication, understanding and co-operation between the people of Ireland, North and South. I was only one of several people involved in organising the conference, and my first debt of gratitude is to the other organisers. Terry Stewart, then President of the Association, first suggested the theme of identity. Mindful of the seemingly endless round of conferences and seminars on the theme of Irish identity, I was initially reluctant to add another. Fortunately, Terry's enthusiasm and his openness to consider an askance approach to a well-worn theme won out over my cynicism. Thanks are also due to the other members of the organising committee: Mary Humphreys, Stephen MacWhite, Catriona Stewart, and Penny Gundry-Beck. Dr Jean Whyte, the current Vice-President of the Association, and other members of its Southern Committee have consistently encouraged me in my efforts to develop the conference papers into a book. I imagine that some of the aforementioned will disagree with some of the various perspectives developed in the book, but I know that they share my view that the issues discussed by the contributors are amongst the most crucial facing Ireland and other societies seeking to cope with cultural diversity.

Máiréad Nic Craith was one of those invited to speak at the conference, and knew of my desire to develop the conference papers for publication. I am very grateful to her for asking me to submit a proposal for a book based on the conference papers for consideration as part of the LIT series on *European Studies in Culture and Policy*. Both Máiréad and her colleague, Ulli Kockel, continued to provide useful advice at crucial moments.

Of the nine contributors, six spoke at the conference: Maurna Crozier, Michael Cronin, Louis de Paor, Piaras Mac

Éinrí, Máiréad Nic Craith and myself. Using these as a starting point I invited further contributions from people whose work I knew and thought would add to the discussion begun at the conference: Gerry Boucher, Gerard Delanty and Robin Whitaker. When inviting people to contribute, first to the conference and then to the book, I was not seeking to arrive at a consensus or to advance a thesis. Rather I wanted to get a variety of perspectives on a common set of issues to do with the development of ideas about Irish identity, cultural diversity and pluralism. In addition to getting the views of authors from different disciplines, I was particularly keen to get contributions from both sides of the Irish border: what Seamus Deane has described as a 'partitionist mentality' continues to structure intellectual debate in Ireland, and though ideas eventually leak across the border in both directions, there is often a considerable time lag. I have enjoyed working with each of the contributors and am grateful to them for forcing me to modify and develop my own views.

Finally I must acknowledge with thanks a grant from the Arts and Social Science Benefaction Fund, Trinity College Dublin, which enabled me to employ a friend and former colleague, Dee Jones, to proof read the manuscript and construct an index. I am grateful not only for her sharp eye, but her patience.

List of Contributors

GERRY BOUCHER is a Research Fellow at the Employment Research Centre in the Department of Sociology at Trinity College Dublin. His interests include European societies, political and economic sociology, nationalism and national identity, ethnic and racial studies and, of course, Ireland.

MAURNA CROZIER is the Director of the Cultural Diversity Programme of the Community Relations Council (Northern Ireland), currently on loan to the Department of Culture, Arts and Leisure as a policy adviser on cultural diversity. She has a PhD in Social Anthropology from the Queen's University of Belfast, where she is an Honorary Fellow. She is on the board of the Arts Council of Northern Ireland, the Northern Ireland Museums Council, the Linen Hall Library, Resource and the British Council Intercultural Advisory Committee.

MICHAEL CRONIN is Associate Professor and Director of the Centre for Translation and Textual Studies, Dublin City University. His most recent works are *Translation and Globalization* (Routledge, 2003), *Time Tracks: Scenes from the Irish Everyday* (New Island, 2003) and two co-edited collections of essays, *Irish Tourism: Image, Culture and Identity* (Channel View Publications, 2003) and *The Languages of Ireland* (Four Courts Press, 2003).

GERARD DELANTY is Professor of Sociology and Head of the Department of Sociology in the University of Liverpool, UK. He is the author of many articles in journals and chapters in books in social theory, the philosophy of the social sciences, the historical and political sociology of European societies. He has edited two volumes and written nine books, which include *Inventing Europe: Idea, Identity, Reality* (Macmillan, 1995), *Social Science: Beyond Constructivism and Realism* (Open University Press, 1997), *Social Theory in a Changing World* (Polity Press, 1999), *Modernity and Postmodernity:*

Knowledge, Power, the Self (Sage, 2000), *Citizenship in the
Global Era* (Open University Press, 2000*)* and *Community*
(Routledge, 2003).

LOUIS DE PAOR is Director of the Centre for Irish Studies at
National University of Ireland, Galway. He has a PhD in
Modern Irish form the National University of Ireland, and
has published articles on a broad range of writing in Irish
from the court poetry of medieval Ireland to the work of
contemporary poets such as Nuala Ní Dhomhnaill and Michael Davitt. His books include a study of narrative technique in the short fiction of Máirtín Ó Cadhain and an anthology of twentieth century poetry in Irish co-edited with
Seán Ó Tuama. He is currently working on a study of the
writings of Flann O'Brien.

ANDREW FINLAY lectures in Sociology at Trinity College Dublin. Originally from Belfast, his PhD thesis (Social Anthropology, University College London) was about class and
sectarianism in Northern Ireland. Subsequently he conducted research on risk and stigma, focussing on injecting
drug use, prostitution and teenage pregnancy. His interest
in Irish studies was rekindled by the experience of living in
Dublin, and he is currently conducting ethnographic work
on cultural differences between Northern Ireland and the
Republic of Ireland.

PIARAS MAC ÉINRÍ was Director from 1997-2003 of the inter-
disciplinary Irish Centre for Migration Studies at University
College Cork, focusing on Irish and comparative international migration research. He is an advisor to the Dublin-
based NGO The Immigrant Council of Ireland and a member
of the National Consultative Committee on Racism and Interculturalism. He has lectured and published extensively in
the fields of Irish and comparative migration studies, with a
particular interest in immigration and integration issues. He
is a Geography lecturer at the university and previously

served in the Irish Department of Foreign Affairs, with postings in Brussels, Beirut and Paris.

MÁIRÉAD NIC CRAITH is Research Professor at the Academy for Irish Cultural Heritages, University of Ulster. Author and editor of several books, she was joint winner of the 2004 Ratcliff Research Prize for her contribution to folklife in Ireland and Britain. Her recent publications include *Communicating Cultures* with Ullrich Kockel (2004), *Culture and Identity Politics in Northern Ireland* (2003) and *Plural Identities: Singular Narratives* (2002). Her research interests include culture and identity politics, minority languages and regional diversity in the context of European integration. She is currently writing a book examining the politics of language in Europe.

ROBIN WHITAKER is Assistant Professor in the Department of Anthropology at Memorial University of Newfoundland. She is currently working on an ethnography of the Northern Ireland Peace Process.

1. Introduction

ANDREW FINLAY

This book is about forms of cultural pluralism in Ireland and the theory that underwrites them; i.e. that Ireland's political problems are the product of underlying confusions and conflicts of cultural identity. In its current form cultural pluralism developed out of a series of debates about Irish identity that began in the 1970s. The problem that pluralism was originally designed to address was the Northern Troubles, which the theory constructed as a conflict between two communities with different cultural identities. In other words, pluralism was initially concerned with accommodating and reconciling the Catholic and Protestant communities in Ireland: for convenience, I will refer to this as the 'old' pluralist agenda. It is old in the sense that it was supposed to have been completed with the ratification of the Good Friday Agreement (GFA) in referenda held concurrently in the two parts of the island in May 1998. The abiding achievement of the Agreement is that it secured ceasefires of a sort, but the old agenda remains incomplete, and the problem that it itemised as the fundamental one has not diminished; on the contrary, communal or sectarian polarisation in parts of Northern Ireland seems worse now than before. In the context of this failure, the book seeks to interrogate the theories and concepts of identity and citizenship that informed the peace process and the GFA.

Beyond that, the purpose of the book is to initiate a discussion about the relationship between the old pluralist agenda and the 'new' agenda that has been opened up by the arrival of immigrants and the hostile reaction to them. The new agenda has been pursued by immigrants, and those who have championed them, mostly in isolation from the old. Insofar as the relationship between the two agendas has been explored, it has tended to be by those associated with the old pluralist agenda. Thus Fintan O'Toole argues that

There are two critical problems confronting contemporary Ireland. One is the task of making a peace settlement in Northern
Ireland and of building a pluralist democracy and an open society beyond it. The other is finding our place in the world now
that the Republic of Ireland has joined the wealthy elite of the
world. We have become rich by riding the tiger of globalisation.
Now we are discovering that globalisation works both ways and
that the global economy that brings foreign investment also
brings ... asylum-seekers. Slowly and inevitably, Ireland will ...
begin to develop as a ... multicultural society. Yet already there
are ominous signs of xenophobia and intolerance ... In a fundamental sense, these are not two problems but one. Both the ...
peace process and the ability of our society to handle its
transition to ethnic and racial diversity are essentially about the
challenge of taking a relatively monolithic culture and making it
accommodate the Other. (O'Toole, 23/7/99)

O'Toole's pioneering effort to explore connections between
the old pluralist agenda and the new and this within an is-
land-wide frame is admirable, and in putting together this
book I have sought to do the same: inviting contributions
from those concerned with each of the two pluralist agendas
and from both parts of Ireland. But, that aside, O'Toole's approach is precisely the kind of approach that I asked contributors to avoid. For O'Toole, Ireland's problems, in this
case racism in the South and sectarianism in the North, are
caused by disorders of cultural identity. In the case of racism in the South (he does not mention racism in the North),
O'Toole avoids suggesting that the arrival of immigrants has
disturbed a static and monolithic cultural identity: that
cultural identity, 'based on Catholicism, nationalism and rural values', was already falling apart, and the problem is that
'[t]he sense of loss, the feeling of insecurity, the uncertainty
about what it means to be Irish ... may be blamed on outsiders' (O'Toole, 2000: 17). Both the peace process and the
transition to ethnic and racial diversity in the South demand
the construction of more open and inclusive Irish identity,
and that is what he proceeds to do.

The theory that Ireland's problems – not just racism and
sectarian conflict but uneasy relations with the European

Union (EU) , the rise of consumerism and so forth – are caused by confusions and conflicts of cultural identity has inspired similar attempts by many other intellectuals to construct, invent, reinvent, imagine or reimagine Ireland and Irishness. More importantly it has also inspired politicians and the policy makers to act. And yet the theory itself remains largely unexamined. Cultural identity as both diagnosis and cure is not beyond question (see Lloyd 1993).

In this chapter I will track back from the GFA to trace the development of cultural pluralism in Ireland, focusing on what theorists mean when they say that Ireland's problems are caused by underlying confusions and conflicts of identity. The use of cultural identity as an idiom for analysis, policy and political practice is not peculiar to Ireland, and I will seek to locate the development of the idiom in Ireland with regard to its development elsewhere in the world. I do this for two reasons. Firstly, as a way of teasing out the assumptions about identity that are implicit in the peace process and the GFA: as will soon become apparent, there are crucial ambiguities here, and there is a lack of conceptual clarity among exponents of the old pluralist agenda. Secondly, because we in Ireland have much to learn from debates elsewhere in the world and we may also have something to contribute. The communal tensions and conflicts that prompted the debate about Irish identity in the 1970s were then aberrant in the Western world, now they are commonplace. As Michael Cronin notes in Chapter Ten, underneath the seemingly endless rehearsals of 'what it means to be Irish' there has also been a serious theoretical and practical engagement with issues to do with belonging, citizenship, cultural difference and conflict: issues which are of marked global significance after the Cold War. It may be that, after all, there is something to be retrieved from the old pluralist agenda that is useful not only to the new agenda in Ireland, but also to other parts of the world where the negotiation of difference is problematic. Certainly, the GFA has been held up to the world, most recently in relation to Iraq, as an example of conflict resolution (see Somasundram 1999).

THE GOOD FRIDAY AGREEMENT AND IDENTITY

Declan Kiberd, one of Ireland's leading cultural critics, be-
lieves that the vagueness of the GFA is one of its virtues: it

> is vague, even "poetic" ... because if offers a version of multiple
> identities, of a kind for which no legal language yet exists ...
> where is the lawyer who can offer a constitutional definition of
> identity as open rather than fixed, as a process rather than a
> conclusion? The ... Agreement effectively sounds a death-knell
> for old style constitutions (2000: 630).

Linked to this he suggests that 'the language of the ...
Agreement is indebted ... to postcolonial theory and to recent
forms of Irish criticism' (2000: 628), and to Anglo-Irish writers such as Charlotte Brook and Maria Edgeworth who had
challenged the fixed, colonial, stereotypical views that the
English had of the Irish.

Now that the lawyers and judges have been brought in to
preserve Ireland from immigrants who, it is claimed, are
taking advantage of the liberal definition of citizenship elaborated as part of the GFA[1], Kiberd's positive spin on the
vagueness of the Agreement's vocabulary of identity seems
in need of re-evaluation. The two most relevant parts of the
Agreement are items 1(v) and 1(vi) of the 'Constitutional Issues'. Here the 'participants endorse the commitment made
by the British and Irish governments that, in a new British-
Irish Agreement replacing the Anglo-Irish Agreement, they
will ...':

---

[1] Following a ruling by the Supreme Court in January 2003, the Irish
Minister for Justice sought to deport the 'non-national' parents of
children who were entitled to citizenship by virtue of their birth on
Irish soil. The Justice Minister subsequently announced a referendum
seeking to qualify the entitlement of any one born on the island to Irish
citizenship, including the children of non-nationals, which was, he
said, an unintended consequence of the rewriting of Article 2 of the
constitution as part of the GFA (*The Irish Times* 18/3/04).

(v) affirm that whatever choice is freely exercised by a majority of the people of Northern Ireland, the power of the sovereign government with jurisdiction there shall be exercised with rigorous impartiality on behalf of all the people in *the diversity of their identities and traditions* and shall be founded on the principles of full respect for, and equality of, civil, political, social and cultural rights, of freedom from discrimination for all citizens, and of parity of esteem and just and equal treatment for the identity, ethos and aspirations *of both communities*;
(vi) recognise the birthright of all the people of Northern Ireland to identify themselves and be accepted as Irish or British, or both, as they may so choose, and accordingly confirm that their right to hold both British and Irish citizenship is accepted by both Governments and would not be affected by any future change in the status of Northern Ireland (1998: 2, my italics).

The reference to a diversity of identities in item 1(v) and to choice in 1(vi) accords with Kiberd's view of the Agreement as generous and open-ended, but this view is contradicted by the contraction in 1(v) such that parity of esteem is accorded to the identities of only two communities. And in practice the only choice that seems to matter is to be British or Irish, unionist or nationalist: in the Assembly set up under the Agreement the votes of those members or putative members who might refuse this choice – liberals, socialists, feminists – do not count (Langhammer: 11/10/2000). And this is to say nothing about Travellers or newer ethnic minorities.

Less utopian defenders of the GFA than Kiberd will argue that Northern Irish, and Irish politics more generally, were always about identity, and that the Agreement is merely a pragmatic recognition of this fact. This is not true. But the argument of this book is not dependent on denying the palpable fact that in everyday life identity-talk and identity politics are real enough and, in some situations, of vital importance. Rather, my argument is that the fact that identity is used as a category of practice does not necessarily mean that we have to use it as a category of analysis or as an instrument of policy. As Brubaker and Cooper argue (2000: 5), 'one can analyze "identity-talk" and identity politics without, as analysts, positing the existence of "identities"'. This is not a trivial point: when analysts and administrators use identity categories they may be constituting categories that they imagine themselves to be merely describing[2]. In other words, by institutionalising a 'two-communities' or 'bicultural' model, the GFA may be encouraging the reification or objectification of cultural identity that is evident in the renewed sectarian polarisation that has occurred since the GFA was signed.

The theory that the conflict in Northern Ireland is one of cultural identity has a history, which is to say it was not always the dominant paradigm. Kiberd was once one of those who cast doubt on the theory, characterising the conflict as originating in a 'rebellion' that 'was primarily a protest against economic oppression and political injustice' (1996: 643). Now he wishes to claim a role for postcolonial theorists like himself in developing the notions of identity that lie at the heart of the GFA. Others have stressed the role of John Hume (Howe, 2000: 238). Like most punters, I am not privy to the processes through which the GFA was arrived at, but in sketching the development of the old pluralist agenda it seems to me that the best starting point is not postcolonial theory, but the 'revisionist' historians and politicians to whom postcolonial theory was a riposte.

THE DEVELOPMENT OF CULTURAL PLURALISM IN IRELAND

F.S.L. Lyons provides a clear statement of the theory at an early stage in its development. In the much-quoted conclusion to *Culture and Anarchy in Ireland 1890-1939* Lyons describes his purpose as having been to

---

2   Cf. Wievorka (1995: 3) 'It can be argued that it is social scientists in their anxiety to use categories and sub-divisions, and by presenting "race" as a category have contributed a great deal to the invention of racism, and to its formulation as doctrine and scholarly theory'.

lay beside the essential unity of Ireland a no less essential diversity. That diversity ... has been a diversity of ways of life which are deeply embedded in the past and of which the much-advertised political differences are but the out-ward and visible sign. This was the true anarchy that beset the country. During the period from the fall of Parnell to the death of Yeats, it was not primarily an anarchy of violence in the streets, of contempt for law and order such as to make the island ... ungovernable. It was rather an anarchy in the mind and the heart, an anarchy which forbade not just a unity of territories, but also a "unity of being", an anarchy that sprang from the collision within a small and intimate island of seemingly irreconcilable cultures, unable to live together or to live apart, caught inextricably in the web of their tragic history (1979: 177).

For Lyons there is no single Irish cultural identity as posited in traditional nationalist historiography, nor are there the two communal identities that are posited by subsequent theorists: there are at least four distinct cultures – English, Irish, Anglo-Irish and Presbyterian – and Lyons suggests that if one were to take a different analytical perspective others might be identified. Lyons's book is deeply pessimistic, and one gets the impression of an Ireland predestined to conflict: his point of reference may be the differences made manifest during the cultural revival that took place at the turn of the nineteenth century, but he brings these into constellation with the conflict that was ongoing at the time when he was writing.

Although Lyons pluralises Irish culture, his pessimism is such that it is unclear what is to be done. Garret FitzGerald gives pluralism a strategic direction in what is one of the earliest published expositions of identity-theory (1976). Fitz-Gerald's thesis is that Ireland suffers from a 'double identity crisis', one in the North and one in the South. The forms taken by these two identity crises are different, but they are the outcome of the same process. They both reflect 'the traumatic psychological impact upon the island of a political division whose significance, and durability, were grossly underestimated by all at the time when it came into being' (1976: 139-140). Partition is thus the proximate cause of a double identity crisis defined in terms of psychological trauma and a morbid preoccupation with history.

Produced by the same event, partition, the two identity crises took different forms. In the South it involved a contradiction in the ideology of a state, which 'claimed to represent in a large sense all the people of Ireland, but whose ideological basis was the narrow one of Gaelic, Catholic nationalism' (1976: 141). Irredentism, the claim on Northern Ireland in Articles 2 and 3 of the Irish Constitution, was a direct response to partition, but the form taken by partition exacerbated the contradiction because it created a state with an 'overwhelmingly Catholic' population. Gaelic became central to national policy because of the role played by the 'Irish language revival' in the movement for independence. Because of partition, the 'Gaelic and Catholic' ideal developed 'unfettered by any challenge from other Irish traditions' (1976: 139).

In relation to Northern Ireland, FitzGerald describes not one but two identity crises, and only one of these is reducible to partition. Notwithstanding the boldness of unionist claims in the 1920s, 'at a deeper level of consciousness, their separation from the rest of the island was for many years seen by them as essentially temporary' (1976: 137), and this feeling persisted even as the state endured. Consequently, the 'inhabitants' of the state never developed any clear sense of identity. In Protestants this feeling of temporariness also created 'a continuing sense of uncertainty and fear about their future' that explains, but does not justify, the discriminatory policies they enacted against local Catholics (1976: 140). It was these policies that led to the collapse of the state. And it was at this point that the Protestant identity crisis 'reached traumatic proportions' (1976: 140). In his discussion of this trauma, FitzGerald alludes to a second kind of identity crisis, one that can only be explained in terms of colonialism, although he does not use that word at this juncture: Protestants never 'felt fully at home ... in the land of their origins ... or in that of their adoption'; i.e. Britain and Ireland respectively.

The identity crisis in the South was less traumatic than in the North. Free from threat, people in the South have been better able to reflect on the internal contradiction between irredentism and the prevailing 'Gaelic and Catholic' ethos. Discussion of this contradiction began in the late 1950s, became a focus of political debate during the 1966 presidential contest, but was given added impetus by the onset of the Troubles in the North. The latter made people in the South think that if they were serious about the claim on the North, maybe they should attempt to 'woo' Protestants 'rather than hector ... them ... because no one could credibly put forward the ideal of a Gaelic Catholic Ireland as an attractive proposition to Northern Protestants.' Out of this debate emerged a different conception of Ireland: 'a pluralist society, in which the different Irish traditions would be given equal importance and standing' (1976: 141).

FitzGerald had already served as Foreign Minister in the Fine Gael/Labour Coalition government 1973-1977, but when he became Taoiseach in 1981 he was able to put his pluralist agenda into practice with a constitutional 'crusade' aimed at changing the provisions in the Irish constitution 'that were interpreted as involving a claim to the territory of Northern Ireland (Articles 2 and 3)' (1991: 376). The crusade was interrupted by the change of government in February 1982, and when FitzGerald returned to office in December 1982, he did not resume the 'crusade', but instead gave priority to the establishment of the New Ireland Forum, which was conceived as a means to bolster constitutional nationalism in the North against the political and electoral success of Sinn Féin in the aftermath of the hunger strikes. FitzGerald explains that he did not pursue the constitutional crusade after the Anglo-Irish Agreement because

> it was too late in the life of our Government to start a general constitutional review process, and in any event the sharp swing to the right in religious as well as political affairs that had marked the first half of the 1980s had created an environment that was more hostile than that of 1981 to the refashioning of the Constitution on pluralist lines (1991: 380).

Here FitzGerald is referring to the Pro-Life Amendment passed in September 1983 and, more generally, to what Luke Gibbons has described as 'the resurgence of a new Catholic fundamentalism' in the 1980s (1991: 567).

Although the constitutional crusade failed, FitzGerald's ideas and those of other revisionists were to have a much greater impact in the North. The Forum paved the way for the Anglo-Irish Agreement of November 1985, which FitzGerald presents as the 'fruit' of the Forum, and in the wake of that Agreement the British government embarked on an ambitious cultural programme, through the Cultural Traditions Group[3], which sought to encourage members of the two communities to explore their cultural identities in the hope that this would foster self-respect and ultimately mutual respect.

We do not have to take FitzGerald at his word regarding the influence of revisionism on the development of a pluralist agenda in Northern Ireland. At the first conference of the Cultural Traditions Group, tellingly entitled *Varieties of Irishness* (Crozier 1989), the key address was by Roy Foster, widely recognised as the heir to the revisionist mantle in historiography. Foster uses his address to redeem Lyons's pessimistic analysis of relations between the members of Ireland's various cultural traditions. Foster suggests that Lyons had read the cultural revival in the light of the bitterness generated by subsequent events: World War I, the shelving of Home Rule, the success of secessionist movements in Ulster, the take-over of the Gaelic League) by the Irish Republican Brotherhood, the execution of the leaders of the Easter Rising history, the Sinn Féin election victory in 1918. For Foster, the written work left by 'the brokers of the different cultural traditions in Ireland' at the end of the nineteenth century reveal that a genuine debate had been opening up: 'they were engaging in dialogue with each other,

---

[3]   The Cultural Traditions Group was established in 1988, initially under the auspices of the Institute of Irish Studies at the Queen's University of Belfast, as an initiative of the Central Community Relations Unit.

however angrily' (1993: 35-6). He suggests, optimistically, that a 'similar process' had been evolving in Ireland at the end of the twentieth century 'in the columns of *The Crane Bag, Fortnight,* the *Irish Review,* The Field Day pamphlets, *Krino, Making Sense* ... There is also the theatre of Friel, Parker, McGuiness, Murphy, Kilroy' (1993: 36). Along with this dialogue, he noted a Europeanisation that might lead to fresh thinking about sovereignty and borders.

Reading the debate about Irish identity that took place in the late 1970s and early 1980s, one is struck by its openness and generosity, but this is only because the debate became so much more bitter in the late 1980s and 1990s (see Foster 1992). Lyons may have been guilty of reading history backwards, but his pessimism seems more prescient than Foster's optimism. In the rancour of the 'revisionist controversy', pluralism seems almost to disappear from the intellectual and political agenda in the Republic.

THE DISAPPEARANCE OF PLURALISM IN THE REPUBLIC

In his biography FitzGerald explains his abandonment of the constitutional crusade in terms of a swing to the right in the early 1980s, but even in 1976 he was pessimistic about the prospects for pluralism in the South. Despite the impetus given to the 'revisionist movement' by the Troubles, FitzGerald was concerned that pluralism had not struck popular roots: it was, he said, too 'abstract' and 'at variance with a traditional inherited value system [that] for historical reasons has not had occasion in the past to distinguish clearly between religious and secular loyalties' (1976: 142).

This explanation is not convincing, and is suggestive of a significant misunderstanding on FitzGerald's part of the broader provenance of pluralism and the notions of cultural identity that he was promoting. Another article in the same issue of *Études Irlandaises* by the historian John A. Murphy suggests a better explanation for the unpopularity of pluralism. Murphy argues against Conor Cruise O'Brien, then

Minister for Post and Telecommunications in the 'revisionist' Fine Gael/Labour government, who had suggested that rather than create a second TV channel, the state broadcasting service, Radio Teilefís Éireann, should simply relay the BBC: 'the fragile nature of Irish distinctiveness calls for a special degree of protection' from the government. Murphy was concerned that the government's policy of muting nationalist commemorations and its favouring of 'a politically-inspired historical revisionism have led ... C.J. Haughey, to defend the nationalist outlook ... and ... claim it for Fianna Fáil' (1976:156).

FitzGerald's pluralism failed in the Republic, not because it was too abstract or intellectual for the masses – it didn't even persuade many intellectuals. Pluralism failed because it was posed in opposition to the continuity of a distinctive Irish identity. For example, in his biography FitzGerald (1991: 64) says that he opposed an Irish language requirement for the public service because it was 'incompatible with any serious attempt to achieve Irish unity by consent... [it] was an obstacle to Northern unionists, to almost all of whom the language was alien' (see Lee 1979: 676-7). The impression was that, to use the words of Luke Gibbons (1994: 29), 'openness towards the other somehow requires obliteration of one's own identity'.

FitzGerald was not alone in his uncertainty about the larger issues that were at stake. The editorial in the second ever issue of the journal *The Crane Bag*, entitled 'A Sense of Nation', is instructive. It was first published in 1977, one year after FitzGerald's article. The issue includes, amongst others, an article by Conor Cruise O'Brien, entitled 'Nationalism and the Reconquest of Ireland', an article by Seamus Deane on Yeats, and an article by Deirdre Bair on Beckett. In the Editorial, Hederman and Kearney start with the question:

What makes you feel Irish? Is it like being Jewish, is it something embedded in your psyche or your physiognomy? Is "Irishness" a certain sediment in the soul or chemistry in the blood stream? Is it something "caught" in the environment?

This issue of Crane Bag attempts to tease out these questions'
(1982: 92).

They summarise O'Brien's article as suggesting that
nationalism is a 'luxury which we cannot afford ... a
dispensable commodity which we can decide in a political
way to abandon, if we feel, as is the case in our country, that
it is being maintained at too high a price' (1982: 92).
O'Brien had argued that the price of nationalism was an aspiration to a united Ireland that sanctioned the Provisional
... [IRA] campaign. He notes that Irish nationalists have held
two theories about Northern Protestants. In one theory, articulated by Tone, Davis, Pearse, and Connolly, Protestants
'whether they know it or not, are part of the Irish nation'
(1982: 97). In the other theory, 'much less publicly formulated ... Protestants are settlers in a land, all of which belongs to us, the native Irish'. He argues that the two theories, 'so remote from one another in theory, amount to the
same thing in practice': they sanction the reconquest of Ireland, albeit by different means. Exponents of the first theory
seek to do this through persuasion. Exponents of the second
theory 'try to bomb and burn the British and the settlers
along with them, out of the occupied six counties' (1982: 98).
Either way, the price for O'Brien is too high.

The editors then note an interview that Seamus Deane
conducted with Seamus Heaney in the first issue of *The
Crane Bag*. Deane had asked Heaney:

> Do you think that the kind of humanism which ... O'Brien
> sponsors is precisely that kind of humanism, totally detached
> from its atavisms, which, though welcome from a rational point
> of view, renders much of what he says either irrelevant or
> simply wrong – particularly in relation to the North where
> bigotry is so much part of the psyche (1982: 92).

Following this, the editors characterise O'Brien as defending rational humanism against the 'native atavisms which ...
find their expression in the terrorism of the IRA' (1982: 92).
They then note Bair's article which claims that Beckett is

Irish despite his 'conscious attempt to repudiate it ... It comes across as an almost subconscious influence which is present and detectable in his work no matter how much he might try to eradicate its traces.' (Cited by Hederman and Kearney, 1982: 92). The editors appear to agree with Deane and Bair, that '[b]eing Irish, therefore, would seem to point beyond the level of conscious decision' (1982: 93). Taking this further, they suggest that this 'primitive atavistic layer of Irishness' goes even 'deeper than psychology', it resides in mythology, and that being so, 'it would be essential to acknowledge it and appropriate it' (1982: 93).

And yet, the editors are not content with this, they want to have it both ways. These articles combined seem to point to a deeply rooted schizophrenia in the Irish psyche'. They summarise this schizophrenia in terms of a series of oppositions: humanism versus atavism, rationalism versus archetypal irrationalism, plural versus singular consciousness, Catholic bourgeois state versus native Gaelic heritage. In conclusion they suggest that

> regardless of whether one calls for the cultivation of the upper layer of what we might call "civilized" Ireland ... or the reconquest and reappropriation of the underlayers of "primitive" Ireland ... one cannot deny that the fissure exists. The present crisis in Northern Ireland stands as irrefutable testament to this rupture ... (1982: 94).

Theoretically, it was not until the 1990s that the apparent contradiction between a revisionist-inspired pluralism and the continuity of a fragile Irish identity was successfully resolved or maybe only finessed by Kiberd's postcolonial theorists. In the meantime, the pluralist project was abandoned in the South and in the North the Cultural Traditions Group pioneered pluralist policies with what Maurna Crozier describes in Chapter Two as an 'instinctive' approach.

The manner in which postcolonial critics resolve the contradiction is ingenious. Like the revisionists, they reject as essentialist or even racist the singular view of Irishness projected in what Kiberd describes as the 'narrow-gauge' nationalism (Sailer 1999) espoused by the Irish state after independence. Unlike the revisionists, they emphasise that this was not the only form of nationalism articulated in the cultural revival that preceded independence, and argue that the fact that it came to dominate in the newly independent state itself owes much to notions of Celticism elaborated in colonial writing (see Gibbons 1991 and Kiberd 1996). Luke Gibbons attaches particular importance to Thomas Mac-Donagh who 'rejected Celticism precisely because its racial provenance carried with it a narrow, exclusivist interpretation of Irishness' (1991: 563). For MacDonagh, Irishness was not a genetic or racial inheritance; rather it was something to be constructed as part of a concerted cultural effort. Francis Mulhern calls this 'prospective nationalism' (1998). In prospective nationalism there is no contradiction between pluralism and the continuity of an Irish identity: as Gibbons suggests, 'openness towards the other' does not, in fact, require the 'obliteration of one's own identity' (1994: 29). Gibbons insists that the open-endedness of nationalism

> has less to do with the "unfinished business" of a united Ireland than with the realisation that there is no possibility of undoing history, of removing the accretions of conquest – the English language, the inscriptions of the Protestant Ascendancy on the landscape and the material culture, and so on. For this reason, there is no prospect of restoring a pristine, pre-colonial identity: the lack of historical closure, therefore, is bound up with a similar incompleteness in the culture itself, so that instead of being based on narrow ideals of racial purity and exclusivism, identity is open-ended and heterogeneous (1996: 179).

Having finessed the apparent opposition between pluralism and the continuity of a distinctive Irish identity in favour of the latter, postcolonial theorists cast the revisionists who had prioritised pluralism as secular, rationalistic liberals in the mould of the European Enlightenment (see Gibbons 1991: 567) whose universal humanistic ideas had been exposed by the intellectual avant-garde in contemporary Europe. In fact, if we look at these broader debates we can see that underneath the rancour the revisionists and post-colonial theorists share more conceptually than either would wish to admit.

MULTICULTURALISM AND THE CRITIQUE OF THE ENLIGHTENMENT

My view of revisionists as the pioneers of pluralism in Ireland is at first sight hard to square with Gibbons's characterisation of them as liberal rationalists, for elsewhere in the world cultural pluralism and multiculturalism developed as radical critiques of the assumptions about humanity, knowledge, power and progress that underpinned the political ideologies – socialism as much as liberalism – that emerged from the European Enlightenment and the French Revolution. The exponents of this critique were from among the peoples colonised by western powers and others who had experienced the rough edge of the Western dream of Progress. The decline of ideology and the rise of identity as the idiom for politics has a lot to do, therefore, with decolonisation and the rise of New Social Movements (NSMs) that are based on identities other than class; i.e. gender, ethnicity, sexuality. These movements asserted themselves by asserting their cultural difference.

In doing so they echoed the first critics of the Enlightenment, notably Johann Herder. The philosophers of Enlightenment in France viewed culture as the universal 'domain in which the creative and spiritual life of Man developed' (Finkielkraut, 1988: 11). Herder disagreed. For him, culture or civilisation was not singular, there was a diversity of cultures which were each the product of different *Volksgeist,* meaning national genius or character. Herder was not merely correcting what he saw as an intellectual error, he was also resisting an imperialism: the philosophers of the Enlightenment thought that their values were of universal significance, Herder said they were not universal, merely French. At the time when Herder was writing, Enlightenment ideas had prestige in Prussia, and his ideas only became popular later, in the aftermath of Napoleon's victory at Jena:

> A Germany, fragmented into a multitude of principalities, regained its sense of unity in the face of French occupation. The exaltation of collective identity compensated for military defeat and the humiliating subjugation which it entailed. The nation made up for the humiliation to which it was being subjected, by the marvellous discovery of its culture (Finkielkraut, 1988: 15).

Herder's ideas form the basis of cultural nationalism, and were influential among French conservatives such as de Maistre who rejected the form of nationalism instituted by the Revolution. 'Misconstruing its own etymology (*nascor* means "I am born") the revolutionary nation uprooted individuals and defined them by their humanity rather than their birth [or heredity]' (1988: 17). Freed from the feudal traditions that bound them, the revolutionaries had formed a political assembly to draft a constitution. For conservatives like de Maistre, the idea that a political assembly could constitute a nation was dangerous nonsense. We are born into constitutions, nations, cultures, languages: 'arrangements which it does not fall to [us] to determine, but only to learn and respect the rules' (1988: 18).

Herder's ideas were also influential in the emerging field of anthropology. Here, particularly in the work of Boas, the idea that 'each of the "peoples" of Africa, South Asia, and the Pacific have a distinct, rational and legitimate way of life which should be valued' was used to question the Enlightenment idea that 'each of these cultures was at a different stage in the evolution of civilization or in a progression towards European rationality' (Wright, 1998: 8). This anthropological definition of culture as the way of life of a people or group is the one used both by Lyons and by Gibbons (1996), and it underpins the old pluralist agenda in Ireland.

Lyons borrowed the title for his book, *Culture and Anarchy in Ireland 1890-1939*, from Matthew Arnold, but he is at pains to explain that his approach to culture is different from Arnold's:

> Arnold's analysis of the role of culture is almost as inadequate as his definition of culture itself ... Culture, he says in a famous passage, seeks to "make the best that has been thought and known in the world current everywhere" and "to make all men live in an atmosphere of sweetness and light ...". When Arnold was composing his essay in the late 1860s, the social sciences were still in their infancy. There were not social anthropologists or social psychologists to compel him to explain himself more intelligibly ... To get closer to Irish realities we shall have to interpret culture in a much broader sense, yet without committing ourselves irrevocably to the devotees of any specific school ... At this stage ... it will be enough to apply it to the different groups in Ireland which either have or have had a distinct and relatively autonomous existence and whose members have shared a recognisably common way of life (1979: 3).

Lyons follows through on the implications of viewing culture as 'the whole mode of life of a community' in a subsequent lecture:

> though our days are filled with the actualities of communal strife, how much do we really know ... about how a community evolves ... We know about community politics, we know about parties and elections ... But about the essence of a community we know ... all too little outside our immediate, personal and highly fallible experience (cited in Gibbons, 1996: 16).

Gibbons comments that this 'observation is central to genuine historical understanding'. The problem is that Lyons does not submit to his own logic:

> no sooner has he emphasised the desirability of "cross[ing] the barriers imaginatively between one community and another" he then proceeds to write off a community's own understanding of itself, the narratives through which it attempts to make sense of its past. These from his perspective as a professional historian, are best construed as simply fiction, " ... false history" (Gibbons, 1996: 16).

When Lyons 'complains that "we can no longer distinguish realities of what has happened on this island from the myths we have chosen to weave around certain symbolic events"' he is suggesting that '[t]ruth lies firmly in the hands of academic historians rather than the benighted cultures they purport to represent' (Gibbons, 1996: 16)

Politically, Lyons and Gibbons are at odds. Gibbons, the radical postcolonial critic, characterises revisionist historiography as being liberal and rationalist, in the Enlightenment mould. Lyons, counterposing communal myth to the fact established by objective historiography, seems to fit the caricature. And yet they both seem to agree a common pluralist definition of culture. Cultural pluralism or multiculturalism might emerge as a critique of the Enlightenment assumptions and the political projects that they inspired, but as Kymlicka (1995) and Joppke and Lukes (1999) have established they are no longer opposed, and the theorist who laid the conceptual groundwork for their reconciliation is Erik Erikson (Balakrishnan 2002).

Although he is not credited in Irish debates of the 1970s[4], there are strong traces of Eriksonian ideas. With the partial exception of Lyons, none of the revisionists discussed above define what they mean by cultural identity or locate their notion of cultural identity in relation to other concepts. Despite this vagueness, Deane, Lyons, FitzGerald, and the editors of *The Crane Bag* seem to share a view of cultural identity as something that is simultaneously both collective and ideational and inward to the individual; something that is continuous and resistant to change; something that is emotionally laden, agonised, and prior to reason and politics. All of this is resonant of Erikson, and the term 'identity crisis' that FitzGerald introduced to the Irish debate and which has

---

[4] *Crane Bag* included one article by Vincent Kenny entitled 'The Post-Colonial Personality' that cites Bateson who was close to the culture and personality school of anthropology. I am unable to provide a full reference, but the article was published between 1981 and 1985.

formed the basis of so many subsequent analyses of both unionist and nationalist politics was coined by Erikson.

Erikson was a Freudian psychologist who worked with members of the culture and personality school of anthropology in the United States (US) in the years before and after World War II. For Erikson, identity was something internal that persists even as the individual changes in response to the developmental tasks associated with biological maturation and the role-requirements associated with his or her cultural milieu. The notion of an identity crisis is used by Erikson to describe the 'climactic turning point in this process ... [which] usually occurs in adolescence, but can also be precipitated by unusual difficulties further along in the life-cycle' (Gleason, 1982: 914). Change and crisis notwithstanding, an individual's identity is at bottom an accrued confidence in the inner sameness and continuity of his/her own being. As such, this inner sameness and continuity is something to be valued and nurtured. Despite his emphasis on identity as something interior to the individual, Erikson regarded identity as inextricably bound up with the communal culture. Indeed in an abidingly influential formulation he reduces individual identity to communal identity: identity was 'a process located in the core of the individual and yet also in the core of his communal culture, a process which establishes ... the identity of those identities' (1968: 22). As Gleason points out, the linkage that Erikson implies between personal identity and an inherited communal culture or way of life makes plausible

> the argument that cultures – especially minority ethnic cultures – require some sort of official recognition if the self-esteem of individuals is not to suffer damage. The respect for the dignity of the individual demanded by democratic ideology is thereby extended to cover ethnic cultures that sustain the sense of personal self worth (1983: 921).

Thus, pluralism or multiculturalism is reconciled to liberalism. Eriksonian theory provides the rationale for the notion of mutual respect and parity of esteem that lie at the heart of the peace process and liberal multiculturalism more generally: to be secure, individual identity needs to be grounded in a strong collective cultural identity, and if the collective cultural identity is not recognised in the broader society, the individual's sense of self-worth or esteem will be damaged (cf. Kymlicka's notion of 'societal culture', 1995).

Notions such as parity of esteem seem impeccable, but, following Gleason, we should note that Erikson's ideas about personal identity depends on an essentialist concept of cultural identity. In Ireland today few intellectuals would admit to using an essentialist concept of identity perhaps because it has unpalatable associations with racial thinking (see Eagleton, 1999). The preferred view is that identities are socially constructed, fluid and multiple. Revisionists and postcolonial critics thought they had consigned essentialism to a less sophisticated, older generation of nationalist, Irish or British, who believed that identity was a primordial inheritance. And yet essentialism lingers. Indeed, it is central to the form of pluralism elaborated as part of the old agenda in Ireland, and to its crowning achievement, the GFA.

An ambiguity between essentialist and constructivist concepts of identity is not restricted to debates about Irish identity, and has been remarked upon by others (Brubaker and Cooper, 2000). Gleason alerts us to another reason for the ambiguity. He shows how, even at an early stage in the development of identity politics in the US, Erikson's ideas were used not just by members of oppressed minority groups but also by 'white ethnic spokesmen unhappy about programs of the affirmative action type' (1983: 920) that were developed as a response to the claims of minority groups. For both kinds of cultural claimant, a strong essentialist argument is not flawless because it might 'suggest ... the conclusion that, if ethnicity is bound to persist anyhow, there is no need for new social policies designed to foster or protect it' (1983: 921). A constructivist view of identity is 'better adapted for arguing in favor of new social policies because it stresses the role of situational factors in shaping ethnic identity'. Gleason might have been referring to the debate about Irish identity when he comments, much as the controversialist may like having terms that mean whatever the rhetorical situation requires, equivocation of this sort is fatal to efforts to achieve a clear theoretical grasp of the issues. It is likewise a grievous handicap to the forging of sound social policy (1983: 921).

DEFINING PLURALISM IN IRELAND

Given this ambiguity, how might the form of pluralism elaborated in the old pluralist agenda be characterised? According to John Whyte, FitzGerald's revisionist analysis of the Northern Ireland problem as a clash of two identities is a Kuhnian 'paradigm shift': traditional nationalist and traditional unionist explanations of the problem stress external agents as the source of the problem. Where as nationalists blame the British and unionists blame Southern irredentism, FitzGerald stresses factors internal to Northern Ireland. The notion of a paradigm shift has been contested from both directions. Referring to the New Ireland Forum, which was FitzGerald's brainchild, Claire O'Halloran suggests that FitzGerald's analysis, for all its self-proclaimed revisionism, 'merely clothed traditional [nationalist] values in a new language of pluralism' (1987: 194) She regards the 'dominant term "identity"' as being 'particularly insidious' for 'it transformed the conflict between nationalism and unionism from the fundamental one of totally opposing political perspectives to one of mere ... cultural differentiation' (1987: 198). Conversely, in a critique of Roy Foster's *Modern Ireland 1600-1972*, Seamus Deane suggests that revisionism

> collaborates – unconsciously – with the very mentality it wants to defeat ... Revisionists are nationalist despite themselves; by refusing to be Irish nationalists, they simply become defenders of Ulster or British nationalism, thereby switching sides in a dispute while believing themselves to be switching the terms of it (1994: 242).

The pluralism that developed out of the old agenda in Ireland is a form of liberal pluralism that, insofar as it draws on Eriksonian ideas about identity, shares much with liberal multiculturalism. There is the same ambiguity about the nature of identity, but key injunctions such as 'parity of esteem' depend on an implicit essentialism. Goldberg characterises liberal multiculturalism as being top-down and managerial: 'glibly' celebrating cultural diversity, and enjoining us to respect other cultures and traditions, it not only 'leaves groups constituted as givens but entrenches the boundaries fixing group demarcations as unalterable' (1994: 7).

We have seen that liberal multiculturalism, with its implicit embrace of an essentialist concept of identity, owes a great deal to cultural nationalism (see also Calhoun 1997). The same can be said of liberal pluralism in Ireland. It may originate as a critique of the narrow-gauge cultural nationalism sponsored by the newly independent Irish state, but it is not, as John Whyte claims, a paradigm shift, for it does not challenge the essentialism of cultural nationalist conceptions of Irish identity, it merely doubles the number of available identity categories. In this sense, Deane's analysis of revisionism can be extended to the liberal pluralism that it sponsors: both 'collaborate ... unconsciously ... with the very mentality [they] want ... to defeat' (1994: 242). Liberal pluralism in Ireland, like liberal multiculturalism elsewhere, is ultimately based on ideas about culture and identity that were first elaborated by the pioneers of cultural nationalism, Johann Herder and French conservatives such as de Maistre, developed in the work of social anthropologists like Tylor and Boas, and reintroduced to the mainstream by Erik Erikson, the anthropologists of the culture and personality school and Levi-Strauss at the founding conference of UNESCO (see Finkielkraut 1988).

In the provenance of the ideas and concepts that underpin it, liberal pluralism in Ireland shares much with liberal multiculturalism elsewhere. This has beguiled otherwise astute observers. Paddy Logue argues that

the peace process has allowed us to snap out of the trance of
the two traditions, that mutual obsession of nationalists and
unionists, the hypnotic focus of a cobra and a mongoose about
to attack each other. As the shouts and din of ancient quarrel
begin to subside, we hear other voices. In Ireland today there
are atheists, Jews, Sikhs, Buddhists, socialists, Chinese,
Travellers, blacks, Moslems, gays, asylum seekers, feminists,
and others, all of whom locate themselves outside the two
traditions and are entitled to parity of esteem and equality of
treatment (2000: xviii).

I wish that this were true. As I have noted, item 1(v) of the
GFA talks about 'the people of Northern Ireland … in the diversity of their traditions', but parity of esteem is reserved
for 'the identity and ethos' of only two communities' (1998:
2).

Since the Agreement was signed, the hypnotic trance of
mongoose and cobra seems to have deepened. This alone is
enough to force a re-assessment of the old agenda, but
equally important to that reassessment is the new agenda
that is now being opened up. The form of pluralism that
emerges from the old agenda is a liberal pluralism that owes
much to liberal multicultural thinking elsewhere but, despite what Logue says, it remains resolutely bicultural in the
way that it privileges the rights of two indigenous communities, each of which is presumed to have its own cultural
identity, conceived in essentialist terms. If the existence of
other indigenous groups, such as Travellers, is barely regis-
tered let alone acknowledged in the biculturalism that
emerges from the old agenda, what are the prospects for
immigrants and those who are increasingly referred to as
'non-nationals'?

Farrell Corcoran has suggested that Irish attempts to ad-
just to the arrival of immigrants are 'uniquely influenced by
the winding-down of "the Troubles" and the search for political initiatives designed finally to deal with the legacy of the
colonial past in Northern Ireland' (2000: 28). Each of the
contributors to this volume would share something with
Corcoran's assessment; beyond that the views differ. The

purpose of the book is not to develop a consensus, but to present a range of views from both sides of the border, and from different disciplinary perspectives.

In the penultimate chapter, Michael Cronin is hopeful that the intellectual and practical efforts that were expended in working through the old pluralist agenda might be useful in the context of the new agenda. In Part One of the book Maurna Crozier (Chapter Two) and Louis de Paor (Chapter Three) suggest that the cultural policies that have been developed to contest sectarianism in Northern Ireland might also prove useful in contesting racism. De Paor also discusses some constructive developments in the interface between one indigenous minority, native Irish speakers, and immigrants

As de Paor points out, Irish cultural nationalism developed as a response to English colonial intolerance. But more than eighty years after independence was won one might wonder what it is that sustains a national project with Irish identity as its central focus, especially as the GFA has supposedly resolved the question of partition. In his analysis of the campaigns waged in the two referenda on the Nice Treaty, Gerry Boucher (Chapter Four) suggests that one of the factors is Ireland's structural position as a small dependent economy on the western fringes of Europe.

Boucher's chapter introduces a series of less sanguine perspectives. In Chapter Five Piaras Mac Éinrí considers the monocultural model of Irishness elaborated by the Irish state after independence, and the extent to which it left Southern Ireland ill-equipped to deal with difference, whether in the form of the indigenous Travelling community or refugees and immigrants. He examines the *ad hoc* and inadequate response of previous Irish administrations to the Jewish refugees who came to Ireland in the 1930s, to the Hungarians after 1956 and the Vietnamese in the 1970s. Although the monocultural model of Irishness has begun to breakdown and the response of the voluntary sector to immigrants has often been exemplary, Mac Éinrí expresses concern that recent initiatives such as the Supreme Court decision to remove *de facto* residence rights in the Republic of Ireland for foreign-born parents of Irish-born children and the recent referendum on citizenship are signs that in some official quarters identity is being reconstructed in line with what Lentin (2002) has called a racialised state.

In Chapter Six, Máiréad Nic Craith suggests that by emphasising communal culture as the basis for citizenship, belonging and equality, the GFA and the sequence of Anglo-Irish agreements that preceded it, unwittingly played to a nationalist rather than a unionist sensibility. Unionists, she suggests, have traditionally been more inclined to conceive belonging and equality in individualistic terms, though, unlike the French, they never developed this into an explicit model of citizenship. In this analysis, the elaboration of an explicit politics of identity by some Northern Protestants is a comparatively recent development, linked to the gradual institutionalisation of communalism.

The history of pluralism in Ireland that I have outlined in this chapter tends to support Nic Craith's argument, as would the work of Brown (1992), Deane (1994) Mulhern (1998) and Finlay (2001). If I have barely mentioned the contribution of unionist thinkers to the development of cultural pluralism in Ireland, it is because their contribution has hitherto been muted. That unionists are less familiar than nationalists with the vocabulary of cultural identity and pluralism should not surprise us given what these owe conceptually to cultural nationalism. In this context, I was surpised to come across a pamphlet entitled, *Republicanism Loyalism and Pluralism in Ireland*, which originated as a series of three reports presented to the General Assembly of the Presbyterian Church in Ireland dating from 1974, 1975 and 1976. Authorship is attributed to the Church's Committee on National and International Problems, but a debt of gratitude is expressed to J.H. Whyte, who was close to Garret FitzGerald, for supplying the bibliography, and it is likely that his contribution was considerably greater[5]. Though

---

5 Personal communication with Nicholas Whyte, 26/3/04.

fascinating, the Presbyterian pamphlet is perhaps one of those exceptions that prove the rule.

The recent proliferation of cultural claims by Protestants in Ireland is picked up in Chapter Six, where Finlay examines the controversy generated by the proposal for an Orange Order parade in Dublin in 2000. What makes this case interesting is that it was one of the first occasions when the old pluralist agenda, concerned with accommodating Catholics and Protestants in Ireland, was publically reworked in relation to the new one, concerned with immigrants. Beyond that, it illuminates more general issues concerning the competitive nature of cultural claims generated in social orders based on cultural pluralism or multiculturalism and the difficulties of arbitrating between them.

In Chapter Eight, Robin Whitaker considers those left out of the 'two-communities', or 'bicultural', model that, following the GFA, is used to map and administer the population of Northern Ireland. Her focus is not on the difficulties experienced by immigrants, but on those experienced by local people who she met through her work with the Women's Coalition. If the GFA focuses on differences between communities, the difficulties experienced by the people Whitaker encountered and by parties like the Women's Coalition might be better understood as arising from differences within subjects. She concludes that such subjects should not be dismissed as troublesome exceptions, for the recognition of such difference is crucial to the creation of new solidarities forged, not through already-settled identities but through political effort.

Following on from Whitaker, Gerard Delanty (Chapter Nine) suggests that the new forms of pluralism that Ireland will need to develop if it is to respond to the challenge of immigration may have little to learn from the old pluralist agenda, and that the impulse for a new politics will have to come from elsewhere. He notes various trends that have undermined the link between national identity and citizenship elaborated in cultural nationalism and the link between nation and state elaborated in republicanism, and argues, following Habermas, that a postnational polity can only be based on a common agreement around basic principles and procedural rules for the resolution of conflict. This is a limited form of patriotism, which involves an identification with a constitution rather than with a territory, a cultural heritage or a state. Such a 'constitutional patriotism' has the potential to reconcile equality and difference, and is sustained, rather than undermined, by the constant negotiation of conflict. Reading this, one cannot help but be reminded of Declan Kiberd's forlorn hope that 'a common bind now uniting the majority North and South who voted for the GFA is 'fidelity to its thirty-five pages, a fidelity that will probably override their actual relation to their respective sovereign powers.' (2000: 630). The fact that this has not happened, I would suggest, is less symptomatic of the weakness of Habermas's ideas than of the extent to which the Agreement falls short of them, particularly in its reliance on old models of identity and identification.

Michael Cronin (Chapter Ten) is, as I have said, more optimistic about the ongoing relevance of Irish debates about identity, not just to the new challenges faced by people in Ireland but by people the world over. Amongst these new challenges, he focuses on the difficulties of forging any kind of personal identity in the uncertain, atomising conditions created by a globalising neo-liberalism. His warning that people may retreat to narrow forms of national identity based less on jingoism – hostility to other nations – than on a xenophobia rooted in ideas about who is, and who is not, entitled to welfare is prescient: in the recent referendum one of the main justifications for restricting Irish citizenship was that immigrants seeking to give birth to an Irish child have placed an intolerable burden on maternity services in Ireland. Beyond that Cronin looks to a future in which, with advances in genetic engineering, robotics, bio-technology and cognitive psychology, the challenge may be not so much to define what it means to be Irish – or British or French or German for that matter – as to define what it means to be human.

REFERENCES

Balakrishnan, G. (2002), 'The Age of Identity' (Review of Lutz
   Niethammer, Kollektive Identitat. Hiemliche Quellen einer
   unheimlichen Konjunktur, Hamburg: Reinback bei, *New
   Left Review* 16, 130-142 (July/August).
Barry, B. (2001), 'Muddles of Multiculturalism', *New Left Re-
   view* 8, 49-72 (March-April).
Brown, T. (1992), 'Identities in Ireland: the Historical Per-
   spective', in J. Lundy and A. Mac Póilin eds, *Styles of Be-
   longing: The Cultural Identities of Ulster.* Belfast: Lagan
   Press, 23-33.
Brubaker, R. and Cooper, F. (2000), 'Beyond "Identity"', *Theory and Society*, 29, 1-47.
Corcoran, F. (2000), 'Technologies of Memory', in E. Slater
   and M. Peillon eds, *Memories of the Present A Sociological
   Chronicle of Ireland 1997-1998.* Dublin: Institute of Public
   Administration.
Calhoun, C. (1997), *Nationalism.* Buckingham: Open University Press.
Committee of the Presbyterian Church in Ireland on National
   and International Problems (c. 1980), *Republicanism, Loy-
   alism and Pluralism in Ireland.* Belfast: General Assembly
   of the Presbyterian Church in Ireland.
Deane, S. (1994), 'Wherever the Green is Read', in C. Brady
   ed., *Interpreting Irish History: The Debate on Historical Re-
   visionism 1938- 1994.* Dublin: Irish Academic Press.
Deane, S. (1997), *Strange Country: Modernity and Nation-
   hood in Irish Writing since 1790.* Oxford: Clarendon.
Eagleton, T. (1999), *The Truth About the Irish.* Dublin: New
   Island Books.
Erikson, E. (1968), *Identity: Youth and Crisis.* New York:
   Norton.
Finkielkraut, A. (1988), *The Undoing of Thought*, London: The
   Claridge Press.
Finlay, A. (2001), 'Defeatism and Northern Protestant "Iden-
   tity"', *The Global Review of Ethnopolitics*, 1, 2, 3-20.
   http://www.ethnopolitics.org

30 Nationalism and Multiculturalism

FitzGerald, G. (1976) 'Ireland's Identity Problems', *Études Irelandaises*, 1, 135-142 (December).

FitzGerald, G. (1991), *All in a Life*. London: Papermak.

Foster, R. (1988), *Modern Ireland 1600-1972*, London: Penguin.

Foster R. (1989), 'Varieties of Irishness', in M. Crozier ed., *Cultural Traditions in Northern Ireland*. Belfast: Institute of Irish Studies.

Foster, R. (1992), 'Nations Yet Again' *Times Literary Supplement* (27/3/1992).

Gibbons, L. (1991), Challenging the Canon: Revisionism and Cultural Criticism, in S. Deane ed., *The Field Day Anthology of Irish Writing, Volume III*. Derry: Field Day Publications.

Gibbons, L. (1994), 'Dialogue Without the Other? A Reply to Francis Mulhern', in *Radical Philosophy*, 67, 28-31.

Gibbons, L. (1996), *Transformations in Irish Culture*. Cork: Field Day and Cork University Press.

Gibbons, L. (2002), 'The Global Cure? History, Therapy and the Celtic Tiger', in P. Kirby, L. Gibbons, and M. Cronin, eds, *Reinventing Ireland: Culture, Society and the Global Economy*. London: Pluto.

Gleason, P. (1983), 'Identifying Identity: A Semantic History', *The Journal of American History*, 69, 4, 910-931.

Goldberg, D.T. ed. (1994), *Multiculturalism A Critical Reader*. Cambridge Massachusetts: Blackwell.

Government of the United Kingdom of Great Britain and Northern Ireland and Government of Ireland (1998), *Agreement Reached in the Multi-Party Negotiations*. Belfast.

Hederman, M.P. and Kearney, R. (1982), 'Editorial: A Sense of Nation', in *The Crane Bag Book of Irish Studies (1977-1981)*. Dublin: Blackwater Press, 92-4 (originally published in *The Crane Bag* 1977, 1, 2).

Howe, S. (2000) *Ireland and Empire, Colonial Legacies in Irish History and Culture*. Oxford: Oxford University Press.

Joppke, C. and Lukes, S. eds, (1999) *Multicultural Questions*. Oxford: Oxford University Press.

Kiberd, D. (1998), 'Romantic Ireland's Dead and Gone: the English-speaking Republic as the Crucible of Modernity', *The Times Literary Supplement*, 4967 (121/6/98).

Kiberd, D. (2000), *Irish Classics*. London: Granta Books.

Kiberd, D. (2001), Strangers in Their Own Country: Multi-Culturalism in Ireland, in A. Pollak ed., *Multi-Culturalism: The View From The Two Irelands*. Cork: Cork University Press and the Centre for Cross-Border Studies.

Kymlicka, W. (1995) *Multicultural Citizenship: A Liberal Theory of Minority Rights*. Oxford: Oxford University Press.

Langhammer, M. (2000) 'Assembly Voting System Referred to Human Rights Commission', *Labour Press Release*, (11/10/00).

Lee, J.J. (1989), *Ireland 1912-1985 Politics and Society*. Cambridge: Cambridge University Press.

Lloyd, D. (1993), *Anomalous States Irish Writing and the Postcolonial Moment*. Dublin: Lilliput.

Lyons, F.S.L. (1979), *Culture and Anarchy in Ireland 1890-1939*. Oxford: Oxford University Press.

Mulhern, F. (1998), *The Present Lasts a Long Time, Essays in Cultural Politics*. Cork: Cork University Press in Association with Field Day.

Murphy, J.A. (1976) 'Identity Change in the Republic of Ireland', *Études* Irlandaises, 1,143-158 (December 1976).

Nic Craith, M. (2002), *Plural Identities, Singular Narratives: The Case of Northern Ireland*. New York: Berghan Books.

O'Halloran, C. (1987) *Partition and the Limits of Irish Nationalism: an Ideology Under Stress*. Dublin: Gill and Macmillan.

O'Toole F. (1999), 'Redefining Irishness Within a Mixed-Race Society', in *The Irish Times* 23/7/99.

O'Toole F. (2000), 'Green, White and Black: Race and Irish Identity', in R. Lentin ed., *Proceedings of a Seminar on Emerging Irish Identities*, MPhil in Ethnic and Racial Studies, Department of Sociology, Trinity College, Dublin, 27/11/99.

Sailer, S.S. (1999), 'Translating Tradition: An Interview with Declan Kiberd', in *Jouvert* 4, 1. www.http//152.1.96.5/ jouvert /v4i1/kib.

Somasundram, M. (1999), *Reimagining Sri Lanka: Northern Ireland Insights*. Columbo: ICES Publications.

Whyte, J. (1990), *Interpreting Northern Ireland*. Oxford: Clarendon.

Wievorka, M. (1995), *The Arena of Racism*. London Sage.

Wilson, R. (2003) 'Am I Me or Am I One of Them? Who has rights: groups or people?' *Fortnight*, 414, 11 (May 2003).

Wright, S. (1998), 'The Politicisation of "Culture"', *Anthropology Today* 14, 1, 7-15.

2. Pre-Political Groundwork and Cultural Identity: the Northern Ireland Experience

MAURNA CROZIER

Political transformation need not refer only to the contemplated, desired or even pending, re-drawing of national boundaries, but may also relate to the changes, or transformations, of what determines political entities, and the relationships between them: not only lines on a map, but also shared values and aspirations for institutionalised standards, held in common. This chapter is concerned with political transformation in this global sense; that is, not in terms of the maintenance or transformation of the twenty-six or thirty-two county state of Ireland, but in terms of what Allolio-Näcke and Kalscheuer (see Wadham-Smith 2002: 13) call 'fading national boundaries'.

Since the early 1990s, cultural exchanges have multiplied massively. Obviously, the reduced price and increased ease of air travel has facilitated both pleasure journeys and the migration of skilled and unskilled workers. Most significantly, every available method of transport has been accessed by desperate imperilled people, in their flight from terrorism, ethnic cleansing and civil strife.

The mass migration of refugees may be one of the outstanding features of the twentieth century when its history is written because of the pain and suffering which it has involved, but the exchange of cultures in a virtual sense through television, the internet – and all their offshoots – is probably even greater. And both real and virtual exchanges are promoted by the global market, which not only uses labour for production on one side of the world to make goods for sale on the other, but now also employs staff on one continent for the service industries on another. Consumer complaints in Ireland, for example, may be dealt with by a call centre in India, and telephone inquiries are dealt with on many continents. Both the transnational companies and international aid agencies are now involved in training their staff to work in other cultures: Australian tourist workers

33

are sent on courses to help improve their service to Japanese holiday-makers, Zambian policemen go on seminars in Vienna to prepare them for work in Bosnia and health professionals learn how to adapt Western and European health strategies to promote HIV prevention programmes in Africa.

These cultural exchanges are across international boundaries, and involve different races, ethnicities and faith-communities. But the prevalence of conflict and intolerance underlines the fact that greater exchange, whether of individuals or groups, does not guarantee an increase in mutual understanding – or the peaceful behaviour which might be the outcome of such understanding. And divisions within internal boundaries continue to exist: in Ireland the differences between the Catholic and Protestant communities reached murderous dimensions at the end of the twentieth century, and divisions in many other parts of the world intensified during the same period, as the great communist bloc crumbled (the former Yugoslavia and Czechoslovakia providing, respectively, tragic and just about sustainable models). Simultaneously, the EU has provided the base for smaller identities to gain confidence: minority language groups are one example. So even a benign approach – designed to address rights issues or recognition of mother tongues – has also served to emphasise difference.

WORLD WIDE INITIATIVES

As these wide examples suggest, both private enterprise and government have strong motives for sharing knowledge about intercultural exchange between countries, and for sharpening understanding about the increased pluralism, or multiculturalism, within state boundaries. Those motives may be Machiavellian or benign, and this chapter is mainly concerned with (apparently) benign initiatives which aim to establish a code of agreed worldwide values. The most fundamental of these is human rights. Efforts to agree a basic code of rights are ongoing in Ireland, North and South.

While there are endless legal complications and certain clauses are disputed by those with particular perspectives, the most difficult issue which is faced by those drafting the necessary legislation is the issue of individual rights as opposed to group rights. Most international codes can, and do, only deal with the rights of the individual, but such a separation rarely represents the needs of real people, who are all, of course, both individuals and family members, and also members of belief, ideological, linguistic and workforce groups, and want their rights in these contexts to be recognised too.

Within states there may be a raft of equality and fair employment legislation, in order to ensure that the general principles of human rights are worked out in the fields of employment, education and training, housing, and general access to resources. This has primarily been instigated to address issues of race, ethnicity and faith, where in many cases inequality of opportunity has been institutionalised (as was the case in Northern Ireland), or is established by practice (as has been the case in Ireland more generally). Currently one of the major issues in Britain and Ireland is that of the fair inclusion of recent immigrants from many different cultures and of those of varied ability.

Because of the complexity of group rights, human rights and equality legislation focus on the individual rather on the community, and within any state there seems to be a need to balance this by an emphasis on responsibility – though this cannot be enshrined in law. This compensatory surge is resulting in the growth of 'citizenship' programmes, principally in the formal education sector. This is no longer primarily a vehicle for promoting the virtue of the nation state, as it was in the not too distant past; rather, it is often sponsored by those seeking to give some shared perspectives to multicultural communities. My (lay) reading of these initiatives is as follows. Human rights are what one needs. Equality is what one should have. Citizenship enshrines the responsibilities we have to each other. But this new emphasis on citizenship may not be sufficient, for within state boundaries there may be many different languages, contested histories, contrary perspectives – in other words, cultural identities – and it is at the level of personal and group exchange and daily interaction that the diversity of resident communities must be publicly recognised and addressed.

ADDRESSING DIVERSITY: CULTURAL DIVERSITY INITIATIVES IN NORTHERN IRELAND

Although the first Fair Employment Act became law in Northern Ireland in 1976, and the second in 1989, there had been no government initiatives to address the general lack of knowledge of 'other' communities. Such ignorance was fostered and encouraged by segregated education, exclusive cultural and sporting activities, demographic division, a largely single-identity police force, and all the other familiar manifestations of a divided community.

The Cultural Traditions Group, which later became the Cultural Diversity Group, was brought together in Northern Ireland in 1988, shortly after the mandatory cross-curricular themes of Education for Mutual Understanding and Cultural Heritage were introduced into all schools. School education in Northern Ireland is almost totally segregated, with state schools having a predominance of Protestant pupils, and Catholic schools catering for the majority of Catholic children of school age. Even today, only five per cent of children attend integrated schools, and the cross-curricular themes were an attempt to ensure that children separated by education had an opportunity to learn more about the culture of the other community. It was supported by many programmes which encouraged children from different schools to work together on projects. These school programmes involved both a cognitive and a contact approach to intercultural understanding.

The Cultural Traditions Group and, later, the Cultural Diversity Group, was tasked to work with the out-of-school community. It was considered that attempts to inform and interest school students in the 'other' community should be complimented by efforts to provide opportunities in the wider community: there was little point in widening the perceptions of children if they were going to be dismissed by their parents and older siblings at home.

The Cultural Traditions Group had been supporting programmes which involved expression (of cultural identity), education, exploration of traditions (one's 'own' and that of the other), exchange (of ideas and people) and debate for some time before there was much discussion in academic literature about ways of promoting attitudinal change, which is the aim of most cultural diversity initiatives.

In 1997, Audigier suggested that to change attitudes and challenge the received wisdom which is embedded in cultural identity, cognitive, experiential and affective approaches are necessary. This multi-dimensional approach is necessary because people engage with new knowledge and experience in different ways, depending on their life experience, their cultural background, their age, or even their mood. For this reason cultural diversity projects or events should offer the opportunity for thinking, doing and feeling, so engaging both the knowledge and the attitudes of participants.

The cultural diversity programme in Northern Ireland – rather instinctively at the start – tried to engage people at each of these levels. It provided funding for resources in the form of documentary publications that shed light on the history of particular aspects of life in the North of Ireland, including Purdie (1990), Bardon (1992), Loftus (1994), Jarman (1999), and McIvor (1996). It supported television and radio programmes which opened up the perspectives prevalent in one community to the other community[1], and funded CDs, animated films and interactive videos[2] which were designed to stimulate group discussion. There was also support for community activity, including local history societies,

---

[1] Examples include *Plain Tales From Northern Ireland; Love Across The Barricades; Whose Music?; Kicking with Both Feet.*

[2] Examples include *Symbols; Ship of Fools, Myth and Memory.*

resident groups, women's and youth organisations, which created occasions for meeting members of the 'other' community.

The 'affective' approach was perhaps best achieved through the arts – plays, exhibitions, and musical groups – which opened the opportunity for empathy with the views of 'others'[3].

I would suggest that the inclusion of newcomers to any part of Ireland needs the same sort of approach: long-term residents need more knowledge of the cultures of those who have just arrived. They also need to know of the history and experience of those who have been in Ireland for some time: the Jewish communities in Dublin and Belfast; the Dutch in Kerry; the Italians in Derry; the Pakistani community in Cookstown; the Chinese in Limerick – and so on.

The general aim of the cultural diversity programme in Northern Ireland was to increase knowledge of the 'other', to provide opportunities for safe contact and to challenge stereotypes, but never to overrule or to eliminate difference. As one of the founding members remarked: 'It's not our business to turn Orange and Green into a sludgy brown'.

In the early 1990s there was a strand of argument which maintained that acknowledging differences served to reinforce stereotypes rather than to challenge them. The more contemporary twenty-first century version of this argument is to consider that teaching about cultural differences does not comply with notions of political correctness that ignore difference and concentrate on individual equalities. It may seem surprising that these ideas survived Glazer and Moynihan's (1970) seminal, and widely discussed, argument that the 'mosaic' not the 'melting pot' was the reality of life in the US.

As a local example of how shared goals and common ground does not eliminate difference, one might cite the fail-

---

[3]   Plays include *The Dock Ward Play* and *Hang All the Harpers*, exhibitions include *Popular Belief*, *The Languages of Ulster* and *History Here and Now*; musical groups include *Pan Arts* and *Different Drums of Ireland*.

ure of the middle ground in Northern Ireland to have any serious political impact. My own perspective, as a worker and policy adviser in the field of cultural diversity in Northern Ireland, is that it is arrogant to work *exclusively* on common ground, while people are still being murdered as a consequence of their perceived differences.

It has been noticeable that in times of despair or celebration in Northern Ireland people have repaired to the places of their fundamental allegiance: all the different churches were filled to capacity after the Omagh bomb, and the flags which were waved at the time of the ceasefires were not the doves of the community relations and peace people but the traditional symbols of partisan affiliation.

So while legislation in the area of human rights and equality is crucial in forming the *base* for a peaceful multicultural world and plural societies, for the *acceptance* that those with diverse cultural identities must learn to live together, it still seems essential that intercultural learning is fostered, at both inter- and intra-national levels.

CULTURAL IDENTITY AND CONFLICT

It is much too simple to say that conflict, in Northern Ireland or anywhere else, is caused by cultural difference or confusions about cultural identity. For one thing, such a perspective focuses on the detail of action or expression, not the underlying assumptions, and interprets aspects of behaviour in accordance with the cultural assumptions of the observer or, indeed, the analyst, not those of the actor. Some examples of the way behaviour can be misinterpreted will serve to illustrate the point.

In the aftermath of the Los Angeles Riots in 1992, which involved considerable conflict between African-American and Asian-American groups, Bailey (1997) analysed the encounters between Korean shopkeepers and their African-American customers, and those same shopkeepers with their Korean customers. The African-Americans had interpreted the restraint and unsmiling service in the shops as hostile racism, but it turned out that the shopkeepers were just as brief and unsociable with Korean customers. The behaviour which had been seen as hostile was little more than a difference of social norms of interaction, but it had significantly fuelled the subsequent racial tension.

More flippantly, the different expectations of the English and the German when they ask 'how are you?' can reinforce the stereotypes: a flippant English answer, 'I'm OK', may seem demeaning to the concerned German questioner, while the intimate health details given by the German generally elicit a detached English nod, which seems pretty unsympathetic to the German.

More seriously, I would refer to one of the assumptions underlying most of the peace initiatives in Ireland over the last twenty years, which has been based on the very capitalist assumption that economic prosperity will 'loosen' or transform cultural and political divisions. This assumption is also reinforced by the factual detail, that is, that most sectarian violence takes place in economically deprived areas of Belfast, just as most drug lawlessness takes place in the poorest estates in Dublin, and not in the suburbs. These facts seem to have been enough to obliterate the manifold evidence world wide that such disputes are unaffected by prosperity. The economic argument propounded by the apartheid regime in South Africa, which suggested that well fed and educated Africans would not challenge the white state was manifestly unfounded. Surely it will not have survived the Twin Towers tragedy in New York on 9/11, though the initial assumptions after that terrible incident, were that it was poor uneducated men who had been bullied into being the perpetrators, a conclusion which proved to be completely unfounded in reality. Similarly, despite the often useful investment which has been made in the 'tough' areas of Belfast, there is little or no evidence that it has softened loyalist or republican attitudes.

CONCLUSION – INTERCULTURAL PERSPECTIVES

Cultural identity is a basic characteristic of human society. The recognition of multiculturalism involves acknowledging that there are many different perspectives, both within and between states. Interculturalism requires us to take them into account, at local, national and international levels. International business has used intercultural concepts for years in the interests of profit (think of Coca Cola advertisements in different cultural milieu) and intercultural specialists are beginning to move into strategic planning and marketing in global companies. Public administration has been slower to put them into practice. There have been small initiatives in some divided societies, including Northern Ireland, though for the most part they have been seen chiefly as relevant to, or the responsibility of, education, rather than as an agenda relevant throughout all organisations and communities.

This is not to suggest that all conflict is cultural, but lack of intercultural knowledge and exchange means that when problems arise they tend to be attributed to the other group's bad intentions, a scenario very familiar to people living in Ireland, and cultural identity is used as a label to claim victimhood, to pin blame, to excuse violence, to behave triumphantly. How cultural groups perceive each other will ultimately determine all political transformations: those which involve the international relationships of major power blocs, such as the Western and Muslim worlds; those which involve the realignment of boundaries and walls; and even political transformation on one smallish island, such as Ireland.

REFERENCES

Audigier, F. (1997), *Practising Cultural Diversity in Education: Project on Democracy, Human Rights, Minorities*. Strasbourg: Council for Cultural Co-operation.

Bailey, B. (1997), 'Communication of Respect in Interethnic Service Encounters', in *Language in Society*, 216, 327-356.

Bardon, J. (1992), *A History of Ulster*. Belfast: Blackstaff.

Glazer, N. and Moynihan, D.P. (1970), *Beyond the Melting Pot: the Negroes, Puerto Ricans, Jews, Italians and Irish of New York City*. London: MIT Press.

Jarman, N. (1999), *Displaying Faith: Orange, Green and Trade Union Banners in Northern Ireland*. Belfast: Institute of Irish Studies, The Queen's University of Belfast.

Loftus, B. (1994), *Mirrors: Orange and Green*. Dundrum: Picture Press.

McIvor, P. (1996) *An Ulster Wean's A to Z*. Belfast: Blackstaff with the Cultural Traditions Group.

Purdie, B. (1990), *Trouble in the Streets: the Origins of the Civil Rights Movement in Northern Ireland*. Belfast: Blackstaff.

Wadham-Smith, N. (2002), Introducing SIETR (Society for Intercultural Education Training and Research), *British Studies Now* 16, 13.

3. Understanding One Another Better: Language, Conflict and Cultural Diversity

LOUIS de PAOR

In most instances of human interaction and communication, the use of a particular language can appear more or less unproblematic. A shared language can facilitate the integration and cohesion of a group or community, whose diversity in other respects can be elided or suspended, temporarily or indefinitely, through the agreed use of one language rather than another. If it cannot finally reconcile or entirely resolve pronounced differences within and between communities, an agreed language can at least provide a vehicle for the articulation and negotiation and, occasionally, the accommodation, of such differences. The precariousness of that facility, and the extent to which language and politics are inextricably linked, becomes apparent if a second language is introduced to such a situation, without prior approval or agreement. If, for instance, I were to continue this chapter in Irish, my decision would seem as needlessly provocative, exclusive, and downright discourteous as my acceptance of English as a proper vehicle for present purposes seems unmotivated and unproblematic, a matter of social courtesy and discursive convenience rather than one of political expediency. In any event, where cultural identity and political allegiance are vigorously contested and the use of one language is privileged over another, the choice, or imposition, of that language rather than any other is likely to be problematic.

This chapter will consider a number of extreme instances of cultural alienation provoked by a conflict of language and the violence that ensues when an individual or group considers its very existence to be threatened by the difference of others. It will consider the extent to which both minorities and majorities are susceptible to such experiences and are likely to resort to exaggerated responses based on a perception of their own vulnerability. Examples will be drawn from both Australia and Ireland, from historical and contemporary experience, to suggest how language is implicated in the processes of power and exclusion and how a more generous and inclusive approach to cultural and linguistic diversity might strengthen the coherence of individual communities without compromising or undermining the separate collective identity of those who share a different set of cultural values and practices.

In his epic history of transportation to Australia, *The Fatal Shore*, Robert Hughes recounts the career of one of the earliest gangs of bushrangers in Van Diemen's Land. The gang comprised two Irishmen, Scanlan and Brown, and an Englishman, Richard Lemon, who took such exception to his companions speaking to one another in Irish that he shot Scanlan dead at their campsite while Brown was away hunting kangaroos:

> He then strung up the corpse by the heels on a gum tree, as if he were hanging a "boomer" (big kangaroo) for skinning. "Now Brown," he laconically observed when his partner returned, "as there are only two of us, we shall understand one another better for the future" (1988: 227-8).

It is an extraordinary but nonetheless exemplary account of the violence that can be generated by the most extreme form of cultural alienation where difference is perceived as a physical as well as a psychological threat to one's very existence. An uneasy stability is then restored by the brutal suppression of that fatal difference.

While the numerical superiority and presumed ethnic solidarity of the two Irishmen might be cited in mitigation of Lemon's murderous intolerance, the same could hardly be said of the Australian government's response to the proposed visit of the radical Czechoslovakian writer and pacifist Egon Kisch in November 1934. Kisch's reputation as a progressive and innovative journalist, alert to the polemical possibilities of his chosen occupation, is founded on a style of reportage which foregrounds the author's involvement and engagement with the subject of his writings. By the time the 'raging reporter' arrived in Australia, he had already published extensively on his experiences as a corporal in the Austrio-Hungarian army in World War I, and as a political activist in China and Vienna. Having been invited to speak at the World Conference Against War and Fascism in Melbourne, Kisch arrived by ship in Fremantle, Western Australia on 6 November 1934. He was refused permission to disembark and subsequently broke his leg while attempting to jump ship in Melbourne. Under the terms of the Immigration Restriction Act of 1901, he was then required to take a dictation test in a European language. The act was the first piece of legislation passed by an Australian government after federation and a crucial element of the White Australia Policy designed to deter non-European immigration. In effect, it provided for an almost complete restriction on the entry of those to whom it applied as the language chosen for the test was at the discretion of the appointed officials and the failure rates remained extraordinarily high during the period of its operation. In 1902-1903, only forty-six of the 805 people required to take the test were successful; between 1904 and 1909, only six people passed from a total of 554.[1] While the act remained in force until 1958, no one passed the dictation test after 1909. Although fluent in several European languages, Kisch failed the dictation test set for him in Scots Gaelic. Following a successful appeal to the High Court, which ruled that Gaelic was not a European language, he travelled extensively in Australia before leaving in March 1935 (Kisch, 1969). That the Australian Prime Minister of the day was an Irish Australian, Joe Lyons, compounds the irony of the story.

The White Australia Policy and its farcical application in this instance indicate the limits of an approach that would insist on a single exclusive definition of national identity, a definition that can only be guaranteed by rigid adherence to prescribed cultural practises and the suppression of unau-

---

[1] A copy of the act along with an account of its application and significance is available at http://www.foundingdocs.gov.au/text_only/places/cth/cth4ii.htm. Accessed 26/11/03.

thorised expressions of difference. It is worth noting that despite the position of Irish, set down as the first official language of the state in the constitution of the Republic of Ireland, successive governments of apparently different political persuasions have refused all opportunities presented since Ireland's entry to the EEC in 1972 to have Irish declared an official working European language. While this is not the first time that Irish has been excluded from the corridors of power, it is nonetheless a spectacular example of 'cultural cringe' when a democratically elected Irish government repeats a pattern of exclusion previously associated with a hostile colonial power. The perception that Irish politicians are more alert to the rhetorical importance of Irish as a token of cultural difference than to its actual potential as a vehicle for the articulation of a shared and distinctive identity is confirmed by their reluctance – hitherto – to insist on its inclusion as a working language of the EU[2].

The legal repudiation of Gaelic as a European language by an Australian court in the case of Egon Kisch is a useful reminder that the authority invested in a particular language is determined by the political context in which that language is used rather than by any absolute value inherent in the language itself. It is worth remembering that for Dáibhidh Ó Bruadair and other remnants of precolonial aristocratic Gaelic Ireland in the seventeenth century, the use of English, or at least of particular forms of English, among the Cromwellian invaders was seen as further confirmation of the lowly social origins of the 'fat-rumped jeerers ... with shaven jaws and English talk and braggart accent ... clownish upstarts ... veterans of cheese and pottage' (Ó Bruadair, 1910: 37). By contrast, comprehension of the more sophisticated forms of literary Irish among the poet's patrons was interpreted as a measure of their continued social standing despite their waning political influence.

---

[2]   In an apparent volte-face, the Irish government announced in July 2004 tht it would be seeking official status for Irish as a working language in the EU.

Perhaps the most striking instance of the connection between language, politics and identity is provided by the Statutes of Kilkenny (1366), which, amongst its many cultural sanctions and prohibitions, ordained that 'every Englishman do use the English language'. As Tony Crowley has pointed out, there is a nice irony here in the fact that the statutes themselves were written in Norman French, an acknowledgement of the minority position of the language they were designed to protect (2000: 12). The rhetorical and legal power thereby invested in English indicates the extent to which the early architects of colonialism in Ireland were alert to the threat posed by cultural hybridity to their political ambitions and the necessity for insisting on a single language of privilege and distinction. Although unsuccessful in the short term in preventing the cultural assimilation of the Anglo-Normans, the Statutes of Kilkenny confirm the colonisers' sensitivity to the potential of language as a vehicle for both the exercise and the subversion or political power.

The dual potential of language for both colonisers and their adversaries is a recurrent motif in Irish cultural and political history. The colonial suspicion evident in Edmund Spenser's remark that 'the speech being Irish, the heart must needs be Irish' (cited in Crowley. 2000: 49) is transformed into an affirmation of cultural nationalism in Pádraig Mac Piarais's aspiration towards an Ireland that would be 'not free merely, but Gaelic as well, not Gaelic merely, but free as well' (Pearse, 1966: 135). Despite their ideological differences, Spenser and Pearse are apparently agreed on the subversive potential of an alternative language where national identity and political allegiance are violently contested. The vehemence of their respective arguments might also be taken as an indication of the perceived weakness of the particular culture or language they would each protect in the very different circumstances in which they found themselves. While Spenser's poems and polemical writing might be seen to provide a cornerstone for received notions of English civility, he has also been described by one of the most perceptive scholars of Irish as a 'sweet poet and bloodthirsty adventurer' (O'Rahilly, 1972: 8). If his participation in the massacre at Dún an Óir in November 1580 provides damning evidence of an abuse of extreme power, the burning of his home at Kilcolman in North Cork in 1598 during Hugh O'Neill's rebellion is a useful reminder of the occasional fragility of the colonial enterprise in the late sixteenth century and of the vulnerability of even the most prominent colonial adventurers at the time. In that light, his apparently triumphalist and exclusive views on the Irish language might be re-read as a much more ambivalent document, forged out of an all-too-familiar siege mentality where the real or imagined threat of capitulation and cultural absorption is such that only the complete annihilation of the detested other can guarantee the survival of one's own precarious sense of identity.

While historians and cultural critics have expressed unease at the contentious and sometimes prescriptive definitions of early cultural nationalists, it is worth pointing out that in each of the instances mentioned thus far, both the resistance to difference and the insistence on its retention occur in situations of extreme pressure where each of the protagonists fears the threat posed by the other to its own cherished and besieged identity. There is also an imbalance of power involved as the more powerful interest in each instance seeks to preserve itself by diminishing or obliterating the less powerful but nonetheless threatening other. In each case, the perceived threat of apparently irreconcilable cultural difference leads ultimately to physical violence on behalf of one or other of the identities in conflict. In defence of cultural nationalists, it should be said that their insistence on language as an arbiter of cultural and political integrity is itself a reaction to sustained colonial pressure that would obliterate a separate Irish culture so that, in the words of Sir John Davies (*A Discovery of the True Causes Why Ireland Was Never Entirely Subdued*, 1612) 'we may conceive and hope that the next generation will in tongue and heart and every way else become English so that there will be no difference or distinction but the Irish Sea betwixt us' (cited in Crowley 2000: 60). Pearse's insistence on an Irish political identity grounded in cultural difference is a reaction then against English colonial intolerance. His aspiration towards an Irish national identity defined by political and cultural independence has, however, been exploited on occasion in very different circumstances to justify further intolerance of cultural diversity. The reactionary views of the quasi-fascist revivalist organisation Glúin na Buaidhe who railed against 'the dirty low nigger culture' of jazz-dancing in the early 1940s and of those who would now refuse entry to Eastern European and West African immigrants on the basis that it might diminish what they imagine to be 'indigenous' Irish culture are a distortion of cultural nationalism, a perversion founded on intolerance of difference and a refusal to share economic, social and political power. As Myles na gCopaleen remarked of the street orators of Glúin na Buaidhe, what is most painful about such exhortations to cultural purity 'is that nobody present laughed' (Cronin, 1990: 136).

If, as has been argued by other contributors to this volume, the acknowledgement of difference enshrined in the Good Friday Agreement is incapable of precipitating an easy acceptance of conflicting identities among communities in the North of Ireland, it is nonetheless a generous and progressive model from which political, cultural and community leaders in the rest of the island have much to learn. There is very little evidence in the Republic of Ireland of any 'top-down multiculturalism' as both urban and rural communities are left to deal with the challenges of inmigration without the benefit of informed and sensitive political leadership and, more importantly, the organised administrative, social, and educational structures that might facilitate inclusion and mitigate the more negative aspects of involuntary integration. Despite justifiable criticism of the GFA, it is remarkable that two sovereign governments should waive what might previously have been insisted on as an inalienable right to command allegiance from the two communities in conflict, thereby disallowing each community's 'right' to bludgeon the other into submission on behalf of the state, or force them to a prescribed conformity. Against the historical backdrop of protracted conflict, justified on both sides by appeal to the authority of a single legitimate state, the notion of alternative or dual allegiance is a strategically generous as well as a practical and creative response to an apparently intractable conflict between embattled and hostile communities.

In terms of cultural production, and the more benign possibilities generated by conflict and difference, it is worth remembering that some of the most productive periods in Irish literature followed from the integration, however reluctant and traumatic, of powerful influences from abroad and that the assimilation of even the most hostile of such influences is characteristic of Irish culture at its most self-confident and adaptive. The courtly love poems of the medieval period, for instance, are a by-product of cultural exchange between Anglo-Norman and Gaelic Irish literature and culture while early Irish literature, following the introduction of Christianity, shows clear evidence of detailed knowledge of classical European literature as indeed does the court poetry of medieval Ireland. In anticipating the necessary conditions for the emergence of a modern literature in Irish in the early twentieth century, Pádraig Mac Piarais insisted on the necessity of a dual approach whereby writers in Irish would be as familiar with the best of contemporary European practice as they were with earlier precedents in the Irish tradition:

> Two influences go into the making of every artist, apart from his own personality, if indeed personality is not in the main only the sum of these influences: the influence of his ancestors and that of his contemporaries. Irish literature if it [is] to grow, must get into contact on the one hand with its own past and on the other with the mind of contemporary Europe (MacPiarais, 1906: 6; see also O'Brien, 1968: 31).

Pearse's prescription for a new literature was extraordinarily prescient. In the development of prose narrative, two of the most important Irish writers of the twentieth century, Tomás Ó Criomhthain and Máirtín Ó Cadhain, were provoked to radical innovations in technique by their own readings of the work of the Russian author, Maxim Gorky (see Nic Craith 1988: 66-72 and de Paor 1990: 51-54). Similarly, the influence of Eliot and Yeats on Máirtín Ó Direáin, and of Blake, Beckett, Ibsen, Yeats, Hopkins and others on Seán Ó Ríordáin was crucial to their poetic development (see Nic Ghearailt, 1988). More recently, the integration of American, European, Indian, African and Asian influences is a significant feature in the contemporary renaissance of poetry in Irish and is evident in the work of writers as diverse as Michael Davitt, Liam Ó Muirthile, Nuala Ní Dhomhnaill, Biddy Jenkinson, Gabriel Rosenstock, Cathal Ó Searcaigh, Colm Breathnach and Gearóid MacLochlainn. The mediation of cultural transfer through creative writing suggests that the dynamic tension between competing cultures can provide an opportunity for the accommodation and integration of difference. At the same time, it is distressingly evident from the near obliteration of Irish and its literature that such a negotiation can only be sustained where there is something approaching parity between the contributing cultures. The destructive possibilities of such an engagement, where one language is almost entirely dominant, is as pertinent to the discussion of newer minority languages introduced through recent immigration as it is to the contemporary position of Irish.

If the flexibility of Irish culture during earlier phases of its development is demonstrated by its accommodation of influences from abroad, the insistence on exclusion of foreign influence in language, sport or any other cultural arena is characteristic of periods of cultural and political uncertainty. In that respect at least, the cultural intolerance which has become evident during the rise and rise of the Celtic Tiger is something of an anomaly. Given the repeated advice of economists that a substantial amount of immigrant labour will be required to sustain Ireland's economic success in the future, it is difficult to identify the particular threat to our national identities posed by the recent influx of immigrants. At the risk of overstating the all too obvious, the extreme violence that preceded the cultural assimilation of Vikings, Normans and English has not been a feature of recent in-

ward migration. Poverty and powerlessness are as characteristic of recent immigrants as wealth and military aggression were of earlier arrivals. It is a strangely hopeful paradox
that the social and economic bias evident in some of the
more extreme negative responses to new migrants may be
more significant in the long run, and more amenable to
resolution, than the irredeemably racist aspect of such discrimination.

Interestingly, the hostility most immediately evident in
racist assaults and murders does not extend to every aspect
of the incoming cultures. A quick glance at the glossy sup-
plements to our weekend newspapers suggests that alternative cuisine, music, and fashion are apparently acceptable
while different religious practices and languages remain
problematic. While the historical context and contemporary
political circumstances are very different in the two jurisdic-
tions in Ireland, there may be some hope to be gleaned from
the ongoing success of Australia's multicultural policies, despite the viciousness of the Howard government's response
to recent immigration. The gradual introduction of European
and non-European names among the Irish and British in the
ranks of prominent public Australians in the area of politics,
broadcasting, literature, and sport suggests a degree of social mobility over time which may anticipate a similar im-
provement in the situation of recently arrived immigrants to
the island of Ireland. On the other hand, the substitution of
one ethnic group for another at the lower end of the socio-
economic ladder, evident in the surnames of those killed in
accidents in the workplace, provides a more distressing indication of social change in a multicultural society where more
recent arrivals continue to be amongst the most vulnerable.

In the face of so much confusion, prevarication and cow-
ardice in public discourse, it is heartening to report occasional signs of a more creative and generous response to the
challenge posed by inward migration. In an address to the
youth organisation Ógras in Galway in February 2002,
Tomás MacRuairí, president of Conradh na Gaeilge (The
Gaelic League), welcomed the linguistic diversity that

characterises contemporary Dublin and argued that Irish language activists' agitation on behalf of a minority language should predispose them to a more pluralist approach to cultural identity. Journalists including Pól Ó Muirí of *The Irish Times* and *Foinse*'s[3] Fachtna Ó Drisceoil have exhorted those involved in the language movement to be proactive in their response to immigrants, to use their own experience as activists on behalf of a linguistic minority to insist on equal rights for newer and more vulnerable minorities in Ireland. Perhaps the most interesting perspective is provided by Alex Hijmans, a Dutch national who came to Ireland in the mid-nineties, learned Irish and went on to take a postgraduate course in applied communications through Irish at the National University of Ireland, Galway. Having spent a number of years as staff journalist with *Foinse*, Hijmans worked on current affairs programmes with Radio na Gaeltachta and TG4, Irish language radio and TV stations respectively, before opening his own café, Bananaphoblacht (Banana republic), perhaps the only genuinely tri-lingual café in Ireland. In an editorial written during his time as editor of the literary and current affairs journal *Comhar*, Hijmans described his own experience of acceptance among Irish-speaking communities in the Gaeltacht and in the Galltacht once he had attained competence in the language. His primary sense of belonging in Ireland derived from a shared language rather than any other form of solidarity or integration:

Ag caint ó mo thaithí féin mar dhuine a tháinig go hÉirinn ó thír eile, is túisce a ghlactar leat mar bhall iomlán den tsochaí má bhíonn tuiscint agat ar nósanna agus teanga na tíre – go mórmhór más í an Ghaeilge atá i gceist. Chuideodh sé leis na teifigh féin agus leis an sochaí trí chéile dá ndéanfaí teifigh a tharraingt isteach sa chultúr Gaelach: bheadh sochaí na hÉireann níos féinmhuiníní as a chultúr féin agus bheadh na teifigh níos féinmhuiníní sa tsochaí. Seans mór gur fearr an

---

3   *Foinse* is an Irish national weekly newspaper

tuiscint a bheadh ag pobal na Gaeilge uaireanta ar chás na dteifeach ná ag dreamanna eile (Hijmans, 2000: 4).

(Speaking from my own experience as someone who came to Ireland from another country, one is more quickly accepted as a full member of the society if one has an understanding of the practices and language of the country - this applies particularly to Irish. It would be helpful for the refugees themselves and for the broader community if they were drawn into the world of Gaelic culture: Irish society would thereby be more self-confident of its own culture and refugees would be more self-confident within Irish society. It may be that the Irish-speaking community sometimes has a better appreciation of the refugees' predicament than other groups have).[4]

His argument that Irish-speakers should be in the vanguard when it comes to integrating recent arrivals to Ireland is predicated on a stated belief that those who speak Irish have a more secure and stable sense of their own cultural identity and should therefore have less to fear from the new possibilities generated by emerging forms of cultural difference. The editorial went on to urge Irish-language organisations to take the initiative in providing opportunities for cultural integration of immigrants and refugees. Hijmans himself has led the way in that regard, along with Siobhán Ní Ghuithín, a project director with Conradh na Gaeilge in Galway, by establishing a class for immigrants in the Galway area in association with the One World Centre. Crucial to both Hijmans's and Ní Ghuithín's sense of the possibilities of cultural regeneration through dialogue and mutual exchange is the need for such initiatives to be open-ended in both directions. In conjunction with the Global Music Project and the Galway Refugee Support Group, Ní Ghuithín has developed further opportunities for such two-way traffic through a series of workshops in African music and dance, as well as continuing classes in the Irish language. Preliminary discussions between language activists and immigrant support groups in Limerick have also stressed the need for

---

[4] My translation.

reciprocal exchange through dialogue between existing and newly introduced forms of cultural production rather than a unifocal approach that would result in passive assimilation of new migrants.[5]

It is easy to support initiatives which encourage others to make the effort to learn or acquire aspects of our own culture. We can, for instance, applaud the cultural resilience of Fionnán MacCártha, a native of County Roscommon, who worked for a time as a schoolteacher in Omagh, Sheffield and London before emigrating to Queensland, Australia in 1918. During his time there, he wrote a collection of poems in Irish, *Amhráin Ó Dheireadh an Domhain*, which were published posthumously by An Gúm (Mac Cártha, 1953). Despite spending more than twenty years in Australia without, as he says himself, hearing as many as twenty words of Irish spoken, his poems show no trace whatsoever of his adopted country. If the poems are a rejection of the reality of his own life as a migrant, they are also an endorsement of his culture of origin and an indication of the powerful sense of security and belonging that culture provided him even in exile. We are understandably proud of those who leave Ireland out of economic necessity but do not abandon our cultural traditions and perhaps unduly so of those such as George Thomson, Robin Flower, Carl Marstrander and others who came here and immersed themselves in certain aspects of Irish culture.[6] Were the same logic to apply, we should be equally encouraging of those who have recently arrived here and would retain their own cultural practices while attempting to adapt to some of ours. In keeping with the spirit of the GFA, and with earlier precedents in Irish cultural history, alle-

---

5   I am grateful to Alex Hijmans and Siobhán Ní Ghuithín and to Máire Ní Ghráda from the Limerick branch of Conradh na Gaeilge for discussing these initiatives with me.

6   The three international scholars were instrumental in the production of a remarkable series of autobiographies produced by the Irish-speaking inhabitants of the Great Blasket off the west coast of County Kerry in the 1920s and '30s, including *An tOileánach*, *Fiche Bliain ag Fás*, and *Peig*.

giance to one culture should not require the suppression or
exclusion of another.

In light of the historical precedents for intolerance, the
alternative is regrettably neither unthinkable nor unimagin-
able. Patrick Galvin's work has always been attuned to what
the philosopher William Desmond (1990: 241) has called the
'ineluctable particular of inward thisness' in those marginalised and ostracised by the insistence on exclusive definitions of belonging. It might be useful then to conclude with a
poem of his which has a more general application beyond its
own immediate occasion. The disturbance at the heart of
'Man in the Porch' (Galvin, 1996: 41-2) is provoked by the
intrusion of a stranger whose only act of hostility is his apparent incomprehension of, or unwillingness to accept, the
overtures made to include him within the community at
whose threshold he has arrived uninvited. The normalisation
of the community's response in Galvin's poem is as disturb-
ingly persuasive as the gruesome story from nineteenth-
century Australia with which we began while the disarming
intimacy of the anonymous spokesperson's address to the
reader presumes on our sympathy so that we are implicated
by our silence and apparent impotence in what follows:

Man on the Porch

In the beginning

We didn't ask who he was
Or what he was doing there
On our front porch
Staring at us

But
You can take so much of a man
Who sits on the front porch
Staring at you

And in the end
We questioned him.

He made no answer.
We made food
Laid it out on a tray
In front of him
And it was good food

But he pushed it aside
And continued to sit there
On our front porch
Staring at us.
We thought he was mad
Or spoke a different language from us.

We made signs in the air.

We drew pictures on the ground
Friendly pictures
Of birds and animals
And lovers kissing under trees.

But
He said nothing
And made no mark
That he understood.

He just sat there on our front porch
Staring at us.

We thought we were mad.

We felt foolish
Standing there
Making signs in the air
And drawing pictures on the ground.

We told him to move.
It wasn't his front porch
It was ours
And we told him that

But he still sat there on our front porch
Staring at us

So we killed him.

We took him to our river
Tied two stones round his neck
And pushed him
Under the water.
We felt safer then – For a time.

REFERENCES

Cronin, A. (1990), *No Laughing Matter: The Life and Times of Flann O'Brien.* London: Paladin.
Crowley, T. (2000), *The Politics of Language in Ireland 1366-1922: A Sourcebook.* London and New York: Routledge.
Davies, J. (1612), *A Discovery of the True Causes Why Ireland Was Never Entirely Subdued.*
de Paor, L. (1990), 'Maxim Gorky, Máirtín Ó Cadhain agus Riastradh na Scéalaíochta', *Comhar* (Nollaig).
Galvin, P. (1996), 'Man on the Porch', in G. Delanty and R. Welch eds, *New and Selected Poems of Patrick Galvin.* Cork: Cork University Press, 41-2.
Desmond, W. (1990), *Philosophy and its Others: Ways of Being and Mind.* Albany: State University of New York Press.
Hijmans, A. (2000), *Comhar* (Meitheamh).
Hughes, R. (1988), *The Fatal Shore.* London: Pan Books.
Kisch, E. (1969), *Australian Landfall.* Sydney: Australasian Book Society.
MacCártha, F. (1953), *Amhráin Ó Dheireadh an Domhain.* Baile Átha Cliath: An Gúm.
MacPiarais, P. (1906), 'About Literature', *An Claidheamh Soluis,* 26 Bealtaine.
Nic Craith, M. (1988), *An tOileánach Léannta.* Baile Átha Cliath: An Clóchomhar.
Nic Ghearailt, E. (1988), *Seán Ó Ríordáin agus 'An Striapach Allúrach'.* Baile Átha Cliath: An Clóchomhar.

O'Brien, F. (1968), *Filíocht Ghaeilge na Linne Seo*, Baile Átha Cliath: An Clóchomhar.

Ó Bruadair, D. (1910), 'Créacht do dháil me im árthach galair', in *Duanaire Dháibhidh Uí Bhruadair: The Poems of David Ó Bruadair*, Rev. J.C. MacErlean S.J. ed., Irish Texts Society, London, 1, 37.

O'Rahilly, T. F. (1972), *Irish Dialects Past and Present with Chapters on Scottish and Manx*. Dublin Institute for Advanced Studies (originally published by Browne and Nolan, Dublin 1932).

Pearse, P.H. (1966), *Political Writings and Speeches*, D. Bell ed., Dublin: Talbot Press.

4. Back to the Future? The Nice Referenda and the Persistence of Irish Discourses of Autonomy

GERRY BOUCHER

The rapid changes in the Republic of Ireland's economy and society during the Celtic Tiger boom have given rise to concern about their effect on 'Irish' culture. In *Changed Utterly*, Michael O'Connell details the creation of a 'new Irish psyche' based on 'rampant consumerism and individualism' (2001: 181). The editors of *Reinventing Ireland* locate such cultural change in the Republic's 'subservient integration into ... Anglo-American informational capitalism' (Kirby *et al.* 2002: 2). To challenge these changes, they argue for political resistance by engaging 'with Ireland's past to identify resources for re-imagining and reinventing a different Ireland of the future' (2002: 2). From these authors, it would appear that Irish culture has dramatically changed for the worse. That millstone on the neck of Ireland's emergence into the 'modern' world, 'traditional' Irish culture, has finally sunk to the bottom of the Irish Sea, only to be replaced by 'postmodern' fetishes of consumption for consumption's sake and selfish selfhood. Worse still, the old enemy of 'traditional' Irish culture, Britain, has been joined in a neo-liberal double team with America, 'traditional' Irish culture's great friend, to seduce the Irish people with 'the market'.

Pity the poor Irish or rather the rich Irish who, having finally achieved economic independence to accompany their political independence, are now sunk by their own greed and selfishness. The only hope is to go back to the future, Celtic style: uncovering fragments of uncorrupted traditional 'Irishness' from the past that can be pieced together, reviving a strong Irish culture to ward off these British and American seducers. Are things really this bleak? The final death knell of the Celtic Tiger after seven years (born circa 1994, died circa 2001) allows some much-needed room for those who study things Irish to take a collective deep breath and reflect on this boom and gloom perspective of Irish cultural change. Perhaps it is better to start by looking at how some characteristics of Irish culture have not really changed and to see how these features continue to shape a contemporary 'Irish' perspective in the Republic of Ireland on traditional issues like identity, nationalism and independence in the twenty-first century.

This chapter focuses on the significance of one specific characteristic remaining the same in Irish culture: discourses of autonomy; a 'cultural survival' (Evans 1988) from Ireland's colonisation by, and integration into, the United Kingdom (UK) and the British Empire. These discourses are embedded in the 'discursive consciousness' (Giddens 1984) of the Irish people, shaping their perspective towards Ireland's external relationships. It is reproduced through the institutions and interactions of agents in daily life as one of the many 'unintended consequences' that become 'the unacknowledged conditions of further acts' (Giddens 1984: 8). These discourses of autonomy shape a contemporary concept of core and surface Irishness, reactive and proactive forms of nationalism, and attitudes towards Ireland's relationships with Britain, the US and the EU. To show the continuing relevance of discourses of autonomy to the Irish experience at the beginning of the twenty-first century, these concepts are applied to an analysis of the Nice Treaty referenda in the Republic of Ireland in June 2001 and October 2002.

IRISH DISCOURSES OF AUTONOMY

The concept of Irish discourses of autonomy emerged from the author's attempt to make sense of an apparent contradiction in interviews with fifty-four high ranking members of the Irish political elite from late 1993 to the spring of 1994[1].

---

[1]   Political elite here refers to higher level representatives of the main political parties, departments of the state and other state bodies,

The apparent contradiction was that discourses used by the political elite celebrated a strong Irish cultural autonomy that had survived through British colonisation and integration, yet they continued to perceive Irish identity, nationalism and Ireland's contemporary external relationships largely in terms of an Irish dependency culture on Britain that was formed during this same period. Specifically, their discourses were structured around a dichotomy of autonomy and dependency in which the autonomy of Irish identity, nationalism and Ireland's external relationships with UK, EU and American globalisation was constantly under threat by the loss of Irish identity, the failure of nationalism to achieve real independence and a general fear of becoming dependent again on any external actor or process of integration. In this sense, the discourses are concerned with 'the reproduction of the structures of domination' (Giddens 1984: 258) or 'power relations ... of autonomy and dependence' (1993: 243) affecting Ireland in an international context. In various guises, these concerns about autonomy can be traced back to discourses in Irish nationalism from the Gaelic Revival in the late nineteenth and early twentieth centuries and further to the Protestant Irish nation arguments of Molyneux and Swift in the late seventeenth and early eighteenth centuries (Hutchinson 1987 and Boyce 1995).

In the dominant discourse of autonomy, the Irish political elite's strategy and identity choices are expressed through a fear that Irish autonomy might be eroded by a dependency similar to the earlier dependence on Britain. From this perspective, the Irish political elite overemphasises Ireland's European integration because the EU preserves more of Ireland's political and economic autonomy relative to the country's relationships to Britain or global American transnational corporations (TNCs). One result of this strategy is that Ireland becomes susceptible to a European dependency.

This discourse of autonomy links Ireland's geographic peripherality to the country's comparative smallness and to the

partnership organisations and official international bodies with whom interviews were conducted during 1993 and 1994 (see Boucher 2001).

belief that the Republic has no viable economic options outside of the EU. This leads to a need to be politically pragmatic and 'good Europeans' in order to maximise the benefits of Ireland's relative dependence on and autonomy within
the EU. However, good Europeanness focuses on pursuing
the Irish national interest within Europe as opposed to
pooling sovereignty for the good of the European common
interest. With respect to identity choices, the Irish political
elite responds in socio-cultural terms to this fear of EU dependency by asserting the existence of a strong Irish culture
with a core Irish identity that has survived through British
colonisation of Ireland. But, this 'strong cultural identity' is
also flexible and adaptive with respect to European and Anglo-American global cultural influences, exporting Irish culture and cultural products abroad while preserving a 'core'
Irishness at home. This core Irishness recombines 'traditional' features of Irish society and culture such as Gaeli-
cism, Catholicism, agrarianism and rurality with 'modern'
features based on urbanism, secularism, liberalism and consumerism. Both the younger and older members of the Irish
political elite agree that the components of the core are in a
transitional period, reflecting a process of incorporating the
changes in Irish society that have occurred since the late
1950s.

The Irish political elite's belief in a contemporary strong
culture based on a renewed self confidence in Irishness implies that there was a period in which Irish identity expressed a lack of confidence, suggestive of the dependency
culture discussed below. For the Irish political elite, the significant point is that a process of transition has occurred
from an inward-looking to a more open Irish society and
culture. This transition from insularity to openness is explained by the members of the Irish political elite as being
the product of mainly internal socio-cultural factors such as
education, television, travelling and the return of emigrants.
By explaining Ireland's transition from an inward-looking to
an open society in this way, the elite minimise the role of
external socio-cultural influences from Britain, Europe and
the US, and retain the notion of a strong and enduring Irish

cultural identity. The 'Irishisation' of external socio-cultural influences protects the essential core while adapting surface Irishness to incorporate European and global cultural influences. In this way, the Irish political elite describes contemporary Irish identity in terms of a core/ surface construct which 'Irishises' external socio-cultural influences as opposed to constructing multiple identities or cultural hybrids from Irish, European and global cultural components.

Among some members of the elite, there is a residual discourse of autonomy, redolent of the de Valera era (1932 to 1958), which focuses less on distinct Irish culture than on an Irish 'dependency culture', derived from the long-term effects of British colonialism in postcolonial, independent Ireland. This dependency culture is expressed in terms of a sense of cultural backwardness, feelings of inferiority and a lack of self-confidence. The residual discourse of autonomy links the dependency culture to Irish emigration, particularly Irish emigration to England in the 1950s. For many, this dependency culture was compounded by anti-Irish prejudice and discrimination encountered in England. Compared with the dominant discourse of autonomy, the residual discourse focuses on Ireland's continued dependent integration into Britain and the negative effects of British cultural influences on Irish identity.

In both the dominant and residual discourses of autonomy, Irish nationalism is primarily used in a defensive fashion as a means to protect Irish cultural identity and sovereignty. The main difference between these two discourses of autonomy is that in the dominant discourse Irish nationalism is also used in a more proactive way: adapting the country's internal national integration to its external British, European and global integrations. However, even in the proactive uses of Irish nationalism, the Irish political elite stresses that the decisions to adapt have been made solely by Irish leaders, organisations and people without reference to external actors with influence in Ireland such as the British government with respect to Northern Ireland and the peace process, and the institutions of the EU and global

American firms located in the country. Thus, there is no reference to the interactions involved between Irish and external actors, the differences between them in international
structures of domination and power relations and the influences that these differences have on Irish 'autonomous' actions to adapt. In this chapter I will argue that the defensive
use of nationalism featured mainly in the campaign against
the Nice Treaty in the first referendum and that this led to a
proactive response in the campaign for the second referendum, largely because of the Irish political elite's fear of the
negative consequences to Ireland of a second rejection of the
Treaty (see below).

Following Giddens's theory of structuration (1984; 1993),
one could argue that Irish discourses of autonomy are reproduced by shaping the discursive consciousness of successive generations of the Irish political elite, influencing the
way they interpret and make sense of social reality. This discursive shaping of consciousness can occur without the actors necessarily being aware of this influence on their perspectives and actions in a wide range of discursive social
settings (Van Dijk 1997), reflecting the mostly unintentional
socialisation processes of becoming 'Irish'. As such, it may
be that the real 'cultural survival' (Evans 1988) of British
rule in Ireland are the discourses of autonomy, not the
strong Irish cultural identity which the discourses inscribe.
Yet even this 'cultural survival' can change or even disappear if it is not continually reproduced by the discursive
practises of the Irish political elite and the Irish people. For
example, certain collective situations such as referenda can
create an 'emotional climate' or 'sets of emotions or feelings'
that are 'shared by groups and individuals' experiencing
'common social structures and processes ... significant in
the formation and maintenance of political or social identities and collective behaviour' (Barbelet 2001: 159). In such
emotional climates, discursive structures like Irish discourses of autonomy may be reshaped by political leaders,
opposition campaigners and the media to change the way
that social groups and individuals in the electorate interpret
issues such as Irish identity, nationalism and Ireland's

external relationships. Arguably, this is what happened between the first Nice Treaty referendum held in June 2001
and the second in October 2002. My discussion will focus on
the political discourse of three Irish Ministers before the first
referendum, and the Taoiseach (or Prime Minister) before the
second.

CELTIC TIGER AND POST-TIGER DISCOURSES OF AUTONOMY

Political discourse in the period before the first Nice Treaty
referendum in June 2001 suggests that the success of Ireland's 'Celtic Tiger' economy led to a reassertion of Irish
political autonomy, particularly with respect to the EU. The
political elite's assertion of an autonomous strong Irish culture aligned with Ireland's new economic autonomy and
political fear of losing power within the EU decision-making
institutions. Further, the Celtic Tiger economy significantly
reduced Ireland's relative economic dependence on EU
transfers, to the point that the country will soon become a
net contributor to the EU budget. As such, there was less
need for the members of the Irish political elite to be political
pragmatists and good Europeans, providing scope for a reaction against the EU. Yet, Ireland's clearly increased economic dependence on the American TNCs that drove the
Celtic Tiger economy did not lead to a cultural reaction by
the Irish political elite. Instead, increased American economic influence in Ireland was interpreted as furthering
Irish national economic sovereignty. This indicates the continuation of the noticeable and yet unexplained silence
among the Irish political elite about this aspect of Ireland's
economic integrations.

Part of the explanation involves interpretations of Ireland's changing relationships with the US and the EU by
members of the Irish government at the time. In the summer
of 2000, two Irish ministers made well-publicised speeches
concerning Ireland's relationships with the EU and the US.
Both these speeches questioned the Irish public political

consensus in favour of continued European economic, political and cultural integration. The first speech was made by Mary Harney, the Tánaiste (or Deputy Prime Minister) and Minister of the Department for Enterprise, Trade and Employment. In the most frequently quoted part of her speech, she directly compared Ireland's European and American relationships, claiming that '[g]eographically we are closer to Berlin than Boston. Spiritually we are probably a lot closer to Boston than Berlin' (Harney 2000). She then focused on Ireland's American economic integration, suggesting that Ireland has used its political autonomy to carve out a 'little America' within Ireland in socio-economic terms, attractive to American TNCs:

> What really makes Ireland attractive to corporate America is the kind of economy that we have created here. When Americans come here they find a country that believes in the incentive power of low taxation. They find a country that believes in economic liberalisation. They find a country that believes in essential regulation but not over-regulation. On looking further afield in Europe they find also that not every European country believes in all of these things (Harney 2000).

What most other European countries believe in is 'the European way ... built on a strong concern for social harmony and social inclusion'. This means that European governments are 'prepared to intervene strongly through the tax and regulatory systems to achieve their desired outcomes'. However, Ireland as a country spiritually closer to Boston has 'tended to steer a course between the two', yet has 'sailed closer to the American shore than the European one'. Having symbolically chosen the American over the European model of economic development, Harney asserts Ireland's political and economic autonomy *vis-à-vis* the EU, claiming that further European integration is against Ireland's national interest:

> We have succeeded because even though we are members of the European Union ... we still retain very substantial freedom to

control our political and economic destiny ... This model works. It allows us to achieve our full economic potential for the first time in our history as an independent state ... There are some who want to create a more centralised Europe, a federal Europe, with key economic decisions being taken at Brussels. I don't think that that would be in Ireland's interests ... I believe in a Europe of independent states, not a United States of Europe.

Thus, Ireland has become economically successful – despite its EU membership – by exercising its political autonomy, and consciously choosing the American over the European model of development. There is no mention of social partnership, reducing the national agreements to neo-liberal tax-cutting exercises. And, somewhere along the way, Ireland's Foreign Direct Investment for exports policy became an American Foreign Direct Investment for American exports policy, necessitating the creation of a little America out of Ireland. After all, who needs a United States of Europe when there is a little United States of Ireland? With respect to autonomy, Harney suggests that Ireland is not economically dependent on America because Ireland has autonomously chosen to become dependent on America as part of its national development strategy. In this way, fear of re-dependency on a British substitute is symbolically transformed into Irish autonomy. American dependency becomes Irish autonomy. Further, Ireland's economic dependency on America is reinterpreted as autonomy because it has 'ended' Ireland's historic economic dependency on Britain, and has buttressed Ireland's political autonomy to choose its own socio-economic policies *vis-à-vis* the EU.

In September 2000, the government's critique of the EU was extended to include a European threat to Irish culture and identity. This second speech by Éamon de Valera's grand-daughter, Síle de Valera, Minister for Arts, Heritage, Gaeltacht and the Islands, was made at Boston College in the US. She begins by arguing that a 'combination' of Irish state policies 'brought about' the Celtic Tiger, before adding that 'our ability to take advantage of our membership of the

European Union has also been an important factor' (de Valera 2000). While she accepts that the EU 'has been good for Ireland', she also claims that 'it is not the cornerstone of what our nation is and should be'. Explaining this point, she acknowledges that 'when we joined [the European Economic Community] in the early 1970s, there were fears that membership would make us less Irish, would damage our unique identity, culture and traditions'. She admits that this did not happen, but adds that it did not occur because the European Economic Community's policy focus 'in those earlier years was on economic progress and development'. However, as the EEC became the European Community and subsequently the EU, 'decisions, other than economic ones, were taken'. Apparently, these decisions were made without the agreement of Irish governments or, if agreed to, 'seemed secondary to us at the time'.

Now, she proclaims, 'we have found that directives and regulations agreed in Brussels can often seriously impinge on our identity, culture and traditions'. This new European threat to Irish culture and identity leads her to reject 'closer integration' as 'a move I would not personally favour' and one that 'is not necessarily in our interests'. Instead, she desires 'a future in which Ireland will exercise a more vigilant, a more questioning attitude to the European Union', while embracing 'our close and very important ties with the United States of America'. These ties include the historical 'deep bonds between us' and recent 'American investment in Ireland'. For de Valera, the unspecified EU cultural directives and regulations have become the new threats to Ireland's cultural autonomy and national identity. The EU's cultural policies are interpreted as political domination over Irish culture, suggesting a fear that Ireland may become culturally dependent on European culture and identity. This is to question the belief, articulated by the dominant discourse of Irish autonomy, that Irish political equality is best achieved within the EU, transforming this equality into potential EU political domination over Ireland.

In this context, it is significant that de Valera and Harney explain Ireland's Celtic Tiger success internally as the result of Irish state policies, including those based on attracting American TNCs. For Harney, the EU is a socialist rock to be avoided preferring instead the American way, while de Valera thinks that EU membership is good for Ireland as long as the Irish take advantage of membership in pursuit of the national interest. This substantially changes the dominant discourse of autonomy, explaining Ireland's socio-economic development as a consequence of the autonomous actions of the Irish state and the political elite, instead of being the product of a strong Irish culture. Ireland's economic dependency on Europe has been turned into Ireland's economic autonomy to choose the 'right' neo-liberal policies, transforming Ireland from a peripheral part of Europe with no options into a dynamic little America in Europe. It is the EU that has become peripheral to Ireland, except as a market for American exports from Ireland. To continue attracting American firms, Ireland must maintain its neo-liberal socio-economic policies, fighting against European social democratic demands to increase economic integration to cover policy areas like taxation. In particular, Ireland must fight to preserve its low corporation tax, arguably the main attraction for American TNCs to locate in Ireland.

Charlie McCreevy, the then Irish Minister for Finance, allied with the British Labour government, was at the forefront of this battle against the EU to harmonise tax policy (*The Irish Times* 16/2/01, 29/5/01 and 11/7/01). He also led Ireland into an official budget reprimand by the European Commission in February 2001 over the supposed inflationary effect of his December 2000 budget, breaking economic policy guidelines agreed by the Minister (*The Irish Times* 14/2/01 and 17/2/01). In waging this political battle, McCreevy made a number of controversial statements, contributing to the 'Eurosceptic' comments of his ministerial colleagues. In one statement, he argued that 'member-states should retain full responsibility for all direct tax policies', before provocatively adding: '[s]ome would say that the attempt to introduce a stamp duty led also to the American revolution' (*The Irish Times* 11/7/01). This bizarre comparison between British imperial taxation of American colonists and Europe's attempt to harmonise taxation policies is revealing. It reinforces the view that the EU wants to dominate Ireland politically, by suggesting that Ireland is like a EU colony being unfairly taxed without equal political representation. It also symbolically reinforces the closer ties between Ireland and the US, associating with America the political equality that the political elite previously associated with the EU in the dominant discourse.

Taken together with the comments by Harney and de Valera, McCreevy's views on taxation symbolically transfer Ireland's British dependency to the EU, and reassign the role of protecting Irish political equality and autonomy to the US. In a final reversal of roles, Britain becomes Ireland's ally in a 'neo-liberal Atlanticist alliance' (*The Irish Times* 17/2/00) against political domination by a social democratic EU. This shows that the symbolic effect of the discourse of autonomy does not depend on the level of Ireland's structural integration with Britain. Even if Ireland is no longer dependent on Britain, it can still fear dependency on other integration processes, and may even ally with Britain as an autonomous equal against these other integrations. Is there not a clearer expression of the Celtic Tiger's discourse of autonomy than this?

However, there are a number of limits to this discussion of the Celtic Tiger's discourse of autonomy. Firstly, the analysis is based solely on published statements from three government Ministers and not on my interviews with fifty-four members of the Irish political elite. Secondly, there are clear political biases in the small sample reflecting the opinions of two neo-liberals (Harney and McCreevy) and one 'traditional' cultural nationalist (de Valera). It is doubtful whether this sample is representative of the present Irish government, let alone the wider political elite. Yet, the results do suggest a change in the present political elite's cultural logic away from the dominant discourse of autonomy that I found when conducting my interviews in the early 1990s: the present elite has reinterpreted Ireland's external relationships to better fit the rapidly changing conditions of the Celtic Tiger. In brief, Europe replaced Britain as the enemy, and America replaced Europe as Ireland's best friend.

It does appear, though, that the political elite's reinterpretation became widely diffused among the Irish population. Specifically, the Irish electorate's rejection of the Nice Treaty referendum on 7 June 2001 by a majority of fifty-four to forty-six per cent indicates a popular change in attitudes towards Ireland's European integration (see *The Irish Times* 9/6/01 and *The Irish Independent* 9/6/01). Admittedly, the low turn out (thirty-five per cent of the electorate) and the fact that fifty-three per cent of the 'Yes' vote in the 1998 Amsterdam referendum did not turn out to vote in the Nice referendum (*The Irish Times* 23/6/01) make it difficult to interpret the meaning of the latter. Nonetheless, there is statistical evidence to suggest that a 'pro-independence' attitude 'was the biggest factor leading to a "No" vote', ahead of other factors such as opposition to Ireland's 'participation in the Rapid Reaction Force and the unacceptability of the provisions on the commissionership and the re-weighting of votes' (*The Irish Times* 9/6/01). This suggests that Ireland's autonomy from, and dependence on, the EU had become a predominant issue among both the Irish political elite and the general population during the period of the Celtic Tiger.

This does not mean that Irish people have turned against the EU or further European integration including enlargement. For example, the *Eurobarometer* survey conducted before the June referendum shows that 'Irish people remain more enthusiastic about EU membership than other Europeans', with seventy-two per cent believing that 'EU membership is a good thing', eighty-three per cent agreeing that the EU has benefited Ireland, and fifty-nine per cent supporting enlargement (*The Irish Times* 18/7/01).

This contradictory evidence of Irish attitudes to the EU may be explained by the salience of Irish national identity in Irish attitudes, and by the significance of discourses of autonomy in structuring these attitudes in the Celtic Tiger. In terms of national identity, Irish national pride in the spring of 2000 was the highest in the EU at ninety-eight per cent compared with an EU average of eighty-three per cent, while the percentage of those feeling Irish only as opposed to European only or Irish and European was fifty-six per cent, the third highest national identification in the EU, significantly above the EU average of forty-one per cent (*Eurobarometer 53*, 2000: 82-3). These figures are not surprising given the socio-economic success of the Celtic Tiger, and indicate the continuing salience of Irish national identity to Irish people, whatever the content of that identity. Yet one can be proud of being Irish and feel Irish only, while believing that EU membership is good for Ireland and that the EU benefits Ireland.

This does not in itself explain the change in Irish attitudes to the EU shown by the Nice Treaty referendum results. What does explain this change in attitudes is the government's reinterpretation of Ireland's external relationships during the Celtic Tiger, and the diffusion of this reinterpretation to the Irish people. Ireland's socio-economic success heightened the salience of Irish national identity and a pro-independence nationalism among the Irish people. The Irish government, as the dominant faction of the political elite, drew on the symbolic resources of Irish identity and nationalism to reinterpret Ireland's British, European and global American integrations along neo-liberal and 'traditional' cultural nationalist lines. In this reinterpretation, the desire for Irish autonomy and fear of dependency has been transferred from Britain to the EU, while the belief articulated in the dominant discourse, that Ireland best exercised its political autonomy within the EU, has been transferred to the country's global American integration. Thus, Irish people can be proud of being Irish, believe that EU membership has been good for Ireland, and fear that the country is surrendering its autonomy to and becoming dependent on the EU. These contradictory attitudes and the fact that they can be held at the same time by individual actors helps us to understand why the Irish electorate chose to vote 'No' to the Nice Treaty or, more significantly, chose not to vote at all.

There are a number of significant differences in the campaign and political discourse leading to the second Nice Treaty referendum in October 2002. Firstly, the coalition government (Fianna Fáil and the Progressive Democrats) was returned to office at the beginning of June, and in the cabinet reshuffle Síle de Valera did not retain her Ministerial post. Secondly, the '[g]overnment made the EU its number one priority' (Ahern 25/6/02) with the passing of the Nice Treaty as its primary goal. Thirdly, the Taoiseach, Bertie Ahern, led the campaign from the front this time around, making a series of official speeches in support of the Treaty and the EU from mid-June until September. Fourthly, the Tánaiste, Mary Harney and the Minister of Finance, Charlie McCreevy remained on the side-lines, both making only one official speech on the Treaty and the EU between June and September, each of which toed the pro-Treaty and EU campaign line. Fifthly, led by the Prime Minister, the government formed a coalition that was cross-party and involved the main social partners in the pro-Treaty campaign. Sixthly, this new coalition invested a lot of time and money to spread the pro-EU Nice Treaty message compared with the first campaign. Finally, the government attempted to address some of the main concerns expressed by those opposed to or uncertain about the Treaty through the establishment of the National Forum on Europe after the first referendum, the so-called 'triple lock' and Seville Declaration on Irish military neutrality[2], and 'enhanced Oireachtas (Parliamentary) scrutiny of European Union issues' (Ahern 25/6/02).

The political discourse was also significantly different, adopting a comprehensive and detailed pro-EU and Treaty perspective, clearly articulated and reiterated by Bertie Ahern in his series of speeches during the campaign. This approach was deemed necessary because in the first campaign, as the Taoiseach admitted, '[c]onfusion reigned and I think the responsibility for much of that lies with all of us

---

[2] The 'triple lock' required that any Irish military involvement in international missions overseas would require a UN mandate and the approval of the Government and the Oireachtas

charged with leadership, both politicians and social partners' (Ahern September 2002a). Turning explicitly against
the Ministerial Euro-scepticism that preceded the first referendum, the government discourse returned to many of the
themes found in the dominant discourse of autonomy. Thus,
Ahern refers to the 'no-economic-options-outside-of-the-EU'
theme, claiming that '[b]ecause we are relatively small and
so trade-dependent, more than any other member state our
economic prospects are tied to an intimate and central involvement in the EU' (July 2002a).

In an earlier speech in June, he addresses this issue of
Ireland's economic options outside the EU to the 'opponents
of the Treaty' asking them to:

> Cast their minds back to the period before our accession to the
> European Union. We were over-dependent on the UK economy.
> We lived and traded in a world where the rules were made by
> others. We had no place at the table where tariffs were set by
> our trading partners; we had no voice when decisions affecting
> our key agricultural and industrial interests were being laid
> down (Ahern 25/6/02).

In response to his own imaging of the past, he adds
'[p]articipation in the EU has been enormously empowering
to us as a nation'. The EU has also been central to Ireland's
socio-economic development:

> Let us be absolutely clear, our current economic prosperity, our
> current standing in the world, the rapid technological, economic
> and social change that Ireland has undergone over the past 30
> years, stems directly from our absolute engagement with
> Europe ...The European Union has been good for Ireland, and
> our active role within Europe has played a vital part in lifting
> our standards of living and our quality of life (Ahern September
> 2002a).

Of course, a key component of this socio-economic development has been Ireland's attraction for mostly American
foreign firms. Thus, Ahern argues:

Ireland also needs a yes vote to increase foreign direct investment in our domestic economy. Foreign firms provide almost
140,000 jobs directly in Ireland, and indirectly support many
thousands more. That is why we truly can promote ourselves as
the gateway to Europe for the United States. Unhindered access
to the European market is a huge attraction for foreign direct
investment, since 70 per cent of our exports are to the European Union (Ahern September 2002a).

At the same time, he rejects his own cabinet colleagues' emphasis on creating a little United States of Ireland in the first
referendum debate, stressing that 'Ireland is fully committed
to the development of a genuine European Social Model'
(Ahern 29/8/02). He further rejects a neo-liberal 'laissez
faire approach to economic development in Europe' that
concentrates 'solely on trade liberalisation'. This he claims
'would not be in Ireland's interest' as a 'peripheral member
state'. Instead, he argues that '[t]he European Union is *the*
model for the regulation of economic globalisation that extends beyond trade' and that to do so 'Europe must have the
ability and the will to develop strong economic and social
policies'. As such, he adds that 'I am a passionate believer in
a strong Ireland in a strong Europe'.

Ahern even directly links Ireland's membership in the EU
to the achievement of nationalist objectives as stated in 'The
Proclamation of the Irish Republic in 1916' (*ibid*), and to an
eventual unity of the island of Ireland: 'the principles that
compel us towards the realisation of the goal of one Irish
nation achieved by mutual consent and mutual understanding are the same principles that inspire a greater
European Union' (September 2002b). In this regard, EU
membership has been beneficial in developing 'the relationship between Ireland and Britain' from one of dependency to
one of equality 'through common membership' and this 'has
been essential to our quest for peace on our own island'.
Significantly, Ahern's use of proactive Irish nationalism here
refers to the influence of British and Irish interactions as
political equals in EU institutions in overcoming the historic

structures of domination between the peoples of the islands, contributing to the development of the peace process.

With respect to the Nice Treaty and EU decision-making, Ahern returns to the theme of Irish political leaders being pragmatic, good Europeans who have been able to manoeuvre 'skillfully to protect and advance [our] national interests in Europe' by 'building alliances and constructing compromises' (September 2002b). Irish political equality in the EU is also stressed, for example, in the statement that 'Irish Ministers and members of the European Parliament work alongside the representatives of other Member States in deciding upon the laws, policies and programmes of the Union' (Ahern 25/6/02). This includes Ireland's full participation in 'the negotiations that led to the Treaty of Nice' (Ahern 20/6/02). The result is that the 'Treaty fully protects our interests' (Ahern 20/6/02) and 'our rights and our standing within the European Union' (Ahern September 2002b). Thus, he argues that '[b]eing able to promote and protect our interests is the true exercise of our sovereignty' (Ahern 20/6/02) and as such that 'there can only be one answer' to the question of voting for or against the Nice Treaty. It is that '[we] stay with the Union all the way ... we do what ensures that our national interests are protected' by managing 'our concerns and issues from a position of full strength and commitment at the heart of the Union' (Ahern 25/06/02).

Finally, he asks the Irish people to consider the position of the accession countries awaiting the outcome of Ireland's second referendum:

> If there is no doubt about the benefit that Ireland has received from our membership in the European Union, then we need to ask the question: Is it right to deny that chance to others? Is it right for us to deny people who desperately want and need the chance to join the rest of Europe to raise their standard of living and secure their social progress? (Ahern September 2002b).

Without stating it directly, Ahern has symbolically turned the accession countries into the Ireland of the early 1970s before it too became an EU member. For the Irish to vote against the Nice Treaty is akin to other more affluent Europeans denying Ireland's right to become a member thirty years ago when Ireland too was poorer and underdeveloped and needed a chance to join Europe.

In this series of speeches, Ahern directly addresses and contradicts much of his own ministerial colleagues' criticisms about the EU in the run-up to the first referendum, responding to their defensive nationalism with a proactive nationalist position. In so doing, he draws on many of themes from the dominant discourse of autonomy such as the belief that Ireland is a small, peripheral country that has no economic options outside the EU and that Irish politicians in Europe must play the game of pragmatic good Europeans in order to secure Ireland's national interests in the EU. At the same time, he goes well beyond the terms of the dominant discourse of autonomy, seeing no political or economic threat at all from the EU. Further, he neither asserts a strong Irish culture to compensate for Ireland's relative economic dependence on the EU and global American TNCs, nor proclaims a core/surface Irish identity that propels European and global American socio-cultural influences onto the surface of Irishness, protecting the core below.

Instead, he embraces the role of the EU in helping Ireland to achieve its traditional nationalist objectives of reducing the country's dependence on the UK, exercising full political sovereignty from a position of equality, achieving a high level of socio-economic development while attracting instead of exporting migrants, and (potentially) realising unity on the island based on mutual consensus rather than force. Ireland's active engagement with the EU also includes the development of the European Social Model in Ireland, not creating a little neo-liberal United States of Ireland. The US is embraced for its foreign direct investment in continuing to develop the country economically, but is not viewed as offering the best socio-economic model to regulate globalisation beyond trade. Further, Ireland's relationship with the UK has developed into one of equality based on common membership of EU such that the two governments were able to work together for a sustainable peace and consensus-based democracy in Northern Ireland.

Overall, Ahern's reshaping of Irish discourses of autonomy in the context of the second Nice Treaty referendum campaign suggests that the political elite's long tradition of interpreting Ireland's external relationships through the prism (or prison) of a dichotomy between autonomy and dependency may be coming to an end. However, it is not plausible to argue from one case that Irish discourses of autonomy have definitively ended, even if that case involves the political leader of the country. The political discourse of the second referendum campaign was a response to the Eurosceptic discourse of the first campaign. It presented a positive perspective on the EU and the Nice Treaty to persuade the electorate to come out to vote and to vote for the Treaty. At the very least, the discourse of Irish sovereignty and equality through active engagement in the EU, along with the concerted cross-party partnership campaign, contributed to dispelling the confusion that much of the electorate felt during the first referendum campaign. This in itself could help explain the higher turnout of forty-nine per cent and the majority of sixty-three per cent for the Nice Treaty in the second referendum (*The Irish Times* 21/10/02).

CONCLUSION: THE SURVIVAL OF IRISH DISCOURSES OF AUTONOMY?

The shift in political discourse by the Irish government from the first to the second Nice Treaty campaign, and its apparent effect on the electorate, shows the resilience and adaptability of Irish discourses of autonomy. It also shows that Irish 'culture' in the boom and post-boom period cannot simply be reduced to rampant consumerism and individualism dominated by Anglo-American informational capitalism (O'Connell, 2001 and Kirby *et al.* 2002). Irish 'actors' at the elite and popular levels of society are not cultural dupes, but like us all are complex individuals in which the structural influences of capitalism – in whatever its form – are one of many societal influences that shape our consciousness and actions and that we shape in return. In this case, Irish discourses of autonomy are one of these many influences, a cultural survival from the past that continues to shape 'Irish' attitudes about identity and nationalism with respect to Ireland's external relationships. Yet it does not fully determine these attitudes. It is closely intertwined with beliefs about Ireland's national economic, political, social and cultural interests. The question is, to what extent does the cultural logic continue to shape 'Irish' beliefs about these interests, influencing Irish actors to interpret Ireland's external relationships through the categories of autonomy and dependency?

Ahern's intervention in the second campaign does not mean that Irish discourses of autonomy have lost their potency. It is more likely that the contradictory attitudes about Irish identity, nationalism and Ireland's external relationships expressed by different members of the Irish cabinet in the two referenda are present at the same time in the discursive consciousness of most Irish people. As such, these contradictory attitudes are present as discursive capacities to be shaped and reshaped depending on the emotional climate of collective events. If so, it replicates the results of the earlier interviews with members of the Irish political elite in which elements of the dominant (Irish autonomy) and residual (dependency) discourses of autonomy were both expressed in a single interview. This suggests that discourses of autonomy have not disappeared from the discursive consciousness of the Irish political elite and people. Instead, they remain dormant as a discursive capacity to be reawakened to shape group and individual attitudes depending on the political context. This makes more sense if Irish discourses of autonomy are viewed, not as independent phenomena, but as related to 'the reproduction of the structures of domination' and 'power relations ... of autonomy and dependence' (Giddens 1984; 1993), reflecting Ireland's changing relational position in the British Isles, Europe and in a global context.

Ahern's proactive nationalism involves a reshaping of the discourse of autonomy to take account of the changing power relationship between the UK and the Republic of Ireland from one of domination to something more like political equality, but contradictions remain. During the second Nice campaign, Ahern argued that improvements in the relationship between Ireland and the UK, mediated by common membership in the EU, have facilitated collaboration between the two governments in the peace process that led to the GFA. Central to the Agreement is provision for dual Irish-British nationality, but Ahern was silent about that. He made no mention of its potential as a model for multiple nationality and identity in a EU context, let alone the implications of multiple identities for the new immigrant communities in the Republic of Ireland. These silences are indicative of the limits of Ahern's discourse: foundering on the core/surface construct of Irish identity and the continuing need to defend a homogenous Irish national identity.

Another contradiction emerges in Ahern's attempt to symbolically relate European social democracy and Irish nationalism as the best means to defend the European Social Model against neo-liberal economic globalisation. On the one hand Ahern's position offers an argument against those like Kirby *et al.* (2002) who claim that only a recovery of uncorrupted fragments of Irish culture can provide effective resistance to Anglo-American neo-liberal capitalism. On the other hand he remains silent again, this time about his coalition government's role in making Ireland one of the best examples in Europe of neo-liberal economic globalisation through Ireland's very successful policies to attract American TNCs. Ahern may have silenced his neo-liberal cabinet colleagues during the second Nice Treaty referendum, but he has not explained how his government's policies can defend the European Social Model in Ireland while implementing American neo-liberal economic globalisation in Ireland at the same time.

Yet, Ahern's contradictory attitudes reflect in many ways Ireland's changing position in international structures of domination and power relations between the UK, the EU and the US. The Republic of Ireland is a small country on a geographically peripheral island located on the northwest fringes of continental Europe. It is next to a larger island and former global imperial power with which it has a complex historical relationship. Economically, it has become a small open economy largely dependent on exports from American TNCs that were attracted to Ireland in part because of Irish access to the larger European market. Ireland's membership of the EU also gives it more political power than its size and location would warrant, allowing its political leaders opportunities to shape European and global policies that protect Ireland's national interests, opportunities it would be less likely to have as a stand-alone country. These features of Ireland's position suggest that power relations of autonomy and dependence in an international context will always be a concern to the Irish political elite and populace and, as such, that discourses of autonomy will remain embedded as part of Irish discursive consciousness in various guises for the foreseeable future. At the same time, Ireland's position is not unique in either a European or a global context. It may be that specific national, regional and local discourses of autonomy can be found, for example, in other smaller European countries in 'Western' Europe and the new accession countries; in historical regions such as Catalonia and Flanders; and even in local urban and rural communities that feel disadvantaged in some way. Discourses of autonomy similar to those discussed here in the Irish case may be alive and kicking, going back to the future, shaping the discursive consciousness of people elsewhere.

REFERENCES

Ahern, B. (20/6/02), *Nice Treaty Essential to Our Role in Europe – Taoiseach at IBEC Biennial President's Dinner.* Dublin: Department of the Taoiseach.
Ahern, B. (25/6/02), *Statement by the Taoiseach, Mr. Bertie Ahern, T.D., On the Seville European Council, Dáil Éireann.* Dublin: Department of the Taoiseach.
Ahern, B. (15/7/02), *A "Yes" Vote to Nice is Vital to Our Prosperity.* Dublin: Department of the Taoiseach.
Ahern, B. (July 2002a), *Taoiseach Calls for Real Debate on Economic Implications of Nice. Condemns Attempts to Censor Contributions to the Debate.* Dublin: Department of the Taoiseach.
Ahern, B. (29/8/02), *Speech by the Taoiseach, Mr. Bertie Ahern T.D. at the Opening of the European Foundation Forum, in Dublin Castle.* Dublin: Department of the Taoiseach.
Ahern, B. (September 2002a), *Taoiseach Speaking at the Launch of the Institute for European Affairs Document on Europe.* Dublin: Department of the Taoiseach.
Ahern, B. (September 2002b), *Nice Treaty Ireland at the Crossroads, Speech by the Taoiseach Mr. Bertie Ahern, T.D., to Dáil Éireann, on the Twenty-Sixth Amendment to the Constitution.* Dublin: Department of the Taoiseach.
Barbalet, J. (2001), *Emotion, Social Theory, and Social Structure: A Macrosociological Approach.* Cambridge: Cambridge University Press.
Boucher, G. (2001), *The Small Island Scarcely Heard: Ireland's Multiple Integrations and Identities.* Unpublished PhD Thesis, University of Dublin, Trinity College Department of Sociology.
Boyce, D.G. (1995) [1982], *Nationalism in Ireland.* London: Routledge.
De Valera, S. (18/9/00), *Address by Síle de Valera T.D., Minister for Arts, Heritage, Gaeltacht and the Islands, Boston College, Massachusetts, U.S.A..* Dublin: Department of Arts, Heritage, Gaeltacht and the Islands.

Eurobarometer 53 (2000), Brussels: Directorate-General Information, Communication, Culture, Audiovisual.

Evans, E.E. (1988) [1967], *Irish Folk Ways*. London: Routledge.

Giddens, A. (1993), *The Giddens Reader*, in P. Cassell ed.. London: Macmillan Press.

Giddens, A. (1984), *The Constitution of Society*. Cambridge: Polity Press.

Harney, M. (21/7/00), *Remarks by Tánaiste, Mary Harney at a Meeting of the American Bar Association in the Law Society of Ireland, Blackhall Place, Dublin*. Dublin: Department of Enterprise, Trade & Employment.

Hutchinson, J. (1987), *The Dynamics of Cultural Nationalism: The Gaelic Revival and the Creation of the Irish Nation State*. London: Allen and Unwin.

The Irish Independent (9/6/01).

The Irish Times (14/2/01; 16/2/01; 17/2/01; 29/5/01; 9/6/01; 23/6/01; 11/7/01; 18/7/01; 21/10/02).

Kirby, P., Gibbons, L. and Cronin, M. eds (2002), *Reinventing Ireland: Culture, Society and Global Economy*. London: Pluto Press.

Moynihan, M. ed. (1980), *Speeches and Statements by Éamon de Valera 1917-73*. Dublin: Gill and Macmillan.

O'Connell, M. (2001), *Changed Utterly: Ireland and the New Irish Psyche*. Dublin: The Liffey Press.

Van Dijk, T. ed. (1997), *Discourse as Social Interaction*, Volume 2. London: Sage.

Williams, R. (1981), *Culture*. London: Fontana.

5. Our Shelter and Ark? Immigrants and the Republic

PIARAS MAC ÉINRÍ

Irish nationalist ideology, particularly as embodied in populist discourses in the post-independence Twenty-Six Counties, has traditionally stressed the concept of a unitary identity and a unitary nation-state, notwithstanding the occasional gestures in favour of more federalist and polyvalent approaches advocated from time to time through such initiatives as Sinn Féin's *Éire Nua* policy of the 1970s (1971). By contrast, what sets the French form of republicanism apart from the Irish nationalist one is its emphasis on political membership of civil society – something all can participate in – rather than the narrow ethnonationalism which has historically characterised much of the rest of Europe, including Ireland (Cullen 2001, Honohan 2001). Wolfe Tone was a French citizen at the time of his arrest off the coast of Donegal in 1798. The ideology of French republicanism accepted that the right to belong was fundamentally a political one, unrelated to blood or soil.

The French model is not, however, satisfactory in all respects, to say the least. A key principle of French Jacobin republicanism was embodied in Clermont-Tonnerre's famous dictum '*[i]l faut tout refuser aux juifs comme nation et tout leur accorder comme individus; il faut qu'ils ne fassent dans l'État ni un corps politique, ni un ordre: il faut qu'ils soient individuellement citoyens*'[1] (Champion 1999). Ethnicity was not then, and is not now, acceptable in France as a constitutive element of public identity. Ethnicity, like religion (illustrated in dramatic form recently in new legislation banning the wearing of the *hijab*, or Islamic scarf, in French public schools), is a matter strictly for the private domain. The French thus rejected the idea that 'the ethnic collectivity

---

[1] One should refuse everything to the Jews as a nation and grant them everything as individuals; they should be, within the State, neither a political body nor a special class, they must be individually citizens.

represents an attempt on the part of men to keep alive, during their pilgrimage from *Gemeinschaft* to *Gesellschaft* ... some of the diffuse, ascriptive, particularistic modes of behaviour that were common to their past' (Moynihan 1969). This emphasis on the sovereignty of the relationship between the individual and the law, and on unity through the elimination of difference (*'la différence positive'*) cannot work in a modern multi-ethnic state, especially where the degree of cultural distance is relatively wide, as has been the case in France since the 1960s, and when a doctrine of universalism masks a hidden hegemony of rationalist European supremacism.

French Republican ideas found an echo here in Ireland, two centuries ago, particularly with those radical Presbyterians who believed in a political Irish nation of Catholic, Protestant and Dissenter (Whelan 1996). It was unfortunate, then, that with the failure of 1798, a narrower, sectarian version of what it was to be Irish should subsequently have been adopted. Nowadays, in evaluating the United Irishmen, it would be appropriate to speak, without going into the more controversial aspects of the Wexford Rising (Dunne 2004), of an ideal of a rights-based democracy which respected diversity. By contrast, many in modern Ireland, which has been characterised by one commentator as a racialised state (Lentin 2002), have tended to see the Irish 'nation' as culturally, religiously or even racially defined (Garner 2004; Fanning 2003), as a narrow, exclusionary 'we'. The instinct of the Irish, it would seem, has been to expel, to corral or to contain, or at least to insist that those who are different should know their place, that is, remain silent or not assert their difference in the public domain.

TRIBAL IDENTITIES

Even in an apparently fixed and unchanging pre-Celtic Tiger Ireland, questions of identity were never simple, secure or monolithic. When I was a child in Dublin, my father used to bring me, a Jackeen[2] born to parents who had migrated from the west of Ireland to the new suburbs of the capital, to the Connacht final – provided, that is, that his county, Mayo, was playing. It was part of a ritual of journeys westward, strong ties with relatives at home and abroad, networks linked by narrative, myth, memory and blood. It was an intimation of how rootless diasporic communities can feel that I grew up for several years totally alienated from the cold, unformed climate of the Dublin suburbs in the late 1950s. When we went to those football finals, whether in Tuam or Castlebar, my memory of them now is my sincere and absolute conviction that one could tell a Galway from a Mayo person, simply by looking at their faces. So much for colour-based difference and the complexities of ethnic differentiation.

There is another side to this warm inchoate feeling of belonging: the exclusion of those who are different, closely linked to the denial of difference or hybridity within ourselves. Communities too often define themselves, not by what they do or by who they are, but rather through the exclusion of those they feel do not resemble them (Barth 1969). Kipling put this in unpleasant but memorable terms in his poem *The Stranger within my Gate* (Kipling 1942):

The Stranger within my gate,
He may be true or kind,
But he does not talk my talk –
I cannot feel his mind.
I see the face and the eyes and the mouth,
But not the soul behind.

The men of my own stock,
They may do ill or well,
But they tell the lies I am wonted to,
They are used to the lies I tell;
And we do not need interpreters
When we go to buy or sell.

---

2   Dublin-born person (slang expression)

The Stranger within my gate,
He may be evil or good,
But I cannot tell what powers control –
What reasons sway his mood;
Nor when the gods of his far-off land,
Shall repossess his blood.

The men of my own stock,
Bitter bad they may be,
But, at least, they hear the things I hear,
And see the things I see;
And whatever I think of them and their likes
They think of the likes of me.

This was my father's belief
And this is also mine:
Let the corn be all of one sheaf –
And the grapes be all one vine,
Ere our children's teeth are set on edge
By bitter bread and wine.

It is interesting that Kipling's poem is probably one of the most widely reproduced of all English-language texts on far-right, racist and white supremacist websites world-wide[3]. But powerful as his vision is, there is a fatal flaw in his view. No society is homogenous: the 'stranger' is always within our gate and within ourselves (Simmel 1950; Kristeva 1991); there is no originary state to which we can return.

The Irish, as a nation of emigrants, should know this better than most. To demonise the stranger is to demonise one's neighbour or oneself. The fact that Irish people in Ireland have sometimes been all too willing to do this in recent times bespeaks a kind of internal denial, a deliberate act of amnesia, a refusal to connect with their own collective history and the narratives of generations of emigrants. In the process, they deny themselves a powerful resource that might enable

---

[3] e.g. White Nationalist Party (UK) http://www. white.org.uk/stranger. html; National Alliance (US) http://www.natvan.com/national-van-guard/099/kipling.html;

them to achieve a degree of empathy with the 'other' without denying the specificity of that other's experiences or the ambivalences of their own position. Such a stance is less easily available, perhaps, to avowedly colonising societies. Perhaps the very resemblance between those others and the ghosts of the Irish Diaspora is a key element in this process of denial. Yet those who say that they do not recognise what Kipling is talking about are not being entirely honest. Ethnicity is kinship writ large, the kind of ties that mean people will put themselves out for others whom they may not personally know, simply because they share a perceived bond with them – the classic 'imagined community' – whereas one may be inclined to ignore the problems of the next-door neighbours if one feels one has nothing in common with them (Anderson 1991).

In the case of Britain it is not too difficult to trace the lineaments of this debate. It is currently again in full swing, opposing multiculturalists to proponents of a return to the core values of Britishness (Philips 2004). A controversial recent article in *Prospect* by David Goodhart (2004) explores this theme, arguing that only those communities with a felt sense of mutuality will pay for welfare, for instance, because they need to recognise themselves in some way in the faces of those whom the welfare state assists. According to this argument (in my view dangerous), it becomes impossible to sustain the necessary sense of social solidarity if the ties of ethnic solidarity do not operate. While in general the terms of this debate have changed little in Britain since the 1960s, few would now deny that immigrants have changed and invigorated British society and are there to stay. The current argument, whether misconceived or not, tends rather to focus on a numbers-driven debate about future levels of immigration, not on the refusal or outright rejection of those already there (Rowthorn 2004). What of Ireland, an ethnically homogenous state with an official monoculture for much of the twentieth century?

Writer and poet, Francis Stuart, was a somewhat atypical Irishman, who at various points of his life swam against the tide. It is not my purpose here to explore his political, ethical and aesthetic choices. But questionable as his political decisions were, it is difficult not to respond to his lyric poem *Ireland*, written in Nazi Germany at Christmas 1944, where Stuart was, like his fellow-citizen William Joyce (Lord Haw-Haw), making occasional ill-judged broadcasts for German radio:

> Over you falls the sea-light, festive yet pale
> As though from the trees hung candles alight in a gale
> To fill with shadows your days, as the distant beat
> Of waves fills the lonely width of many a western street.
> Bare and grey and hung with berries of mountain ash
> Drifting through ages with tilted fields awash,
> Steeped with your few lost lights in the long Atlantic dark,
> Sea-birds' shelter, our shelter and ark.

This poem is filled with an intense yearning and imbued with a strong sense of the texture of the Irish landscape. It is interesting to juxtapose the images Stuart invokes with those in de Valera's famous vision, uttered less than two years before, of happy maidens and sturdy youths and the virtues of simple self-sufficient rural living (in Deane 1991). Stuart has evidently not adjusted to life in Berlin, in spite of his decision to choose the heart of darkness as his place of abode. Like de Valera, the painter Paul Henry, J.M. Synge and others before them, Stuart's Ireland is the rural west. His image of a whole country listing like a lost ship, 'drifting through ages ... in the long Atlantic dark,' conveys desolation, longing and belonging in equal measure. Yet this is also a troubling vision, with its theme of the saved and the lost. Not everyone was welcomed into the 'ark' (Keogh 1998). Moreover, this can be read as a classically anti-modern text, a refusal of the world and a retreat to a spatially and chronologically othered place of purity and escape. The least that can be said is that it scarcely offers a useful reading of Irish society today.

Nevertheless, it is possible to detect, in the bitterness and aggression of many who attack the new Ireland with its cap-

puccinos and clubs, its hollow rhetoric of diversity, its overnight wealth and the uneven distribution of these new
riches[4], a cry of pain and loss not dissimilar to Stuart's. The
Ireland these people mourn is as far away from them now as
Stuart's was from him in Berlin, sinking beneath the waves
of modernity and change. As Marx and Engels put it in a
different context, all that is solid melts into air.

Let us take a case in point. The 2003 Saint Patrick's Day
Parade in Dublin led to an interesting exchange of views
between elements of the old and new Ireland. On the one
hand, the *Irish Catholic* newspaper complained that there
was no religious participation in the parade even though it
was said to be about 'Irish identity'. The parade organiser,
when pressed to concede that the Catholic religion was a
major part of Irish cultural identity, said that 'we don't
manifest some aspects of our identity within the parade ...
there are no groups at all involved of any religious persuasion ... Participation is entirely based on entertainment
value' (*The Irish Times* 18/3/03). There are a number of
nettles which need to be grasped here. Unitary identity,
especially the old Catholic, ruralist, 'not-British' one which
typified de Valera's vision, has indeed become greatly at-
tenuated. But it is scarcely possible to address the vacuum
about the meaning of contemporary Irishness by the postmodern move of reducing identity to 'entertainment value',
or by denying the role of religion in many people's sense of
their own identities. It would seem that for some in Ireland
now the 'old country' has become a relic, to which the necessary obeisance will be paid when appropriate, but at best in
a commercial or playfully performative context in which
what were previously regarded as essential realities have definitively slipped their moorings. Modern Ireland has now
floated free of its own past.

---

[4]   For an example of the new discourse, see Patrick West (17/6/02). 'The
new Ireland kicks ass: the English now agonise about their identity,
while the Irish, from Ryanair to the World Cup team, are supremely
confident'.

In the midst of this rapid change and such postmodern moves to accommodate it, there are darker forces at work. A group of Irish racists, for instance, discussed the appointment of Samantha Mumba, who is of mixed Irish/African ethnicity, as Grand Master of the Saint Patrick's Day Parade in 2003:

> The so called "Irish" superstar, Samantha Mumba, is to lead the parade of our country's patron saint! Now, I am not at all religious, but what I find repulsive about this is that mumba jumba is a mud and I'll eat shit before I accept that she is Irish. You have to be Pure White to be Irish, she is naught but a half-breed bitch whose Irish parent is an utter disgrace to all Whites. Mumba fills the role that has been previously filled by the likes of ex-Boyzone members, Ronan Keating and Keith Duffy but, hey, at least they are White and actually Irish. Personally I am outraged at this and what the hell will visiting White tourists, who come here for Irelands remaining, if dwindling Whiteness, think when they see our National "Proud to be Irish" parade being led by a mud, who has the audacity to call herself a national, in a open top car?[5]

Comment would be superfluous, except to say that while those who express such views (at least in public) are probably few, there are politicians willing to exploit them. A prominent example of such political opportunism is Cork TD Noel O'Flynn of Fianna Fáil who is reported to have described asylum seekers as 'freeloaders' (*The Irish Times*, 29/1/02). And what should one make of journalist John Waters who wrote in an *Irish Times* opinion piece: '[t]here is a stark choice for those who live in the West, speak English and have white skin: we can join with America and Britain or take our chances alone' (24/3/03).

Waters' s view is divisive and supremacist and is at odds with his own commendable stated opposition to the government referendum on citizenship. He calls for nothing less than a crusade against the rest of the world: as he puts it, 'if

---

Contribution to *Stormfront* (racist website), http://www.stormfront.org /forum/showthread.php?t=57440-1, accessed 7 May 2004.

the West did not eliminate its enemies, they would eliminate the West'. Should this campaign of elimination begin, perhaps, with those in Ireland who do not have 'white skin': Samantha Mumba; or the star footballers and hurlers, brothers Seán Óg and Setanta Ó hAilpín; or soccer-hero Paul McGrath; or Galway singer/songwriter Sharon Murphy (all of mixed ethnicity)? It is clear where such division of people by categories – ethnicity, religion, skin colour – has led in the past. Ireland's history as a colonised country – albeit one that has sometimes found itself on the colonising side as well – might point to a different way forward in the present conjuncture.

Is Ireland a Monocultural State?

Consider the following:

> No thoughtful Irishman or woman can view without apprehension the continuous influx of Jews into Ireland and the continuous efflux of the native population. The stalwart men and bright-eyed women of our race pass from our land in a never-ending stream, and in their place we are getting strange people, alien to us in thought, alien to us in sympathy, from Russia, Poland, Germany and Austria ... people who come to live amongst us, but who never become of us ... (*United Irishman*, 23/4/1904, cited in Keogh, 1998: 42).

This was Arthur Griffith's view, expressed in 1904. To paraphrase Foucault, all societies may be defined by those on the margins. Who has no power? Who is in jail? Who is regarded as mad? Who is excluded? In the case of this state, exclusion has been a key theme. The official cultural identity of the Southern jurisdiction, for the first forty years of its existence, reflected a dominant, unitary concept of Irishness. Apart from its explicit content – the ending of Partition, the restoration of the Irish language, Catholic domination, the secondary status of women, the privileging of rural over urban identities – there was an underlying assumption that difference meant inferiority, or at least, that those who were different should be isolated or remain silent. Douglas Hyde, a Protestant, may have been the first President of the Irish Free State, but no (Roman Catholic) government minister dared darken the doors of the church during his funeral; they remained outside as the service took place[6].

The ruling structures of the newly independent state also reflected the realities of power and class. A relatively small middle class, urban and rural, inherited the earth. The marginal, the socially radical, the poor, the landless, women, minorities, were disproportionately represented in the ranks of emigrants, taking with them some of the energy which would have been required if the domination of the few was to be seriously challenged. In the mid-1950s Alexis Fitzgerald actually saw emigration as useful because it 'releases social tensions which would otherwise be the subject of radical change' (Commission on Emigration and Other Population Problems: 1955). The net effect of these processes of exclusion was the preservation of apparently unifying but essentially archaic and coercive social norms, to the exclusion of most forms of meaningful dialogue or dissent. This false consensus contrasts with dynamic societies elsewhere in Europe, where there was a continuing dialectic between opposing views and identities. In political terms it was reflected in a widespread adherence to corporatism of one kind or another, coupled with a desire to deny the existence of real differences, such as those of ideology, class and gender (O'Carroll 2002). It was commonplace to hear it asserted that Ireland was 'a classless society' (Healy 1978). During World War II and the postwar period the country was uniquely insulated from the winds of change which had

---

6   A regulation of the Roman Catholic Church then in force forbade its members from attending any Protestant Church service. Poet Austin Clarke wrote savagely 'At the last bench/Two Catholics, the French/ Ambassador and I, knelt down./The vergers waited. Outside./The hush of Dublin town,/Professors of cap and gown,/Costello, his Cabinet,/In government cars, hiding/Around the corner, ready/Tall hat in hand, dreading/Our Father in English. Better/Not hear that 'which' for 'who'/And risk eternal doom.' (from 'Burial of an Irish President' 1963).

swept the rest of the continent. Southern Irish society remained officially oblivious to the fact that, despite that neutrality, it provided tens of thousands of soldiers and workers, male and female, to the war economy of Britain, and continued to export its people there as labour fodder in the 1950s and beyond. Secretly, some civil servants were glad to see the back of these migrants. Insofar as they considered the matter at all, it was not their departure but the danger of their return, perhaps infected by British thinking about social justice, which was a cause for concern (Delaney 2000).

Coming into the latter half of the twentieth century, Ireland was thus one of the countries least able to respond to messages about plural cultural identities, still less to consider the political alterations which might flow from such discourses. It had a culture which privileged tradition and feared change. In the 1950s and 1960s European traumas of decolonisation, immigration and the once-for-all ethnicisation of society found little echo in Ireland. From the Fethard-on-Sea boycott (Whyte 1980) to the banning of books and the suppression of women's rights, Ireland proudly pursued its own lonely path, obsessed with the decadence of others. There were many, and not just the poor, who were less than equal in this society. The broadcaster and novelist Brian Cleeve was dropped as presenter of Radio Telefis Éireann's *Discovery* series in 1966, the year of the commemoration of the Easter Rising, because 'his "Ascendancy" accent was considered unsuitable for broadcasting' (*The Irish Times*, 22/3/03). The Remembrance Garden for those Irish who fought in World War I was allowed to fall into a state of neglect for decades. Some golf clubs excluded Roman Catholics, others Jews. Most denied women full membership until the fairly recent past and some continue to do so.

MOVING TOWARDS CHANGE: THE PLACE OF THE OTHER

The economic and social changes which define modern Ireland are generally dated from T.K. Whitaker's proposals for economic development in 1958 (Lee 1989). Apart from the perceived need for new economic and social policies (a topic which is beyond the scope of this chapter), one of the main initial targets of those who in the 1960s favoured change was, understandably, the reverential and exclusive version of nationalism which had become the official credo of the South. Though the revisionist-nationalist contestations of the 1980s and 1990s have often been bitter, there have been efforts in both quarters to develop a more inclusive version of Irishness in terms of the disparate traditions within the state, albeit from different starting-points. By and large they have inevitably focused on differences within, rather than on the place of the other in, Irish society.

Let us, then, turn specifically to how Ireland regarded the arrival of newcomers to Irish society. Those few immigrants who came as refugees in the period before the 1990s encountered incomprehension, lack of policy and support, but above all a desire to exclude. In 1956 Hungarians, fresh from an unequal fight against Soviet oppression, found themselves effectively interned in a military camp at Knockalisheen in County Clare, isolated (a common theme in Ireland when dealing with difference) and badly looked after. Even though these people were presented in official rhetoric as anti-Communist heroes, the state had neither the social services nor the openness to address their needs, which were left to a voluntary body, the Irish Red Cross. The treatment meted out to the Hungarians was a textbook example of a policy of containment. Even though they were supposedly in Ireland as invited refugees, every effort was made to minimise the effects of their presence. They were prevented from working as far as possible. They were, in effect, confined to their accommodation under threat of possible arrest if they left without permission, even though any such act would have been of dubious legality. Those who protested at their conditions of confinement and who subsequently went on hunger strike because of the appalling conditions were vilified (Fanning 2002: 90-94). Eventually they left for Canada, where they received a warmer welcome.

This unedifying episode confirmed the xenophobic response already evident in the lamentable attitude of the Irish state towards Jewish refugees (Keogh 1998) and repeated in the views of prominent Cork Bishop Cornelius Lucey in the Commission on Emigration ('immigration we rule out'). Such determined insularity was to change little in the following quarter of a century. Ironically, Knockalisheen was later proposed as a resettlement camp for Travellers in the 1960s and is now a reception centre for asylum seekers and refugees. When Chilean refugees from the US-inspired coup in 1973 came to Ireland, they found goodwill towards them, especially in radical and left-wing Catholic circles, but very little in the way of support from the statutory services – even basic language training was not provided until 1977 (Fanning *et al.* 2000). The notion of the specificity of the needs of the migrant – especially the forced migrant – was still foreign. By the time the Vietnamese Boat People arrived in the late 1970s and early 1980s there were some ideas about their needs, at least concerning language training and other basic services, but little understanding of how to encourage social inclusion while respecting Vietnamese cultural heritage. Their experience was largely one of being distanced from mainstream Irish society. The well-meaning but disastrous attempt to promote their integration through their dispersal around the country on a one-family-per-town basis soon broke down as these families inevitably drifted back to Dublin, the one place where some kind of critical social and cultural mass existed for them (Fanning *et al.* 2000). Moreover, public discourse tended to present them as exceptional, an attitude which still remains dominant. There was thus no perceived need to develop a structural response, or to recognise that such movements of people challenged not only the lack of services for them, but also the very nature of Irish society. Identity construction in Ireland remained rooted, literally, in place, exclusive and hermetic.

It is clear, then, that policy towards those seen as culturally different, whether Traveller or immigrant, has accordingly stressed assimilation rather than integration (e.g. the

'Itinerant Resettlement' programme of the 1960s). For those incomers born outside Ireland, 'Irishness' in the sense of full acceptance is still really only acquired through parental connection. And even then it is doubtful if those who are Irish by parentage but English or American by accent are ever really experienced, or treated, as Irish by the native-born. Unlike Canada, the USA, Australia or even Britain, Ireland offers no easy way to 'become' Irish; citizenship does not in itself convey belonging.

Nonetheless, the monolithic cultural identity gradually began to break down during the 1980s. Instead of an ethos which focused on a Catholic, consensus-based rural ideal, recent years have seen the secularisation of Irish life and society, the impact of the women's movement, a strengthening of individualism and consumerism, a more fluid relationship between Ireland and its own Diaspora (including the return of large numbers of migrants), the arrival in some numbers of new immigrants with a variety of new cultures, the ubiquitous spread of the information society, and a growing confidence and willingness to experiment and adopt new ideas and customs.

ANTINOMIES OF IRISH POSTMODERNITY

In the light of these changes, it has become fashionable to endorse a new self-confident postmodern Celtic Tiger identity as somehow divorced from the past: self-referential, free-floating and forward- rather than backward- looking. The iconic geographical reference is Dublin, which has apparently slipped its older moorings to become a global city in which (as I have suggested above) the past, Joycean or other, is little more than a commodified cultural product which serves as a backdrop to today's 'happening' city. However, serious questions arise about this postmodern, 'whatever-you're-having-yourself' Irish identity, which sugg-est it should not attract unquestioning endorsement.

How are new cultural identities being mediated in the political domain, if indeed they are? And if not, is a new nihilism emerging, or something more subversive and creative? Who are the new stakeholders? Who are the losers? Whose voices are still not being heard? It would be rather difficult to explain to a newly enfranchised Irish citizen from another ethnic background – French, Rwandan or Palestinian, say – the differences between Irish political parties and whom they might wish to vote for. Is Ireland a republican society in the French meaning of the term? It certainly seems that Irish cultural identity is no longer a monolith, but if so, what new, multifaceted models are emerging?

Societies which are already genuinely committed to a rigorous respect for difference, whether in terms of cultural identity or political options, also acquire an awareness that in political, financial and practical terms, diversity costs, even if it also conveys enormous benefits in the long term. Yet many 'echt' (authentic) Irish people have themselves encountered the feeling that to be different in any way is to be a nuisance. This is not even a question of being Black, or a Traveller, or an asylum seeker. It may be a question of being Irish-speaking, or a cyclist, or lesbian, or a poor or blind person, or a person with a disability, or an anti-globalist. Difference is exceptionally poorly tolerated in Ireland. This Irish intolerance of so-called 'cranks' of any description contrasts markedly with British or Dutch traditions of internal dissent and the acceptance of eccentricity. The seriousness of the 2003 debate on Iraq in the British House of Commons, on both sides, illustrated the difference between a country where public political morality is taken passionately and seriously, and the tendency for much Irish public, even parliamentary, speech to be characterised by shiftiness, doublethink and self-interest.

Ireland likes to think of itself nowadays as a go-ahead entrepreneurial society, and is regularly presented as such by its governing politicians. But its attitudes do not encourage, still less reward, innovation and risk-taking in the *social* domain. There is an absence of productive confrontation, of the dialectical processes through which ideas are opposed one to another and something new and creative emerges from the interactive process that this entails. Thus, society itself is changing, but some of the old norms have not, and the process of social provision for that change is not being engaged upon.

Take schooling as an example: in Ireland it is almost entirely confessional. There are Roman Catholic, Protestant, Jewish and now Muslim schools. That might seem like choice: but many people do not support faith-based schools, even if they have a specific confessional belief themselves. The proportion of agnostics or atheists is also growing[7], but no provision is being made in the public sector for the growing diversity among the state's population. On the contrary, equality legislation has a specific exception for schools. In practice there is often no choice at all because there is only one local, faith-based school. An example from the late 1990s will illustrate the situation. My stepson attended the local primary school. It had an admirably open stated policy and worked actively to ensure that racism or sectarianism were not acceptable and that those black, Asian, Muslim and 'other' boys who were present by then in every class, albeit in small numbers, were accepted as equals. Until, that is, the sixth-class school photograph – the photograph which would sum up a boy's life to date, eight years of primary schooling and socialisation. This coincided, as it always had, with the week of the Roman Catholic ceremony of Confirmation. Only one photograph was taken, and despite the presence of my agnostic son and his Pakistani Muslim colleague in the class, they were not in the picture: a small but telling and irreparable erasure of those who were different.

It is a moot point whether the 'Protestant state for a Protestant people' of Northern Ireland was more or less exclusionary than its Southern equivalent. Still, David Trim-

---

7   According to the Census, the number of persons with 'no religion' or 'not stated' rose from 6,732 in 1961 to 217,358 in 2002 (Central Statistics Office Ireland 2004).

ble's remarks about a 'mono-ethnic, monocultural society' notwithstanding (*The Irish Times* 11/3/02), the Republic has definitively crossed a line from the near 'theocracy of the de Valera era' (Akenson 1999) to the modern, or postmodern, multi-ethnic and partly secularised Irish state of today. Nevertheless, although Irish cultural identity is in a state of flux, it remains unclear whether a parallel process of social and political transformation, with all that this would imply in terms of power and policies, is taking place.

MULTICULTURALISM IN IRELAND

Turning to multiculturalism or interculturalism, to use the official term (which no-one does), there have been a number of significant initiatives in recent years. These include, the establishment of a National Consultative Committee on Racism and Interculturalism (NCCRI) and a *Know Racism* campaign. *Integration: a Two-Way Process* (Department of Justice, Equality and Law Reform 1999) presents a blueprint for future policy, but it is largely aspirational. Civil society, as distinct from the state, and in particular the voluntary sector, has shown a remarkable capacity to rise to new challenges. Thus, for instance, the government's policy of dispersing asylum-seekers was resisted at first by some local communities, but I do not know of a single place where serious resistance continued once the new people had actually arrived. On the contrary: a plethora of voluntary groups sprang up overnight and the umbrella organisation, Integrating Ireland, now lists up to one hundred and sixty members. Moreover, many of these groups can be said largely to espouse a rights-based and not a charitable approach.

But there are negative features as well. Racism is not endemic but it is far from absent and if anything seems to be increasing (Millward Brown 2004). The failure of the state to attend to issues of ongoing social exclusion risks increasing social tension, as the most disadvantaged members of society, rather than cooperating, may be tempted to struggle

against one another. Little attempt is being made to explain
the reality of multi-ethnicity in Ireland today and the fact
that it is here to stay, and adequate responses on the policy
level are conspicuously lacking. In the voluntary sector there
is a significant gap between those working with 'new communities' – for the most part mainstream and middle-class
Irish – and disadvantaged working-class Irish people. It is
perhaps symptomatic that few middle-class Irish people will
ever have heard of the range of state-backed initiatives such
as the Community Development Programmes (CDPs) designed to combat social exclusion. Indeed, there is a more
general divide between the middle- and working-classes in
Ireland: only Gardaí (police), civil servants, teachers, social
workers and a few others cross this divide, and then mainly
as gatekeepers. Movement in the other direction is even
rarer. In other northern European countries this gap is narrower as civil society, public spaces and public services bind
all together. Even within those very sectors where a more
inclusive attitude might be expected, new communities are
underrepresented. Some non-governmental organisations
working with asylum seekers and refugees frequently do not
see it as part of their mission to transfer power to those with
whom they work. On the official side, only a handful of CDPs
directly address new community needs and fewer still are
directly run by incomers. In fact (apart from Traveller initiatives) there is only one, the Bosnian CDP, with a specific
ethnic focus, although other CDPs do address minority issues as part of their broader remit. In short, although the
language and grammar of inclusion exists, it is not yet being
employed in a sufficiently meaningful way.

CURRENT DEVELOPMENTS

Recent developments illustrate both the positive and the
negative potential immanent in the moment at which Ireland
now finds itself. On the negative side, a majority Supreme
Court decision in 2003 removed *de facto* residence rights in

Ireland for foreign-born parents of Irish-born children. The Minister argued that a situation had developed whereby substantial numbers of women were travelling to Ireland to give birth expressly to facilitate the family's case for residency here. However, the merits of his case, insofar as there were any, were greatly vitiated by the government's subsequent attitude towards those who were already in the country and had already applied for residency before the court case was decided. The decision rendered indeterminate the situation of approximately 11,000 persons; more than one year later, many are still in limbo and a number have been deported. Yet if the government had shown a degree of magnanimity by regularising the position of those already in the system, their future policy would not have been affected in any way and the integration of this known number could have proceeded. The refusal to regularise their position had, then, the clear aspect of a punitive measure, and can be seen as an example of *de facto* institutional racism.

In a further negative development, the government decided to hold a referendum in mid-2004 concerning the children themselves, with the intended effect of removing the automaticity of Irish citizenship, the basis of all previous Irish legislation and incorporated into the provisions of the 1998 Agreement. The measure was justified by allegations that a significant number of foreign women were still arriving in Irish hospitals in late pregnancy to ensure that their infants would have citizenship. These women were alleged by Minister Michael McDowell, in a pejorative phrase, to be engaged in 'citizenship shopping', though the government failed to produce detailed statistics indicating what proportion of the births were simply to foreign-born women already living in Ireland: for instance, spouses or partners of the large cohort of labour migrants, or themselves legitimate workers, or persons with refugee status already living in Ireland (Irish Council for Civil Liberties 2004). The least that can be argued is that these two developments, taken together, suggest a certain construction of identity in official quarters based on a racialised state.

Two other recent events are more positive, although not completely so in one case. The first is the decision of the government to maintain a reasonably open regime for labour migrants from the new Accession States. At one point at least five Member States had adopted this position (Netherlands, Sweden, Denmark, Britain, Ireland) but three fell away, leaving only Britain and Ireland. It is true that Britain then introduced draconian limitations on welfare claims by new Accession State labour migrants, using the 'habitual residence' rule as the basis for a new and strict regime[8]. Ireland followed suit, keeping the labour market open but introducing into Irish welfare regulations a concept of 'habitual residence' which did not previously exist in Irish policy. It remains to be seen whether the regulations introduced in Ireland, which appear to have been framed in a way designed to exclude returning Irish migrants from their draconian provisions, will fall foul of the European Court if challenged by the EU Commission or by an individual. The Irish government's position was to some extent understandable and even unavoidable, as the Common Travel Area arrangement between the UK and Ireland effectively obliges the latter to align its policies to those of the former (the reverse never happens!). But it was, regrettably, accompanied by public statements which appeared to legitimate the unproven and arguably quite spurious 'benefit tourism' rhetoric of the British tabloid press. Nonetheless, it has to be seen as basically a positive move that the government has chosen to keep the door open to migrant workers. That said, it is more likely that this reflects a markedly pro-employer attitude in the Department of Enterprise, Trade and Employment rather than a pro-migrant stance for its own sake. In this context, there is some concern that Accession may be seen as an opportunity for Ireland to source future labour migrants from

---

[8]   It is difficult to avoid the conclusion that the change of policy in the UK was motivated in part by a virulent and openly racist campaign in the tabloid press, directed at so-called 'benefit tourists' and targeting Roma in particular.

'desirable' (White? European?) sources, thus reducing the need to find them in other places.

Finally, local elections in June 2004 led to the new phenomenon of immigrant candidates standing in a number of areas around the country. If there is hope for the future it lies in part in the willingness of migrants themselves to engage with the political process and to find their own voices within it.

The Way Forward

I begin by identifying and distinguishing between a number of different ways to proceed in implementing a workable pluralist policy: taking preventative action against racism; creating a top-down prescriptive legislative framework; voluntarist awareness-raising campaigns; specific sectoral integration and diversity programmes, preferably bottom-up and based on the participation and empowerment of all. The British case typifies the preventative approach. Virtually all states apply the third, voluntarist approach, and current Irish initiatives seem to be heading in this direction as well. Continental countries tend to apply a mixture of top-down and preventative approaches, but lack participation and empowerment. Only Canada and Australia have applied a more holistic approach, combining all of these perspectives. It is probably true to say, however, that it is not part of Irish political culture to adopt a radical perspective. Furthermore, one might argue that such perspectives were probably adopted in Australia and Canada for lack of other options. In the Canadian instance, a hugely complex internal configuration of ethnic groups, encompassing tensions between English and French language communities, First Nations communities and new immigrants, and a degree of fragility within the Canadian federal system which may yet break the country apart, made it imperative to find new solutions. In Australia some of the same ingredients are present: a shameful history of past mistreatment of aboriginal and Torres Strait Islander peoples, a 'White Australia' immigration policy until the 1970s and an increasingly diverse new population. Moreover, there has been resistance in both countries to multiculturalism, although the rather dramatic collapse in 2002 of Pauline Hanson's racist One Nation movement and the relative lack of support for similar causes in Canada may give cause for optimism.

A vaguely benevolent multiculturalism which ignores social inequality will not last. During the late 1990s tenants of A public housing project in Cork hung out a banner saying 'we wish we were refugees'. This poignant and depressing incident shows how alienated, excluded and angry some people felt, even if they placed the blame for their predicament in the wrong quarter. It also illustrates the real potential for social conflict in Ireland, in the absence of focused policy developments. The classic liberal model, with its tendency to understate the operation of power and inequality in society, cannot in itself ensure equality. Not to grasp this is to fail to understand the rise of populist politicians such as the Dutch Pim Fortuyn, murdered in 2002, and the consequent hardening even of mainstream approaches to multi-ethnicity. Ireland has an opportunity to avoid such polarisation, but it will require creative thinking as well as a willingness to dig into its own past and find those resonances which might help to deal with the new realities. I would argue that the country has one major psychosocial asset to hand which it has not, so far, used to the extent that it migh: the collective experience of those millions of Irish emigrants who made their way in other societies and coped with intercultural tensions, difference and sometimes prejudice and outright discrimination. This is however a complex issue which cannot be tackled simply by claiming some overall identity of interest between 'us' and 'them' which would neither be true nor justified, nor serve as a meaningful approach to pluralism.

CONCLUSIONS

Conventional criticisms of nationalism usually focus on ethnic cleansing, cultural exclusivism and other practices which have characterised the narrowly fanatic nationalisms of the late twentieth century. Ideas and models of national identity can, however, be founded upon democracy and conceived as inclusive and respectful of diversity and difference, yet still remain positive and compelling. But a civic nationalism that makes a claim to respecting cultural differences does not in itself guarantee that the state will refrain from coercive assimilationist policies. In other words, democratic forms of nationalism cannot be defended simply through a formal appeal *à la française* to abstract, liberal principles. How nationalism and the nation state enact democracy must be determined, in part, through the access which diverse cultural groups have to shared structures of power that organise commanding legal, economic, and cultural institutions at the local, state, and national level. This will require a new kind of republicanism, which accepts that all those who live in Irish society, irrespective of their origins, shall have equal rights and equal opportunities. There will have to be real power sharing, across classes as well as across communities. Ireland has the prosperity, the potential and the capacity to bring about such positive and decisive change; it is at present not clear whether it has the necessary will.

REFERENCES

Akenson, D. (1999), 'New Scriptures Needed', *Annual Conference of The Irish Association*, Carrickfergus (14/11/99) http://www.irish-association.org/archives/don_atkenson11_99.html (Accessed 7/5/02).

Anderson, B. (1991), *Imagined Communities: Reflections on the Origin and Spread of Nationalism*. London: Verso.

Barth, F. (1969), *Ethnic Groups and Boundaries: the Social Organization of Culture Difference.* Bergen: Universitets Forlaget.

Champion, F. (1999), 'De la Diversité des Pluralismes Religieux', *MOST Journal on Multicultural Societies* 1, 2. http://www.unesco.org/most/vl1n2chf.htm (accessed 27/4/04).

Central Statistics Office Ireland (2004), *Census 2002 Volume 12 Religion.* Dublin. http://www.cso.ie/census/vol12_index.htm (accessed 7/5/04).

Clarke, A. (1963), 'Burial of an Irish President' in *Flight to Africa.* Dublin: Dolmen Press.

Commission on Emigration and other Population Problems 1948-1954 (1955), *Reports.* Dublin: Stationery Office.

Cullen, F. (2000), 'Beyond Nationalism: Time to Reclaim the Republican Ideal', *The Republic* 1, 7-14.

Delaney, E. (2000), *Demography, State and Society: Irish Migration to Britain 1921-1971.* Liverpool: Liverpool University Press.

Department of Justice, Equality and Law Reform (1999), *Integration: a Two Way Process.* Dublin.

De Valera, E. (1991), 'The Ireland That We Dreamed Of', (Radio Éireann 17/3/43). In S. Deane ed., *The Field Day Anthology of Irish Writing,* Vol. 3. Derry: Field Day Publications.

Dunne, T. (2004), *Rebellions: Memoir, Memory and 1798.* Dublin: Lilliput.

Fanning, B., Loyal, S. and Staunton, C. (2000), *Asylum Seekers and the Right to Work in Ireland.* Dublin: Irish Refugee Council.

Fanning, B. (2002), *Racism and Social Change in the Republic of Ireland,* Manchester: Manchester University Press.

Garner, S. (2004), *Racism in the Irish Experience.* London: Pluto.

Goodhart, D. (2004), 'Discomfort of Strangers', *Prospect* (February). Also accessible online at http://politics.

guardian.co.uk/comment/story/0,9115,1154687,00.html
(Accessed 7/5/04).

Healy, J. (1978), *Nineteen Acres*, Galway: Kennys.

Honohan, I. (2001), 'Freedom as Citizenship: The Republican
Tradition in Political Theory', *The Republic* 2, 7-24.

Irish Council for Civil Liberties (2004), *ICCL Briefing on
Proposal For Referendum On Citizenship*. Dublin: Irish
Council for Civil Liberties.

The Irish Times, 11/3/02, 18/3/03 and 22/3/03.

Keogh, D. (1998), *Jews In Twentieth-Century Ireland:
Refugees, Anti-Semitism and the Holocaust*. Cork: Cork
University Press.

Kipling, R. (1942), *Rudyard Kipling's Verse: Definitive
Edition*. London: Hodder and Stoughton.

Kristeva, J. (1991), *Étrangers à Nous-mêmes*. Paris: Fayard.

Lee, J.J. (1989), *Ireland 1912-1985: Politics and Society*.
Cambridge: Cambridge University Press.

Lentin, R. (2002) 'Anti-Racist Responses to the Racialisation
of Irishness: Disavowed Multiculturalism and its Discontents', in R. Lentin and R. McVeigh eds, *Racism and
Anti-Racism in Ireland*. Belfast: Beyond the Pale
Publications.

Millward Brown IMS (2004), *Research Findings Opinions on
Racism and Attitudes to Minority Groups*. Dublin: Know
Racism Campaign. http://www.knowracism.i/pdfs/
Presentation_26th_Feb_04.ppt (accessed 7/5/04).

Moynihan, D.P. (1968), 'The New Racialism', *Atlantic Monthly*
222, 2; 35-40. http://www.theatlantic.com/politics/race/
moynihan.htm (Accessed 6 May 2004).

National Consultative Committee on Racism and Inter-
culturalism (no date), *About the Consultative Committee on
Racism and Interculturalism, Its Role and Activities*.
Dublin: NCCRI.

O'Carroll, J.P. (2002), 'Cultural Lag and Democratic Deficit
in Ireland, or "dat's outside the terms of d'agreement"',
Community Development Journal 37, 1, 10-19.

6. Conceptions of Equality: The Case Of Northern Ireland

MÁIRÉAD NIC CRAITH

Unionists and nationalists in Northern Ireland place different degrees of emphasis on individual and communal conceptions of belonging to the state. In keeping with a largely Protestant religious tradition which emphasises the personal relationship with God, unionists focus primarily on individual citizens. For nationalists, the communal, cultural context is of far greater significance – a perspective which is reinforced by the historical communality of Catholicism. This chapter argues that the variance in focus on citizenship and culture has impacted on different interpretations of the concept of equality in Northern Ireland and has generated an interesting response from the unionist community in particular.

CITIZENSHIP AND CULTURE

Citizenship has traditionally emphasised a reciprocal relationship between individual and state. Individuals affirm their obligations to the state and recognition of state authority confers certain rights and privileges in return on citizens. Lister (1997: 35) has suggested that citizenship is a process of participation: 'citizenship as rights enables people to act as agents'. Historically the concept of citizenship has been viewed as a political rather than a cultural concept, which may stem in part from the significance of the individual relationship, but also derives from the emphasis of social theorists such as T.H. Marshall (1992 [1950]) on the civil, political and social aspects of citizenship. However some more recent sociological definitions recognize a cultural dimension, explaining citizenship as a 'set of practices (juridical, political, economic and cultural) which define a person as a component member of society' (Turner 1993: 2).

In contrast, culture presupposes the communal context and 'culture is a shared and negotiated system of meaning' in an ongoing process of development (Lassiter 2002: 40). Anthropologists typically define culture as a way of life: 'as simply a way of talking about collective identities' (Kuper 1999: 3). Culture is a matter of ideas, a pattern of meanings, which are embedded in symbolic forms through which people communicate with one another (Thompson 1990: 132). Geertz (1973) construed forms of culture as 'webs of significance' in which people interact and with which they identify. The nature of such patterns or webs is constantly re-negotiated and culture is an ongoing process in which collectives participate and renew their sense of identity.

Notions of citizenship and culture place different degrees of emphasis on the concept of community. Citizenship primarily encapsulates an individualistic element but it does imply a communal context, which is the political entity. The autonomy of the citizen is based on the rights and privileges which citizenship confers on individuals who recognise the legitimacy of the political agency for the collective unit. As culture is inherently a shared concept, it places far greater emphasis on belonging to the community, although individuals may play different roles in the process of renewing or reviving different patterns of culture.

CIVIC AND ETHNIC CONCEPTIONS OF BELONGING

Tensions between individuals and collectives are also inherent in civic and ethnic models of nationalism. France is usually cited as a prime example of civic nationalism which places far greater emphasis on individual citizens rather than on communal cultures. In theory at least, people in France choose to belong to the French State, regardless of their language, race or creed. They become citizens (as Tom Paine did). At the heart of the French Revolution was a new conception of citizenship as an active and radical process, one which emphasised the universal and egalitarian potential of the citizen. Emphasis was placed on the individual rather than on the communal context, and rights would reside in persons rather than in minorities or groups. The French Revolution can be perceived as an event which asserted the primacy of citizenship over culture, of universalism over specificity, and France is regarded as a prime illustration of an approach to social membership which is political more than cultural. The key to membership in France is the acceptance of its secular republican values on the part of would-be citizens.

But there are problems with this example. When the state set out to create a French nation within its territorial boundaries, unity was equated with uniformity. The voluntaristic notion of nationhood merged with the ethnic or cultural, and inclusion in the nation inevitably entailed assimilation to the majority culture. In theory civic nations such as France are culturally neutral, yet this is hardly the case. The French Revolution introduced the notion of secular citizenship, but it also provided a strong impetus for linguistic and cultural unification. Although a language census in 1790 revealed that less than 12.5 per cent of the population spoke French as their mother tongue, the message of the Revolution was carried in French (Wright 2000: 38). In subsequent decades and centuries, the nation-state pursued an official assimilationist policy (Ager 1999, Judge and Judge 2000). French was authorised as the sole medium of communication in public life. Cultures and languages such as Breton, Basque or Occitan, were regarded as divisive and a danger to the territorial unity of the nation-state.

Even in contemporary times, France does not cope well with expressions of ethnic identity from different cultural groups. For example, Muslims who wish to wear the *Hijab* (veil) in state schools generate symbolic problems for the state (McCrone 1998: 39) and recent changes in state legislation have removed the right of school children to wear symbols of religious affiliation in state schools. This should not be interpreted as a lack of appreciation for symbols of culture. As Smith (1988) quite rightly points out, the original

Jacobin Revolutionaries were not unconcerned with culture. In fact they were so enamoured with the French language and civilisation that they wished to enhance it at the expense of all other regional identities! A unified French identity is dependent on a capacity to assimilate migrants and the culturally different (Loughlin 1998). In this example of 'civic' nationalism, there was (and is) an inextricable link between language, culture and imagined community.

Unlike France, Germany (the usual example of ethnic nationalism) has traditionally stressed ethnic origins rather than political commitment when defining legitimate membership of the nation and Germany's citizenship law in 1913 established the ethnic basis of citizenship for almost a century. National consciousness in nineteenth-century Germany was derived from the ideology of the Grimm brothers and Herder who emphasised the importance of German *Volk* culture. Of primary significance was the indigenous language and its oral literature. Ultimately, German nationality is in one's genetic family and in theory at least one recognizes 'family relatives' through the use of a common language, but there are some complications with this line of reasoning.

During Herder's lifetime, the territory that was to become the German nation-state hardly comprised a single recognizable language. Instead there were several mutually unintelligible forms of 'German speech', none of which had established its own legitimacy as the 'standard' form (Billig 1995: 32-3). In reality, print rather than spoken languages united people and 'permitted the continued existence of very dissimilar spoken varieties of the language in the different regions of the state' (Wright 2000: 41).

The German language is still considered of great importance in contemporary Germany. Migrants from Russia who come to Germany speaking an unintelligible dialect of 'German' are considered part of the German community if their ancestors were German. Moreover, Germany extends membership of its *Kulturnation* to German speakers outside of its territorial boundaries. In 1995, for example, the German government offered the right to a German passport to 70,000 Germans resident in the Polish region of Silesia.

Yet German language and culture are of limited importance in defining citizenship of the 'imagined community' (Anderson 1983). Second- and third-generation Turkish immigrants speaking perfectly fluent German and immersed in German culture are considered *Ausländer* (outsiders). Their fluency in German does not guarantee membership of the German community (Watson 2000: 31). Instead, it serves to emphasise difference, as despite proficiency in the language, one may never be accepted as a member of the German nation.

However, recent events have indicated the demise of ethno-cultural exclusion in Germany in the process of acquiring citizenship. In May 1999 the German parliament opted to revise traditional citizenship policies and the new law offers automatic citizenship rights to immigrant children born on German soil who are permitted to retain two passports until the age of twenty-three, when they must choose their preferred citizenship (Kivisto 2002: 169). This differs starkly from the situation in France, where children of immigrants must now apply for citizenship and the idea of a secular France, which ignores cultural and religious particularity, is largely a myth.

THE CIVIC/CULTURAL AXIS IN NORTHERN IRELAND

Unionists and nationalists in Northern Ireland have different senses of place and have traditionally placed different emphasis on concepts of citizenship and culture. Unionists view themselves as part of the UK whereas nationalists see themselves in the context of a thirty-two county Ireland. Liberal unionists imagine themselves as members of the Great British State whereas nationalists think in terms of the Irish cultural nation. Not only do unionists and nationalists think in terms of different geographical territories, there are different senses of nation-state for each. Unionists primarily think

in terms of an imagined political community, whereas nationalists have a stronger sense of cultural nationhood.

Unionists and nationalists have espoused different
conceptions of belonging to a nation-state. Although some
cultural unionists assert the primacy of culture, liberal unionists have traditionally endorsed the principles of citizenship and think in terms of a civic, individual perspective.
Citizenship is the central tenet of British unionism although
the British never developed the concept of citizenship as the
French did. Instead, British citizenship developed from the
pre-modern definition of people as subjects of the Crown.
Citizenship is usually perceived in contrast with, rather than
as a form of, nationalism – a dichotomy which is reinforced
in part by a common insistence on 'two communities' whose
aspirations are perceived as being in opposition to one another. British unionists regard their Britishness as a reflection of citizenship rather than nationality. 'There are only
British citizens who happen to be English, Scottish, Welsh,
Irish and some who would be none of these' (Aughey 1995:
12). Issues of equality, rights and the calibre of citizenship
within the Union strongly motivate them and they believe
that a nationalist obsession with concepts of culture and
nation are confusing and detrimental.

In contrast with unionists, nationalists think primarily in
communitarian terms; a perspective that has been reinforced historically and religiously. Irish nationalism borrows,
simultaneously, from the Republican traditions of the
French Revolution, but also, and contradictorily, from the
ethnic traditions of Irishness such as language, music and
religion. The Constitution of the Irish Republic, drafted in
1937, expressed great certainty with regard to the nature
and extent of the Irish ethnic community. Article 1 established the inalienable right of the nation to political sovereignty and identified the 'national territory' as Éire.

More contentiously the second Article affirmed that the
territory of this ethnic nation 'consists of the whole island of
Ireland, its islands and the territorial seas'. In this manner,
the Constitution of the Republic of Ireland claimed to apply

to the entire nation on the island. Cultural symbols of this ethnic nation were clearly defined, and included the tricolour, the Irish language and Roman Catholicism. Hall (1992) has applied the term 'discourse' to the concept of national culture, enabling communities to produce an impression of unity on a fragmented and differentiated reality.

Theoretically at least, all nationalist groups aspire to the re-unification of Ireland. In common with their constitutional colleagues, republicans now endorse the political process as the best method of achieving this aim. While they accept the current partition of Ireland, many of them view it as being of a temporary nature. Their political ideology holds that the boundaries of the nation-state should be coterminous with an ethnic group. For them the Irish ethnic nation has always extended to the entire thirty-two counties. Characteristics such as language and religion already operate as important cultural affirmations of this Irish ethnicity. By promoting Irish culture in Northern Ireland, they strengthen their affiliation with the Republic.

EQUALITY OF COMMUNITIES AND IDENTITIES

Different senses of place have generated inevitable ongoing tensions in Northern Ireland. For unionists, Northern Ireland is inherently British and must remain part of the UK. Nationalists have always held the view that partition was artificial and Northern Ireland culturally and politically belonged with the rest of the island. In the final decades of the twentieth century, British and Irish governments increasingly sought to develop a new model of accommodation deriving from different senses of belonging of unionists and nationalists. Essentially the two governments sought to accommodate both perspectives by redefining Northern Ireland as a region of two communities with two distinct conceptions of belonging. The UK and Irish governments were also keen to promote the concept of equality for each of the communities.

The development of the notion of two equal communities emerged in a series of agreements between the two states. In the Anglo-Irish Agreement of 1985, the two governments agreed to recognize and respect 'the identities of the two communities in Northern Ireland, and the right of each to pursue its aspirations by peaceful and constitutional means' (in O'Day 1997: 189-90). Article 5 of the 1985 Agreement asserted that the government would concern itself with procedures to recognize and to accommodate the identities and rights of both traditions in Northern Ireland (Department of Foreign Affairs 1985: 5). While nationalists welcomed the Anglo-Irish Agreement, there was a virulent reaction from many unionists to the document primarily because it affirmed a role for the Irish government in the affairs of Northern Ireland.

Despite unionist hostility and reservations regarding the recognition of two communities, the British and Irish governments continued to endorse the communal model. In 1993, the Downing Street Declaration reconceptualised the role of the British government as a facilitator of a peace process. The British government would support the achievement of consensus through co-operation and a process of dialogue, which would be 'based on full respect for the rights and identities of both traditions in Ireland' (in O'Day 1997: 194). Similarly the Irish government undertook to 'respect the democratic dignity and civil rights and liberties of both communities' (in O'Day 1997: 194-5).

Two years later the Framework Document endorsed a balance of legitimacy between the two communities. The governments agreed that relationships within Northern Ireland itself and those between the governments of Britain and Ireland should recognize and 'respect the full and equal legitimacy and worth of the identity, sense of allegiance, aspiration and ethos of both unionist and nationalist communities'. Both governments agreed to the principle that 'institutions and arrangements in Northern Ireland and North/South institutions should afford both communities secure and satisfactory political, administrative and symbolic expression and protection' (in O'Day 1997: 202-3).

This principle of duality was reinforced in 1998 when signatories to the GFA affirmed 'substantial differences' between the 'continuing and equally legitimate, political aspirations' of unionists and nationalists (Government of the United Kingdom of Great Britain and Northern Ireland and Government of Ireland 1998: 1). Parties to the GFA accepted the legitimacy of the wish for a united Ireland, but they also affirmed the wish of the current majority to maintain the Union (*ibid.* 1998: 2).

Participants in the talks accepted the freedom of the people of Northern Ireland to choose their political jurisdiction and acknowledged their right to identify themselves as British or Irish or both if that was their desire. Essentially this meant that unionists could no longer be secure in their relationship with Britain and the foundations of their home appeared to be shifting. The GFA inevitably provoked consternation among hard-line unionists who viewed it as symptomatic of the British government's increasing lack of commitment to Northern Ireland. In contrast, nationalists felt a little closer to home.

While nationalists welcomed the progress made in the GFA, republicans were not necessarily reconciled to the notion of parity of esteem for British as well as Irish cultural identities. For them, Northern Ireland was Irish and a formal recognition of Britishness impacted on that sense of Irishness. Cultural unionists adopted a similar single-minded approach. For them Northern Ireland was a British province and the formal recognition of two cultural identities implied a dilution in Britishness and generated increased insecurity. Neither party disputed the need for equality or parity of esteem between the various traditions but their interpretation of this concept differed greatly, a factor that has not yet been recognised by various parties to the process.

CONCEPTS OF EQUALITY

Different interpretations of concepts of equality and parity of esteem between unionists and nationalists engender serious misunderstandings that are not appreciated. For unionists, the phrase 'parity of esteem' implies that equality should apply at an individual level. This is in accordance with the traditional emphasis on individual relationships in their religious and political ideologies. From their perspective each Northern Irish citizen is considered equal before the law. This applies to all members of society who uphold the sovereignty of the British state. If members do not benefit from this system, it is usually as a result of their contempt for the British state.

Nationalists interpret the notion of parity of esteem in a completely different manner. They understand it in communal terms. From this perspective, parity of esteem implies equality at a collective rather than an individual level and relates in particular to recognition for Irish cultural traditions in Northern Ireland. These differing interpretations reflect the ongoing tensions between notions of individualism versus collectivism, citizenship versus culture. They also reflect a differing sense of morality among Catholics and Protestants. Essentially they point to different modes of recognition.

Charles Taylor (1994) draws attention to two alternative approaches to equality, which he terms the politics of universalism and the politics of difference. The politics of universalism require that every citizen has identical rights. In contrast, the politics of difference emphasises the distinctiveness of each individual and focuses on positive discriminatory practices in order to ensure equality.

> With the politics of equal dignity, what is established is meant to be universally the same, an identical basket of rights and immunities; with the politics of difference, what we are asked to recognize is the unique identity of this individual or group, their distinctness from everyone else (Taylor 1994: 38).

Proponents of the politics of universalism seek non-discrimination so that every individual receives similar treatment. They 'seek to protect against harm caused by prejudice and discrimination, and therefore to restore and maintain a level playing field' (Packer 1999: 259). This process is perceived as essentially neutral and could be regarded as 'culture-blind'. In contrast, advocates of the politics of difference seek positive or reverse discrimination for collectives in order to ensure that no-one suffers discrimination. Their concern is 'to protect against harm caused by identity through the effects of the normal majority rule, and also to facilitate the equal opportunity for persons belonging to minorities to maintain and develop their identity/ies' (Packer 1999: 259).

Different processes of recognition are at the heart of many crisis points. In 1933, for example, the Albanian government abolished all private schools including those of the Greek minority. When the Greeks reacted against this decision, the Albanians argued that every individual was receiving equal treatment and that the Greeks could hardly have greater expectations than the Albanian majority. Two years later the case was brought before the Permanent Court of International Justice, which ruled that there was a difference between equality *de juro* and equality *de facto*. While the former might preclude discrimination of any kind, the latter might require some differential treatment in order to establish an equilibrium between different situations.

Both the politics of universalism and the politics of difference have the concept of potential at their roots, but their emphasis is different. The politics of universalism focus on the individual and require equal treatment of everyone because of the universal human potential in which every person shares. The equal treatment of all individuals is possible only in a 'difference-blind' fashion. Society at large does not recognise collective identities or group rights, and the public sphere is deemed to be culturally neutral. In fact the majority context is perceived as civic and non-cultural. In contrast, the ideology of the politics of difference seeks to ensure that every individual or group has the potential to develop to full capacity and circumstances may require that some individuals receive differential treatment in order to achieve this.

EQUALITY, CULTURE AND CITIZENSHIP

In the context of Northern Ireland, 'parity of esteem' is generally assumed to imply the unquestionable existence of two separate traditions, which should be recognised and respected in equal terms. From the unionist perspective, all peoples in Northern Ireland are British citizens and unionists prefer to rely on the concept of citizenship to ensure equality. Many liberals, particularly in the post World War II era, believe that the common right of citizenship protects membership of cultural traditions. If the necessary infrastructure is in place, minorities do not need any 'extra rights'. Instead of granting special protection to vulnerable groups, basic civil rights are guaranteed to all individuals regardless of group membership. Inherent in this model of recognition is the implication that minority groups cannot legitimately demand special protection as all individuals enjoy equality of treatment. In public this principle of citizenship should reflect itself in terms of loyalty to the state. Privately, individuals are free to espouse their own cultural traditions.

Nationalists, however, do not agree with the logic of such arguments and make the case for the operation of the principle of equality on a collective rather than on an individual basis. They lend weight to this collective issue with an emphasis on their indigeneity. From the nationalist perspective, the fact that they are an indigenous, rather than an immigrant, group further necessitates full government recognition of Irish cultural traditions in Northern Ireland. Will Kymlicka (1995) has argued that rights of indigenous minorities are far more robust than those of migrants, although many, myself included, disagree with this contention.

The focus on equality at a collective rather than an individual level has generated several interesting responses from unionists. To some unionists, the size of the collective has become an issue and it is simply not fair that a minority, however large, should be treated in equal terms with the majority. Nationalists reject such arguments on the basis that the terms 'minority' and 'majority' are inappropriate as nationalists constitute more than forty per cent of the population and their numbers are expected to rise. From their point of view nationalists make up such a large proportion of the population that they can hardly be considered a minority.

Unionists are keen to establish that minority in many other countries appear happy when proportional public recognition is given to their ethnic identity. Antony Alcock (1975) cites the example of the Croat and Slovene minorities in Austria. While designated secondary schools in the provinces of Carinthia, Burgenland and Styria cater on a proportional basis to these ethnic groups, they do not receive full equality in all aspects of the public sector. Alcock also refers to the German minority in the province of North Schleswig, which has its own separate educational institutions and is represented proportionally in the political sector. Similarly the Danish minority in the Province of Schleswig-Holstein appear to be happy with their proportional representation on local government committees.

But of course there are major differences between the circumstances of these minorities and those of the Irish in Northern Ireland (Kockel 1999), and those espousing an Irish identity in Northern Ireland could emphasise the magnitude of their community. Proportionally they represent a far greater minority than the respective German or Danish groups. In fact the size of those ethnic minorities in continental Europe is no longer easily established as census forms in Denmark and Germany do not query the ethnic identity of respondents.

If both communities were placed on an entirely equal footing, the nationalist minority in Northern Ireland would operate in a manner similar to those espousing a German iden-

tity in the province of Bolzano and the neighbouring bi-
lingual towns in the province of Trento, Italy. In these regions the cultural traditions of German-speakers are given
equal status with those of Italians and a variety of safeguards serves to ensure that the German ethnic and cultural
character is preserved.

But there is one vital difference between the circumstances of nationalists in Northern Ireland and those of
German-speakers in South Tyrol. Austria has completely renounced its claim to the territory of South Tyrol and these
German-speakers view their future solely in an Italian context. Although the Irish Republic has renounced its constitutional claim to the six counties, this will not deter some
Northern Irish nationalists from aspiring to the reunification
of the thirty-two counties, a factor that disturbs many unionists.

Unionists argue that equality for Irish cultural traditions
is a dividend of the peace process rather than an entitlement
of a substantial minority group. Equal status is merited
rather than granted.

> In Northern Ireland we are now being subject to the latest pro-
> paganda "in" phrase – "parity of esteem for the two traditions".
> Esteem is not a "right" which can be granted. It must be earned
> and it is only by their deeds and words that republicans will be
> so rewarded' (Finney 1995: 57).

Porter (1996) proposes that the concept of parity of esteem has severe limitations, not least of which is the fact
that one is being asked to affirm the intrinsic value of another's identity and way of life. He suggests that it is inappropriate to expect Catholics to have esteem for an Orange
culture that they view as inherently triumphalist. It is
equally absurd to assume that Protestants will admire the
expression of an Irish identity that they perceive as threatening. It is also the case that there are elements in 'both traditions' in Northern Ireland that liberals cannot or should not
regard with esteem. For these reasons Porter argues that

'due recognition' is a more appropriate phrase as it implies an absence of hierarchy and affirms relations of reciprocity.

THE EMERGENCE OF ULSTER-BRITISH CULTURE

The focus on two communities in the final decades of the twentieth century inevitably gave weight to the communal rather than the individual context and in a sense catered unwittingly to nationalist rather than to unionist ideologies. It also served as the catalyst for a gradual shift in focus from citizenship to culture among members of the unionist community and the emergence of distinctly British forms of culture in Ulster.

One of the more significant initiatives was the establishment of the Ulster Society for the Promotion of British Heritage and Culture in the summer of 1985. The first chairman of the society was David Trimble who was quick to discern the implications of government attention to cultural matters. Anticipating that respect for nationalist culture would entail funding for the Irish language, music, games etc., he argued that culture was going to become the 'new battlefield' in Northern Irish politics. It would be extremely important for unionists to develop a non-sectarian, non-political front if they were to gain any financial benefits for the promotion of an Ulster-British cultural identity.

The establishment of the society offered a new source of confidence for unionists. This was important as nationalists had regenerated Irish culture in previous decades and had galvanised significant support for the Irish language in particular. More significantly, republicans taunted unionists about their lack of culture, which was a source of great insecurity to many Protestants. The Ulster Society offered them a mechanism for developing a voice for their culture. As one member put it: 'Trimble gave us a new sense of identity beyond singing "God save the Queen" at the end of every party conference and marching on the Twelfth of July'. Yet it was an identity with which unionists were not entirely comfortable and many liberal unionists in particular have reverted

to the significance of citizenship while continuing to emphasise the importance of Protestant culture.

A shift in focus to the communal context among the Protestant community may also have prompted the emergence of
a revival of emblems of Scottishness in the region. In the late
1970s and early 1980s, there was little public awareness of
the speech-form known as Ullans or Ulster-Scots. Adams
(1977) referred to it simply as a variety of English spoken in
particular regions of Ulster. Ian Adamson (1991: 78) classified Ullans as a version of English at this time stating that

> there are many parts of Ulster, therefore, where people are still
> bilingual in two varieties of the English language. They use
> Ulster Lallans while speaking among themselves and the
> approximation of the regional standard of Ulster English, in
> talking to strangers.

Native speakers usually refer to this speech form as 'Scotch'
and it has also been termed 'Ullans' by some writers.

Since the early 1990s the people of Northern Ireland have
become increasingly aware of the Ulster-Scots phenomenon
and the construction of an Ulster-Scots ethnolinguistic
identity. As Montgomery (1999) points out, several mile-
stones occurred in the process In 1992 the Ulster-Scots Language Society was established with the specific intention of
promoting the study, application and use of Ulster-Scots.
The society's journal was inaugurated in the following year.
Ullans: the Magazine for Ulster-Scots provides an outlet for
the publication of literary and linguistic items. Essentially
this constituted the reinvention of an Ulster-Scots print
community and several novels in Ulster-Scots have since
been issued (e.g. Robinson 1997, 1998).

Ulster-Scots culture is hardly confined to the question of
language and in recent years cultural activists have broad-
ened their scope of activities to include questions relating to
the distinctiveness of Ulster-Scots music and identity. Other
emblems of Scottish culture in Ulster have also been profiled
– such as the historical narrative of emigration to Canada
which emphasises Protestant suffering in Irish history – an

experience that has primarily been claimed by Catholics. There has also been an increase in the number of Scottish piping bands and Scottish country dancing and the development of an Ulster-Scots profile in the media.

CONCLUSION

In recent years, there has been some attempt to shift the focus from collective cultures back to individual citizens and there is some recognition of the difficulties associated with too great an emphasis on the communal, cultural context. One specific counter-initiative was the introduction of a programme on citizenship in schools and the establishment of a Northern Ireland Human Rights Commission to confirm rights supplementary to that of the European Convention for Human Rights. However there have been many problems inherent in a process which endeavours to change focus from collective cultures to individual rights – particularly as formal recognition for the collective context has only recently been acquired.

Essentially the Anglo-Irish Agreement and subsequent government declarations revised the concept of public space in Northern Ireland and significantly altered the emphasis from citizenship to culture in the public realm. This requires far greater consideration of questions that have previously been relegated to the cultural arena. Citizens will need to concern themselves with questions such as which kinds of 'culture' are deserving of public protection? Which policies are most likely to fulfil these objectives? The deconstruction of Britishness and the reconstruction of Irishness has been accompanied by an endeavour to widen the social, inclusive fabric of society and to create space for difference and for otherness. Yet many are insecure in this new situation and genuinely fail to understand alternative perspectives – a factor which may explain the increasing unwillingness to compromise.

REFERENCES

Adams, G.B. (1977), 'The Dialects of Ulster' in D. Ó Muirithe ed., *The English Language in Ireland*. Dublin and Cork: Mercier Press, 56-70.

Adamson, I. (1991), *The Identity of Ulster: the Land, the Language and the People*. Bangor: Pretani Press.

Ager, D. (1999), *Identity, Insecurity and Image: France and Language*. Clevedon: Multilingual Matters.

Alcock, A. (1975), *Protection of Minorities: Three Case Studies South Tyrol, Cyprus, Quebec*. Belfast: Northern Ireland Constitutional Convention.

Anderson, B. (1983), *Imagined Communities*. London: Verso.

Aughey, A. (1995), 'The Idea of the Union', in J.W. Foster ed., *The Idea of the Union: Statements and Critiques in Support of the Unions of Great Britain and Northern Ireland*. Vancouver, Canada: Belcouver Press, 8-19.

Finney, B. (1995) 'An Englishman on the Union', in J. W. Foster ed., *The Idea of the Union: Statements and Critiques in Support of the Union of Great Britain and Northern Ireland*. Canada, Vancouver: Belcouver Press, 53-9.

Government of the United Kingdom of Great Britain and Northern Ireland and Government of Ireland (1998), *Agreement Reached in the Multi-Party Negotiations*. Belfast.

Geertz, C. (1973), *The Interpretation of Culture*. New York: Basic Books.

Hall, S. (1992), 'The Question of Cultural Identity', in S. Hall, D. Held and T. McGrew eds, *Modernity and Its Futures*. Cambridge: Polity Press, 273-316.

Judge, A. and Judge, S. (2000), 'Linguistic Policies in France and Contemporary Issues: the Signing of the Charter for Regional or Minority Languages', *International Journal of Francophone Studies* 3, 2, 106-27.

Kivisto, P. (2002), *Multiculturalism in a Global Society*. London: Blackwell.

Kockel, U. (1999), *Borderline Cases: the Ethnic Frontiers of European Integration.* Liverpool: Liverpool University Press.

Kuper, A. (1999), *Culture: the Anthropologists' Account.* Cambridge, Mass. and London: Harvard University Press.

Kymlicka, W. (1995), *Multicultural Citizenship.* Oxford: Oxford University Press.

Lassiter, L.E. (2002), *Invitation to Anthropology.* Walnut Creek: AltaMira Press.

Lister, R. (1997), *Citizenship: Feminist Perspectives.* Basingstoke: Macmillan.

Loughlin, J. (1998), 'Culture, Nation and Region in Western Europe: a Comparative Approach', Paper delivered at Cardiff University (September).

Marshall, T. (1992), 'Citizenship and Social Class', in T. Marshall, and T. Bottomore eds, *Citizenship and Social Class.* London: Pluto Press, 1-51.

McCrone, D. (1998), *The Sociology of Nationalism: Tomorrow's Ancestors.* London: Routledge.

Montgomery, M. (1999), 'The Position of Ulster Scots', *Ulster Folklife* 45, 86-107.

O'Day, A. (1997), *Political Violence in Northern Ireland: Conflict and Conflict Resolution.* Westport, Connecticut and London: Praeger.

Packer, J. (1999), 'Problems in Defining Minorities', in D. Fottrell and B. Bowring eds, *Minority and Group Rights in the New Millennium.* Amsterdam: Kluwer Law International, 223-74.

Porter, N. (1996), *Rethinking Unionism: an Alternative Vision for Northern Ireland.* Belfast: Blackstaff Press.

Robinson, P. (1997), *Esther, Queen o tha Ulidian Pechts.* Belfast: Ullans Press.

Robinson, P. (1998), *Wake the Tribe O'Dan.* Belfast: Ullans Press.

Smith, A. (1988), 'The Myth of the "Modern Nation" and the Myths of Nations', *Ethnic and Racial Studies* 11, 1, 1-26.

Taylor, C. (1994), 'The Politics of Recognition', in C. Taylor ed., *Multiculturalism: Examining the Politics of Recognition*. Princeton: Princeton University Press, 25-73.

Thompson, J. (1990), *Ideology and Modern Culture*. Cambridge: Polity Press.

Turner, B. (1993), 'Contemporary Problems in the Theory of Citizenship', in B. Turner ed., *Citizenship and Social Theory*. London and New Delhi: Sage, 1-18.

Watson, C. (2000), *Multiculturalism*, Buckingham, and Philadelphia: Open University Press.

Wright, S. (2000), *Community and Communication: the Role of Language in Nation State Building and European Integration*. Clevedon: Multilingual Matters.

7. Me Too: Victimhood and the Proliferation of Cultural Claims in Ireland

ANDREW FINLAY

The pivot around which this chapter turns is a recent episode of what, following Joppke and Lukes (1999), might be called multicultural claims-making. Although the claim was made in the Republic of Ireland by Irish citizens it came from the Orange Order, an organisation which is based mainly in Northern Ireland, and it was an attempt by them and their supporters to extend, or to return, to the Republic the challenge presented by the liberal pluralist notion of parity of esteem that lies at the heart of the GFA. The controversy generated by the Orange Order's claim – they wished to parade in Dublin – was possibly the first practical reworking of the old pluralist agenda, concerned with Protestants and Catholics, in relation to the new agenda, that concerned with immigrants.

Out of this reworking, new forms of pluralism began to emerge, notably something akin to what Goldberg might call 'critical' multiculturalism. Critical multiculturalism defines itself against the relativism of liberal multiculturalism which enjoins us to respect or tolerate the cultural traditions of others. As Goldberg (1994: 7) says liberal multiculturalism is 'unconcerned ... with the redistribution of power and resources'. The critical forms of multiculturalism that Goldberg would prefer are concerned with defending minorities that are, to use Joppke and Luke's terms, oppressed on the basis of an immutable ascribed characteristic (see also Hall, 2000).

The Orange Order's parade proposal and responses to it thus have something to tell us about the prospects for a multicultural order emerging in Ireland as a whole beyond the biculturalism institutionalised in the GFA. It also raises more general issues. Firstly, issues to do with the tendency in a multicultural social order for cultural claims to proliferate. Some, like Joppke and Lukes, see this as problematic; others see it as a positive development. Among the latter is

Toni Morrison, the Nobel-prize-winning African-American novelist who says that she was well aware that women's issues were being set aside by the Black Power movement, and implies that this did not overly concern her. 'One liberation movement leads to another – always has. Abolition led to the suffragettes; civil rights to women's lib, which led to a black women's movement. Groups say, "what about me?"' (*The Guardian* 15/11/03). For Morrison, the proliferation of cultural claims among oppressed groups is an expanding project of liberation.

If only it were so straightforward. The multicultural order that seems to be emerging in Ireland after the paramilitary ceasefires and the GFA shows us a pattern of proliferation that is more complicated than that described by Morrison. The pattern is complicated by Ireland's colonial history and its fractured experience of nation-building which created what Harold Jackson called a 'double minority problem' (1979 [1971]): Protestants are a minority in Ireland but partition created a Catholic minority in Northern Ireland. Thus, the organisers of the proposed Orange Order parade in Dublin come from a minority in Ireland, but to the extent that they constitute a cohesive group (which is questionable) it is one that in the Republic of Ireland is identified with the former Anglo-Irish ruling class, and that is still over-represented among the professional classes (Foster, 1988 and Pilkington, 2002). Nevertheless, the organisers sought to justify the proposed parade as emblematic of a minority tradition that had been marginalised.

The proposal for a parade in Dublin and the campaign against it – which invoked prior claims to oppression – suggest that cultural claims do not simply proliferate, they proliferate in an exclusivist, competitive, zero-sum manner in which one group's cultural claim is off-set against, or negated by, the claims of others. Paul Gilroy, again writing in a North American context, has expressed concerns about the 'many dangers involved in the vacuous "me too-ism" or some other equally pointless and immoral competition over which peoples, nations, populations, or ethnic groups have suf-

fered the most; over whose identities have been most severely damaged' (2000: 113). So the case of the Orange Order in Dublin raises a second set of issues that seem to be
problematic in social orders based on multiculturalist or
pluralist principles, whether in Ireland or elsewhere: how to
reconcile, or arbitrate between, competing cultural claims. It
also suggests that both liberal and critical conceptions of
pluralism or multiculturalism are to be found wanting here.

CULTURAL CLAIM AND RESPONSE[1]

The Orange Order was founded in 1795 during conflicts over
land between Catholics and Protestants near Portadown, in
what is now Northern Ireland, but it grew as an all-Ireland
organisation, and became a bulwark of the Protestant
Ascendancy. The proposed parade in Dawson Street in Dublin would have been the first since 1936, and was planned to
coincide with the unveiling of a plaque commemorating the
bicentenary of the first meeting of the Grand Lodge of Ireland in Dublin on 9 April 1798. When plans for the parade
were made public in March 2000, the opposition was such
that the plans were postponed and later cancelled. In the
end, the plaque was unveiled by the Lord Mayor of Dublin
with little ceremony, in the absence of any Orangemen.

The idea of a plaque to mark the original premises of the
Grand Lodge of Ireland came from the then Education Offi-
cer of the Orange Order, Reverend Brian Kennaway who,
though based in Belfast, had established good relations with
some politicians in Dublin, notably the Lord Mayor, Mary
Freehill, and Senator Mary Henry. The idea of a parade to
coincide with the unveiling of the plaque came from the

---

[1] This chapter draws on an analysis of documentary sources and on
interviews with some of the main protagonists, which were conducted
after the controversy had abated. Most of the interviews were carried
out by Natalie McDonnell; see N. McDonnell, (2000), and Finlay and
McDonnell (2003).

Dublin and Wicklow Loyal Orange Lodge 1313. The Lord Mayor and Senator Henry supported the proposed parade not because they approved of the Orange Order, but as a logical outworking in the South of the GFA. Senator Mary Henry wrote to *The Irish Times*:

> True to her motto "Building Bridges", President McAleese has had the Orange Order to tea. The Lord Mayor, Mary Freehill, welcomes them to Dawson Street ... we ask so much of both communities in Northern Ireland in the name of reconciliation. This march will say more about us here than about the Orange-men ... no matter what our views on the Orange marches, the process of reconciliation and the development of a tolerant Irish society has to take place here as well as in Northern Ireland (29/3/00).

In a similar vein, the Lord Mayor explained:

> It's nothing to do with whether I agree or disagree with the Orange Order. I voted for the Good Friday Agreement and in that agreement I voted for parity of esteem and ... people exist on this island, I mean what are you going to do, push them off, I mean they're there (interview: 23/8/00).

Supporters of the proposed parade also invoked general liberal-pluralist principles such as the toleration of cultural diversity, and drew parallels between Orangemen and asylum seekers and refugees.

> The forthcoming unison of the *bodhran* and the Lambeg drum[2] deserves loud and genuine applause. So too does Lord Mayor Freehill for extending the "hand of friendship" to the Dublin-Wicklow Lodge. By so doing the Lord Mayor has portrayed us as tolerant and mature citizens. If we do not tolerate the customs and traditions of our next-door neighbours, one can truly ask what chance have the refugees? (Carey 23/4/00).

---

[2] The *bodhrán* drum is used in traditional Irish music and the Lambeg is used in Orange parades, especially in rural areas.

Another contributor to the letters pages of *The Irish Times* expressed his disappointment at the cancellation of the Orange parade in similar terms: 'with all the furore over refugees, I suggest that just as charity begins at home, so too should tolerance' (O'Shea 5/5/00). Mary Freehill also deployed this type of argument: '[i]t's all about tolerance and openness. It's important that we cherish diversity, whether we are talking about refugees or the Orange Order.' *(The Sunday Business Post* 6/4/00). When asked in interview whether she felt issues such as these would continue to arise, the former Lord Mayor expressed her view that:

> We're hugely intolerant as a nation. We don't even seem to be able to separate the issue of immigrants and asylum seekers and refugees and respect for individuals, that's another thing ... we can't even cope with cultures on this island (interview 23/8/00).

Opposition to the parade was led, but not confined to, Sinn Féin Councillors on Dublin City Council. They attempted to dismiss the parade as a publicity stunt orchestrated by 'Northern brethren' for a political purpose: to undermine the mostly successful campaigns by nationalist residents in Belfast and Portadown to prevent Orange parades from going through their areas. Initially Sinn Féin said that they would protest against the proposed Dublin parade, but this was reformulated as a solidarity meeting in Dublin with nationalists living on Garvaghy Road in Portadown[3]. The need to show solidarity with Northern nationalists remained a constant theme throughout the campaign, but Sinn Féin also engaged with the pluralist arguments put forward by supporters of the parade. They sought to establish their pluralist credentials by advocating tolerance of

---

[3] Starting in 1996, the refusal of residents of the Garvaghy Road in Portadown to allow Orangemen returning from an annual church service in Drumcree church to pass through what had become a nationalist part of a mainly Protestant town, became a focus of loyalist disaffection with the peace process. For a time the violence of loyalist reaction attracted the attention of the international media.

cultural diversity, and having done so, to show why this tolerance should not be extended such as to allow an Orange parade on the streets of Dublin.

At the April meeting of Dublin City Council, Sinn Féin put forward the following motion which was successfully carried:

> That Dublin City Council defends the right to freedom of speech and assembly which includes the rights of bodies such as the Orange Order to parade peacefully in the streets of the city. In the spirit of mutual respect for diverse traditions and the right of communities and mindful of the planned Orange parade and plaque unveiling in Dublin, the City Council calls on the Orange Order to enter into direct dialogue with the chosen represent-atives of the people of the Garvaghy road in Portadown to lift the siege of that beleaguered [community] to finally resolve the issue through real negotiation (3/4/00).

Thus Sinn Féin establishes its support for freedom of expression, respect for tradition and the rights of communities, and makes Dublin City Council's endorsement of the parade in Dawson Street conditional on the Orange Order granting those same rights to nationalists in Portadown. Later in April Sinn Féin toughened its stance:

> The Orange Order march cannot be seen in isolation from the siege of the Garvaghy Road and other contentious parades throughout the Six Counties. That nightmare siege has been going on for two years with no let-up by the Orange Order, the same people who are asking for the freedom to march through the city of Dublin. It has to be remembered that in a matter of weeks after parading in Dublin, the Orange Order will try to bulldoze their way through a nationalist area against the wishes of the people who live there. For the Lord Mayor of Dublin to invite the Orange Order to march in Dublin is like the state governor inviting the Ku Klux Klan to march in Alabama (Sinn Féin Press Statement April 2000).

The comparison with the Ku Klux Klan was reiterated by Sinn Féin Councillor Nicky Kehoe:

> The Orangemen state that they are an expression of "Protest-
> ant" culture in the same way that racists state that their views
> and actions are an expression of "white" culture. Orangemen
> and racists have a constitutional right to march but the rest of
> us have a constitutional right to say what we think of the
> organisation organising the march (*The Irish Times* 14/4/00).

He added that '[i]t is not necessary to be tolerant of bigotry
while also being tolerant of its right to exist ... It might be
difficult for an apologist for Orangeism to spot it but this is
pluralism in action'. The point of the comparison with the
Ku Klux Klan is to suggest that the Orange Order is an irredeemably supremacist organisation. That this is indeed the
point was confirmed by Kehoe's colleague, Councillor Larry
O'Toole, who when asked in interview about the nature of
his objections to the proposed parade, said: 'I think we seem
to be a long way away from where we can say that the Orange Order and Orangeism is something that can be celebrated because, unfortunately, it's still an Order which
practices supremacy' (interview: 29/8/00).

Given the effective use of liberal pluralist rhetoric by supporters of the Orange Order's claim, those who were opposed
to the parade, particularly Sinn Féin, began, knowingly or
otherwise, to gravitate towards a rhetoric that is more akin
to the 'critical' multiculturalism described by Goldberg; i.e.
one which, amongst other things, seeks to address imbal-
ances in power and resources. In an interview carried out
sometime after the controversy, Larry O'Toole defended his
multicultural credentials:

> I'd be a firm believer and defender of people's rights to express
> their culture and their past. I'd love to see Orange marches
> where they weren't a threat to anybody and they'd be welcome
> ... now the Travelling community and, secondly, asylum seekers
> and refugees are a minority that are being treated very badly
> and Sinn Féin would always defend – and are doing so daily –
> the rights of these people' (interview 29/8/00).

Larry O'Toole is willing to defend the cultural rights of
minorities that have been ill-treated, but this does not in-

clude the Orange Order, which in Northern Ireland is, for
O'Toole, a threat to the minority community; nor does it include the Republic's Protestant minority because it has not
been ill-treated. For Sinn Féin it would appear that entry
into Ireland's emerging multicultural order is dependent on
one's ability to claim social or cultural victimhood (cf. Wray
and Newitz, 1997).

Significantly, this is a point on which Sinn Féin and the
parade organisers would seem to agree. Notwithstanding the
latter's claim that it was merely a cultural event, the proposed parade clearly had a political purpose, but this was
not simply, as its opponents argued, a counter-move against
campaigns by Northern nationalists to prevent Orange parades going through their areas. Rather it was a reactive
form of identity politics or politics of recognition or multicultural claims-making that was aimed as much at Southern
nationalism as at Northern nationalism. A spokesman for
the Dublin and Wicklow Loyal Orange Lodge, Ian Cox, a
young Southern Protestant, told a journalist (Humphries
2000) that he had joined the Orange Order because he 'was
a bit fed up with the Church of Ireland … It has really let
Protestants down. It's become so timid that Protestants don't
know what it means to be Protestant anymore. The Orange
Order brings it back to basics.' According to the journalist,
part of Orangeism's appeal to Cox was 'its rejection of guilt,
its refusal to be tied down by real or imaginary sins of the
past'. Cox is quoted as saying '[a] lot of Protestants feel they
have to apologise for the Famine or what happened to
Catholics 200 years ago. That's no way to live your life.' Cox
was tired of being made to feel guilty – the Orange Order was
unapologetic. For him the parade, had it been allowed,
would have been recognition of a minority cultural tradition
that had been silenced, shamed and marginalised in the Republic. Cox is reported to have explained that the parade
had been cancelled because of 'intimidation and a lack of
political support' (*The Irish Times* 5/5/00). Backstage at an
Orange Order event in Northern Ireland, he was reported to
be

Still angry about the role of the Mansion House[4], the Church of Ireland and the government in the events which led to his cancelling the Dublin parade, he said the last thing he needed was his face on television. There had been angry protests outside his house during the Dawson Street saga, and he "had to go to the doctor after the whole thing" (*The Irish Times* 13/7/00).

Thus the claim to victimhood on the part of the parade organisers, which was expressed as a reaction to prior nationalist claims to victimhood, was trumped by an assertion of solidarity with people (asylum seekers, refugees and Travellers) who had really been 'badly treated', and the fact that the parade was cancelled compounded the organisers' alienation.

The proposal for an Orange Order parade in Dublin was justified in terms of the GFA, and it provides an example of how, once pluralist or multicultural principles are institutionalised, there is a tendency for cultural claims to proliferate. The parade proposal, and the opposition to it, also exemplifies the form that such proliferation can – and, to judge from Gilroy (2000), Wray and Newitz (1997) and others, often does – take; i.e. competing claims to victimhood in which one claimant seeks to negate that of another. Once institutionalised, as in the case of the GFA, multicultural or pluralist principles encourage competing cultural claims, but are, at the same time, inadequate to resolving, reconciling or arbitrating them. As the example of the Orange Order parade shows, this weakness is most evident in the case of liberal

---

4   Lord Mayor's Office. The Lord Mayor said she was 'surprised' at the suggestion that she had distanced herself from the proposed parade: she said that she had been 'strongly supportive of the right of the Orange Order to march in Dublin ... However, as a woman and a socialist I do not and could not be expected to endorse the aims and objectives of the Orange Order'. She also indicated that she too had received threatening phone calls and letters from people opposed to the parade (*The Irish Times* 5/5/00).

forms of multiculturalism or pluralism[5], but I will argue that critical multiculturalism is also inadequate in this regard. I will start with the limits of the former.

THE LIMITS OF LIBERAL PLURALISM

For critics like Goldberg and others the problem with liberal multiculturalism is not only that it fails to deal with issues of unequal power and resources, but that it is based on an essentialist concept of identity. With this in mind, one might expect supporters of the parade with their liberal-pluralist notions of parity of esteem to hold essentialist views of identity. On the other hand, given the evidence that the principal opponents of the parade were gravitating towards something akin to Goldberg's critical multiculturalism, one might expect to see them questioning essentialism. In practice this does not quite happen.

For the organisers of the parade, their supporters and most of their opponents, Orangeism remains the quintessential cultural expression of a single Protestant 'identity' (cf. Coulter, 1996). Both Councillor Kehoe and Ian Cox say as much (*The Irish Times* 14/2/00). Supporters of the proposed parade do not say as much, but they imply it: if Orangeism were not the, or a, main expression of Protestant culture, why else would they put so much effort into cultivating it? After the postponement of the parade, Kevin Haddick-Flynn complained, 'it tells us something about Irish hypocrisy when political leaders and other public figures – men and women who stand to attention before a flag with an orange panel – refuse to come out and support the rights of the so-called "second tradition"' (*The Irish Times* 4/5/00). Invoking the symbolism of the national flag appears to have become

---

[5] Perhaps in response to this kind of issue, some liberal multiculturalists (e.g. Kymlicka 1995) now tend to give priority to the claims of indigenous minorities over those of immigrants. It is interesting that defenders of the GFA did not invoke this kind of argument to counter Sinn Féin's favouring immigrants over an indigenous minority.

attractive to others who wish to assert the rights of Protestants in an all-Ireland context after the GFA, but this is to obscure the fact that Orangeism was always a minority pursuit among Protestants, in the North as well as in the South (see *The New Irelander*, 1998 and Murphy 2002). During the whole of the controversy, we found only two references to the fact that the Protestant 'tradition' and Orangeism are not co-equal. One such example[6] is Finian McGrath, an Independent Councillor on Dublin City Council who argued:

> The history of the Orange Order is closely associated with sectarianism. They are a group of people who have always excluded Catholics and have made a major contribution to division on this island. *There are many people from the Protestant tradition that would have nothing to do with the Order.* It is important that the people of Dublin show that sectarian organisations have nothing to do with respecting other traditions. Triumphalism is not linked to equality. People on the Garvaghy Road and the Ormeau Road have to live with this reality every day. I now call on the Lord Mayor to dissociate herself from this group and to put up a plaque to honour all the people that have given their lives fighting sectarianism and injustice. (McGrath, 2000, my italics).

There is an implicit critique of essentialism here, but opponents of the parade do not develop this. To have done so would have been to pose a direct challenge to the GFA and the notion of parity of esteem that lies at its heart. As Finlay points out in the Introduction, it is essentialist theory that provides the rationale for parity of esteem, for it suggests that to be secure, an individual's identity needs to be grounded in a strong collective cultural identity, and consequently if the collective, cultural identity is not recognised in the broader society, the individual's sense of self-worth, es-

---

6   The other person to make this point was a caller to the Marian Finucane Show, Radio One, RTE, 25/5/00. Neither McGrath nor the caller to the Marian Finucane Show reflected on the implications of their argument for the symbolism of the national flag.

teem or dignity may be damaged. In a democracy lip-service must be paid to the dignity of the individual, and essentialist theory extends this to the ethnic cultures that supposedly sustain a sense of personal self-worth (Gleason 1983: 921). To doubt the theory that an individual's sense of self-worth needs to be grounded in a strong communal culture is to recognise the weakness of the notion of parity of esteem: if one really held another culture in high esteem would one not make that culture and the values that it embodies one's own? (Michaels, 1995).

But in this instance, it is not in the interests of the opponents of the parade to admit the possibility of change, for their opposition to the parade depends precisely on the argument that the Orange Order is an unchanging, inherently bigoted and triumphalist organisation, the cultural expression of an enduringly privileged community. In this view there is no difference between a march on the Garvaghy Road in Portadown or in Dublin's Dawson Street[7].

THE LIMITS OF CRITICAL MULTICULTURALISM

For opponents of the proposed parade, invoking the criteria of oppression was a successful rejoinder to the relativism that enabled supporters of the parade to suggest some sort of equivalence between the indigenous Protestant minority and new minorities being formed through immigration. In its constitution and practice, the Republic of Ireland may have favoured Catholicism, but the parade organiser's claim to form part of a marginalised or oppressed minority group was weakened by the identification of Southern Protestants with the former Anglo-Irish ruling class, something that seems to

---

[7] Cf. Bryan and Jarman (1997) who point out that parading is a tradition, but its nature and meaning are open to interpretation and change and must be located in context; it is not a constant, unchanging display.

have become stronger since independence[8], and by the over-representation of Protestants in the professions; worse, the claim was disputed by others who also claimed to speak for 'Irish Protestants' (Pilkington 2002, Finlay and McDonnell 2003).

But what of the prior claim to oppression or victimhood implied in the of the otherwise obtuse set of comparisons that Sinn Féin sought to make between Ireland and the Southern States of the US (Sinn Féin Press Statement: April 2000) and in the equivalence that opponents of the parade generally sought to establish between the Garvaghy Road in Portadown and Dawson Street in Dublin?

Efforts on the part of opponents of the parade to elide the palpable differences in the respective positions of residents on the Garvaghy Road in Portadown in Northern Ireland and the residents of Dawson Street[9] in Dublin implicitly turns on the idea that despite the success of nationalists in winning independence for the twenty-six counties that now form the Republic of Ireland, and despite the economic success and unprecedented prosperity of the last decade, the trauma of the colonial era lingers in Dublin. In this sense, the majority community in Ireland is made into a cultural claimant,

---

[8]   The Protestant population of the Republic is half what it was in 1911. The decline in numbers is due to various factors. Many left shortly after independence. These included some who left voluntarily – e.g. those who had worked for the British administration and military – and some whose departure was involuntary or forced (Hart 1996). Those who left in this period were mainly from the working- and lower-middle classes. Thereafter, the decline in numbers was facilitated by the *Ne Temere* decree through which the Catholic Church required the Catholic partner in a mixed faith marriage to promise that any children would be raised as Catholics (see Bury 2004).

[9]   Dawson Street is a prosperous commercial street that runs parallel with Grafton Street in the centre of Dublin. Nevertheless it does have a few residents. In addition to the Lord Mayor of Dublin, *The Sunday Business Post*, a Dublin newspaper that combines republican politics with neo-liberal economics and was strongly opposed to the parade, identified five residents. Their journalist was only able to contact one of these, who said that 'he had no strong feelings on the march' (*The Sunday Business Post* 16/4/00).

whose dignity would be infringed by the sight of Orangemen parading on Dawson Street.

From the foregoing we can concur with Joppke and Lukes (1999: 11) when they argue that deciding 'when ... a "group" qualif[ies] for membership in the multicultural club ... is trickier than it seems', and that this problem is not resolved by critical multiculturalism. The problem is not just in deciding what counts as oppression, but also in deciding when oppression begins and when it ends. Discussing this issue, Joppke and Lukes cite two examples of multicultural claims-making: one is that of Chinese Americans; the other of non-native, Indian Americans. Chinese Americans were subject to a racist immigration and citizenship law at the beginning of the twentieth century, but most of them came to the US after 1965 when the law was removed: '[i]f Chinese Americans have experienced oppression in the context of a racist immigration and citizenship law at the turn of the century, does this still make them an "oppressed" minority today?' (Joppke and Lukes 1999: 12). In the other example, non-native Indian Americans are a group whose educational and occupational achievements exceed those of white Americans. Both claims were successful. Under American Civil Rights law, Chinese Americans were included as 'Asians' into one of the protected classes. After lobbying, non-native Indian Americans secured separate minority recognition in the 1980 census questionnaire, and access to the benefits of affirmative action as a 'prophylactic measure' to protect future immigrants who may not have the same professional qualifications as first generation Indians who came to the US under occupational quotas[10].

The cultural claim made by Sinn Féin implicitly turns on the notion of an inherited trauma, and it is notable that the debate between revisionism and nationalism out of which pluralism in Ireland emerged was in some measure a dispute

---

[10] Part of the subtext of the GFA is that the principle of parity of esteem would be a prophylactic measure for a Protestant minority in some putative future united Ireland. Supporters of the proposed parade allude to this, but do not make it explicit.

about trauma in Irish history and 'communal memory'. In an influential essay, Brendan Bradshaw rejects the reliance of revisionist historians on supposedly 'value-free' methodologies, 'which have the effect of filtering out ... trauma' (1988: 338), which is still keenly felt in 'the communal memory'. Subsequently, the lingering effects of the pain of Irish history have been theorised in terms of colonial discourse theory. Thus Declan Kiberd argues that 'the effects of cultural dependency remained palpable long after the formal withdrawal of the British military: it was less easy to decolonise the mind than the territory' (1996: 6). And Luke Gibbons famously described Ireland as being a 'First World country ... with a Third World memory' (1996: 3). It is the trauma of colonialism and the damage it did to Irish identity, not the unfinished business of partition, that makes a nationalist project with Irish identity as its focus of enduring importance.

As Haslam (1999, paragraph 27) notes, 'Gibbons's maxim ingeniously sidesteps the objections of critics like Liam Kennedy, who have attacked naïve invocations of Ireland's supposed Third World status'. Kennedy (1996) had used the acronym MOPE (Most Oppressed People Ever) to refer to the salience of victimhood in representations of the Irish past. Roy Foster has been equally scathing of 'commentaries on the Great Famine during commemorations of the mid-1990s', and particularly of the tendency, engendered by essentialism, for individual and group identities to be conflated such that, one

> bestselling and highly talented author, born in the Republic in 1955, can still claim in 2000 that his youthful difficulties with women should be blamed on growing up in "a small country, trying to find its own identity in the face of British oppression" (2001: xv).

Foster suggests that the 'elision of the personal and the national' (2001: xi) in narratives of 'victimhood and tyranny' (2001: xv) is a peculiarly Irish phenomenon and suggests a number of reasons for its current salience: '[s]ometimes it is hard to avoid the feeling that the new, modernised, liberated Irish consciousness feels a sneaking nostalgia for the verities of the old victim-culture: which was also, in its way, a culture of superiority' (2001: xv-xvi).

Gibbons has responded to such criticisms by invoking the international literature on trauma, mourning and memory, which 'indicates ... [that] the experience of pain and suffering may not coincide with its moment of articulation, often leaving a considerable time-lag before a catastrophe or a shock to the system achieves any kind of symbolic form' (2002: 95). He discusses the example of Roger Casement and other nationalists who, he says, drew on Irish experience to express solidarity with other oppressed peoples:

> the point ... is not to claim that they were representative of Irish people in general or even mainstream Irish nationalism, but rather to contest the common assumption that preoccupation with one's culture and one's past, particularly an oppressive past, militates against international solidarity and an embrace of cultural diversity in a modern social polity (2002: 102).

He rejects the argument that 'to reclaim the memory of those who have been forgotten or who have been written out of history' is to 'indulge in the self-absorption of victim-culture'. Rather it is to 'engage in an act of ethical imagination in which one's own uneven development becomes not just a way in, but a way out, a means of empathising with other peoples and societies in similar situations today' (2002: 104).

The vexed question regarding the extent to which a preoccupation with the painful history of one's ancestors inures one to the pain of others or fosters a feeling solidarity with them seems to me to be one that can only be addressed through contextualised, empirical investigation. In the present context, I would suggest that Sinn Féin's embrace of asylum seekers and Travellers seems to be less like the 'ethical' empathy of one oppressed group with another that Gibbons describes than a tactic to exclude the Orange Order and, by essentialist extension, Protestants from the emerging multicultural order in Ireland. Equally we can see similar tactics being imagined by the strategists of Orange Order. Some time after the parade controversy, at an academic seminar in Belfast, I encountered a member of the Orange Order, who had some involvement with the proposed parade in Dublin. I asked him about the cancellation of the parade. He was still chafing at the comparison that Sinn Féin had drawn between an Orange Order parade in Dublin and a Ku Klux Klan event in Alabama. Although he thought with hindsight that the parade proposal was a mistake, and that the Orange Order should have contented itself with a plaque, he was sorry that the parade had not gone ahead, because 'we would have snookered them. If [the parade] had gone ahead, do you know who would have been at the front? A big, black brother from Liverpool[11]' (fieldnote 28/9/01).

Competing claims to victimhood like those that animated the organisers of the proposed Orange Order parade in Dublin and its opponents seem to have proliferated in Ireland, particularly Northern Ireland, since the onset of the peace process and the signing of the GFA. Fintan O'Toole has suggested that the two are linked. He suggests that the violence at the interfaces between Protestant and Catholic areas of north Belfast expose 'the great weakness of the ... [GFA] ... the way it institutionalises sectarianism'. He notes that in north Belfast, both sides see themselves as victims rather than perpetrators, and adds that

> For all its genuine greatness, the peace process has tended to give universal currency to [a] sense of victim-hood. Its language of "two-traditions" has been made manifest on the ground by increasing segregation in urban working-class areas (*The Irish Times* 14/01/2002).

In cases such as those alluded to by Fintan O'Toole, the claims to victimhood and trauma relate to a much more recent past than that which was at stake in the revisionist

---

[11] The Orange Order has long had members and lodges in Liverpool and some other British cities.

controversy, and it is useful to look elsewhere for guidance in approaching them.

TRAUMA, GRIEF AND CULTURAL IDENTITY

Despite what Roy Foster suggests, a preoccupation with victimhood is not a peculiarly Irish phenomenon. Jay Winter (2002), Bernhard Giesen (2000) and others have noted that in the late twentieth century various collectivities have moved from an identification with a glorious, heroic past to an identification with a traumatic past. Jay Winter focuses on the way in which Gallipoli is figured in the construction of Australian national identity. He points out that wars have long been commemorated. That has not increased. But wars seem to be commemorated in a different way than they used to be. Commemorations of war used to focus on heroics; today they are more likely to focus on trauma and victimhood. Winters calls this a 'memory boom' (2002: 26). Although Anzac day is his immediate focus, he notes that the 'memory boom' is a broader phenomenon which has, he suggests, three sources. 'It began to emerge in the 1980s when victims of the Holocaust finally found that their stories could be told, recorded and preserved'. Veterans of the Vietnam war are another group whose 'predicament helped bring issues of memory to public attention ... those who suffered from post-traumatic stress disorder had their pension claims validated by the American medical profession'. Other victims, including those of 'sexual abuse, of chronic urban conflict, or of brutal campaigns against civilians in a host of civil wars also began to speak of their memories' and more and more people felt moved to listen.

I do not believe that Winters has exhausted the sources of the 'memory boom'. I would argue that crucial to the contemporary mood has been the manner in which progress has been rendered problematic in the mid- to late-twentieth century. As Alain Finkielkraut (1988) and others have noted, all of the conflicting political ideologies that emerged from the Enlightenment and that mobilised the masses in the West in the nineteenth and early twentieth centuries revolved around a belief in the possibility of Progress, of life getting better. There is a risk for those whose ethic is Progress: the ethical promise must be kept. The nineteenth century had seen enormities such as slavery, and the obliteration of native Americans and other indigenous peoples, but throughout 'the nineteenth century, up to World War I enough was gained by enough people to support the doctrine that held its own well into the twentieth century' (Lemert 1999: 192-3). Even those who had reason to distrust the promises of Western culture still believed in Progress or were silenced by the conventions that had been promoted by Adam Smith and others from the seventeenth century onwards which militated against the expression of pain and injury in the public sphere. In the aftermath of two World Wars, the inter-war crisis in the international capitalist system, the Holocaust, decolonisation and the collapse of the Soviet Union, belief in the doctrine of Progress faltered, and the conventions which restricted suffering to the private sphere loosened (Gibbons 2003). No longer could the voices of those who had suffered be off-set against the gains of Progress, real or projected.

Tracing the origins of the 'memory boom' is not the most important issue here. More important are its implications for the emerging pluralist or multicultural order in an Ireland which must now come to terms with more than thirty years of armed conflict. Joy Damousi's study (2001) of war widows in Australia is instructive here. By comparing the experiences of widows bereaved in World War II with those bereaved in World War I, Damousi shows that what Winter calls the 'memory boom' has compensations: the bereaved can express their feelings publicly and more people are willing to listen. The conventions mentioned above limiting the appropriate display of grief to the private sphere made the tasks of recovery more difficult for widows of World War I. Without the chance to express their anguish publicly, these women were trapped in an isolation which both bred nostalgia and was reinforced by it. Nostalgia is problematic in this context because it tends to conjure up perfect memories of imperfect worlds. When wistfulness dominates mourning, the survivor may remain frozen in an idealised past. By contrast, later conflicts produced losses which were just as devastating, but which, Damousi argues, could be spoken of in public. This alternative to a kind of stoical repression seemed to help some women to endure their losses and begin to live again. Thus, the memory boom that Winter refers to provides a supportive context in so far as it enables people who have suffered or who have been bereaved to express their feelings and to have them heard.

CONCLUSION

Bearing in mind what Damousi says about the dangers of repressing, and the positive benefits of expressing grief and suffering in the public sphere[12], the post-ceasefire proliferation of talk about bereavement and loss should not be dismissed as a rehearsal of an older Irish trait. Some distinctions might be in order, though. Paraphrasing Naomi Wolf (in Stringer 2000), we should listen attentively and with respect when people who have been bereaved or who have suffered specify and articulate publicly their grief and suffering, while at the same time being very circumspect about attempts to mould individual suffering into a collective identity. Such efforts are evident on the part of some activists claiming to speak for each of the two main 'communities' in Northern Ireland, but the example of the 'Long March' from Derry to Portadown in June and July 1999 will suffice. One of the organisers explained that the main aim of the march was to raise awareness of the 'forgotten victims' of the Trou-

---

[12] The benefits are not unqualified. Some who were bereaved or injured in Northern Ireland chose not to speak. In some cases this reticence was based on a desire not to add to the bitterness that fueled violence. In other cases one might speculate that such reticence has something to do with the lingering effects of the old convention that pain be confined to the private sphere (cf. Simpson and Donnan 2004).

bles. The individual stories of those who had been maimed in bombs or whose relatives had been murdered by the IRA are traumatic, but the spokesman for the Long March sought to link these individual stories to a broader collective project: '[w]e are looking for respect for victims, for parity of esteem for Protestant culture and heritage and for support for deprived unionist communities' (*The Irish Times* 2/7/99). The organisers planned the march to arrive in Portadown in time for the annual confrontation between the Orange Order and nationalist residents at the Garvaghy Road.

Joppke and Lukes argue that once multiculturalism is institutionalised, with positive benefits accruing to minority group status, there is an inherent tendency to the proliferation of cultural claims: '[t]he recognition of a minority group divides the world into three segments: majority, recognized minorities and not-yet-minorities' (1999: 22). Fintan O'Toole suggests that the institutionalisation of biculturalism in the GFA has encouraged increasing recourse in Northern Ireland to a rhetoric of victimhood. In fact, as Foster notes (2001), this tendency has long been evident in nationalist politics. As the examples of the proposed Orange Order parade in Dublin and the Long March from Derry to Portadown would suggest, some politicians and activists who claim to speak for Protestant seem to be following suit. Fintan O'Toole may be correct when he suggests that this trend has been intensified by the GFA, but there is clear evidence that it predates it (see Finlay 2001 and Fleischmann, 1995).

The problem with the competitive proliferation of such cultural claims is threefold. Firstly, they produce disputes that are difficult to adjudicate. Secondly, the preoccupation with suffering, often of distant ancestors, that they encourage may inure one to the suffering of others. Thirdly, as the example of the proposed Orange parade in Dublin suggests, the experiences of people who do not fit the narrative, such as immigrants in today's Ireland, may be occluded or worse, pressed into service to fit the needs of whatever dispute is ongoing, with the result that, as Joppke and Lukes (1999) suggest, legitimate claims are trivialised.

Paul Gilroy has also highlighted the dangers of 'me-too-ism'. He argues that 'there is much to be learned by fore-grounding that experience of being victimized and using it to challenge the wilful ignorance of some Europe-centred ac-counts of modernity's pleasures and problems' (2000: 113). But he worries about a social order in which the 'identity of the victim, sealed off and presented as an essential, un-changing state, has become ... a prized political possession'. He quotes James Baldwin: '[t]he testimony of the victim as victim corroborates, simply, the reality of the chains that bind him – confirms, and as it were, consoles the jailer' (in Gilroy, 2000: 113).

At the outset of this chapter I suggested that in the multi-cultural order emerging in Ireland after the paramilitary ceasefires and the GFA the proliferation of cultural claims reveals a pattern that is complicated by Ireland's colonial history and its fractured experience of nation building, which created what Harold Jackson called a 'double minority problem' (1979 [1971]). In the light of Gilroy's discussion and of the arguments developed by the opponents of the proposed Orange parade in Dublin and of the rhetoric of some loyalist and unionist politicians in Northern Ireland who have sought to draw a hard and fast line between the 'real', the 'innocent' or the 'forgotten' victims of the Troubles and others (see Morrissey and Smyth 2002), the pattern of proliferation seems, on reflection, more simple. Its underly-ing logic is a reductive opposition, in which activists claim-ing to represent each of two substantial indigenous commu-nities seek to portray their community as the victims, and members of the other community as the perpetrators. En-duringly bicultural rather than multicultural, this Manichaean schema is inhospitable to newcomers and to people who would wish to identify themselves in terms other than Catholic or Protestant, unionist or nationalist. It is also inimical to peace and reconciliation between those who do identify themselves in the latter terms. For it is not only, as Gilroy suggests, the identity of victim that is essentialised as an unchanging state, but also that of perpetrator: there is no succour for the former or redemption for the latter.

REFERENCES

Bradshaw, B. (1989), 'Nationalism and Historical Scholarship in Modern Ireland', *Irish Historical Studies* XXVI, 104 (November): 329-51.

Bryan, D. and Jarman, N. (1997), 'Parading Tradition, Protesting Triumphalism: Utilizing Anthropology in Public Policy' in H. Donnan and G. McFarlane eds, *Culture and Policy in Northern Ireland; Anthropology in the Public Arena*. Institute of Irish Studies, The Queen's University of Belfast.

Bury, R. (2004), 'Time For Our Largest Minority to Celebrate', *The Irish Times* 17/5/04.

Carey, P. (23/4/00) in 'Letters to the Editor', *The Irish Times*.

Carol, C. (1996), Preface to M. Hyndman ed., *Further Afield Journeys from a Protestant Past*. Belfast: Beyond the Pale.

Damousi, J. (2001), *Living With the Aftermath Trauma, Nostalgia and Grief in Post-War Australia*. Cambridge: Cambridge University Press.

Donnan, H. and Simpson, K. (2004) 'Borders and Bounded Emotions: Silence and Suffering Among Northern Ireland Protestants', *Borders and Emotions Conference*. Centre for International Borders Research, The Queens University of Belfast, 27 and 28/5/04.

Finlay, A. (2001), 'Defeatism and Northern Protestant "Identity"', *The Global Review of Ethnopolitics* 1, 2, 3-20. http://www.ethnopolitics.org

Finlay, A. and McDonnell, N. (2003), 'Partition, Pluralism and the Response to a Proposed Orange Parade in Dublin', *Irish Studies Review* 11, 1, 17-32.

Finkielkraut, A. (1988), *The Undoing of Thought*. London: Claridge Press.

Fleischmann, R. (1995), '"The Blood Our Fathers Spilt" – Rhetoric and Poetry', in T.A. Westendorp and J. Mallinson eds, *Politics and the Rhetoric of Poetry – Perspectives on Modern Anglo-Irish Poetry*. Amsterdam: Rodopi.

Foster, R.F. (1988), *Modern Ireland 1600-1972*. London: Penguin.

Foster, R.F. (2001), *The Irish Story Telling Tales and Making It Up In Ireland*. London: Penguin.

Freehill, M. (23/8/00) Interviewed by Natalie McDonnell.

Gilroy, P. (2000), *Against Race: Imagining Political Culture Beyond the Color Line*. Cambridge, Mass.: Belknap Press of Harvard University Press, 2000.

Gleason, P. (1983), 'Identifying Identity: A Semantic History', *The Journal of American History* 69, 4, 910-931.

Gibbons, L. (1996), *Transformations in Irish Culture*. Cork: Field Day and Cork University Press.

Gibbons, L. (2003), 'Gaelic Gothic Race, Whiteness and Irish Culture', *Department of Sociology/M.Phil in Ethnic and Racial Studies Seminar*, 20/11/03.

Giesen, B. (2000), 'Cultural Trauma and National Identity: the Case of Post-War Germany', a paper delivered at a Conference, *Cultural Trauma and National Identity*, Dublin City University, 28-9/4/00.

Goldberg, D. (1994), 'Introduction', in D. Goldberg ed., *Multiculturalism: A Critical Reader*. Oxford: Blackwell.

Hall, S. (2000), 'Conclusion: the Multicultural Question', in B. Hesse ed., *Un/Settled Muliculturalisms: Diasporas, Entanglements, "Transruptions"*. London: Zed Books.

Hart, P. (1996), 'The Protestant Experience of Revolution in Southern Ireland' in R. English and G. Walker eds, *Unionism in Modern Ireland*. Basingstoke: Macmillan.

Haslam, R. (1999), '"A Race Bashed in the Face": Imagining Ireland as a Damaged Child', *Jouvert: A Journal of Postcolonial Studies Special Issue Ireland 2000*, 4, 1.

Henry, M. (29/3/00), in 'Letters to the Editor', *The Irish Times*.

Howe, S. (2000), *Ireland and Empire, Colonial Legacies in Irish History and Culture*. Oxford: Oxford University Press.

Humphreys, J. (2000), 'Church of Ireland "Has Let Protestants down"', *The Irish Times*, 25/3/00.

The Irish Times 14/2/00, 14/4/00, 4/5/00, 5/5/00, 13/7/00.

Jackson, H. (1979) [1971], *The Two Irelands: The Problem of the Double Minority – A Dual Study of Inter-Group Tensions*. London: Minority Rights Group.

Joppke, C. and Lukes, S. eds (1999), *Multicultural Questions*. Oxford: Oxford University Press.

Kehoe, K. (14/4/00), in 'Letters to the Editor' *The Irish Times*.

Kennedy, L. (1996), *Colonialism, Religion and Nationalism in Ireland*. Belfast: Institute of Irish Studies, The Queen's University.

Kiberd, D. (1996), *Inventing Ireland The Literature of the Modern Nation*. London: Vintage.

Kirby, P., Gibbons, L. and Cronin, M. (2002), *Reinventing Ireland: Culture, Society and the Global Economy*. London: Pluto Press.

Kymlicka, W. (1995), *Multicultural Citizenship*. Oxford: Oxford University Press.

Lemert, C. (1999) ed., *Social Theory: The Multicultural and Classical Readings*. Oxford: Westview Press.

Michaels, W.B. (1995), 'Race into Culture: A Critical Genealogy of Cultural Identity', in K.A Appiah. and H.L. Gates eds, *Identities*. Chicago: University of Chicago Press.

McDonnell, N. (2000), *Dublin Says No? An Analysis of the Responses to the Proposed Orange Parade in Dublin*. Unpublished MPhil Dissertation, University of Dublin, Trinity College.

McGrath, F. (2000), in *The Irish Times* 25/3/00.

McLennan, G. (2001), 'Problematic Multiculturalism', *Sociology* 35, 4

Morrissey, M. and Smyth, M. (2002), *Northern Ireland After the Good Friday Agreement: Victims, Grievance and Blame*. London: Pluto Press.

Morrison, T. (2003), *The Guardian*, 15/11/03.

Murphy, J.A. 'Time to Reclaim the Tricolour from Sinn Féin', *The Sunday Independent* 9/6/02.

The New Irelander, 1998, 6.

O'Shea, T. (5/5/00), in 'Letters to the Editor', *The Irish Times*.

O'Toole, L. (29/8/00), Interview with Natalie McDonnell.

Pilkington, L. (2002), 'Religion and the Celtic Tiger: The Cultural Legacies of Anti-Catholicism in Ireland', in P. Kirby, L. Gibbons and M. Cronin eds, *Reinventing Ireland: Culture, Society and the Global Economy*. London: Pluto

Stringer, R. (2000), '"A Nietzschean Breed" Feminism, Victimology, Ressentiment', in A. Schrift ed., *Why Nietzsche Still? Reflections on Drama, Culture and Politics*. Berkeley: University of California Press.

Sinn Féin (3/4/00), Motion to Dublin City Council.

Sinn Féin Press Office (2000), Press Statement (April).

Winter, J. (2002), 'Their Name Liveth For Evermore', *The Times Literary Supplement*, 5169, 26/4/02.

Wray, M. and Newitz, A. (1997) eds, *White Trash: Race and Class in America*. New York and London: Routledge.

8. Where Difference Lies: Democracy and the Ethnographic Imagination in Northern Ireland[1]

ROBIN WHITAKER

> There [are] two truths in Northern Ireland, "a Protestant   truth
> and a Catholic truth"
> *David Dunseith*[2]

> The "two communities" model of Northern society has become
> so widely accepted that to challenge it is to invite derision
> McCann (2000).

What difference should unrepresentative subjects make to our analysis of Northern Ireland politics? What difference should they make to 'post-conflict' attempts to build inclusive democracy? Not much, to judge by comments from some politicians in the run-up to the 1996 elections to the Forum and multi-party talks. Speaking on RTÉ's *Prime Time*, Séamus Mallon of the Social Democratic and Labour Party (SDLP) suggested that the new Northern Ireland Women's Coalition was in danger of becoming a 'cult-factor' and 'single-issue'. He added:

> What we must realise is that these negotiations ... are going to
> be very hard-nosed and they are going to be real and it's going
> to be down to political judgement in terms of the Ulster Union-
> ist Party, the SDLP, Sinn Féin ... and the   DUP   [Democratic
> Unionist Party] ... The real weight of political opinion will be
> shown through those political parties and I hope that weight is
> shaped by women within those parties (in Fearon 1996: 14-5).

---

[1] Many thanks to Andrew Finlay, Peter Hart and Nicole Power for helpful feedback on this chapter. My research was made possible by the generous support of a Social Sciences and Humanities Research Council of Canada Doctoral Fellowship. The Canadian and International Federations of University Women, the Woodrow Wilson Foundation and the Institute of Social and Economic Research at Memorial University all offered additional support at various junctures. I am grateful to all.

[2] In McKay (2000: 26). Dunseith is host of a popular lunchtime call-in show, *Talkback*, on BBC Radio Ulster.

Peter Robinson of the DUP agreed: the Coalition women 'haven't been at the forefront of the battle when shots were being fired or when the constitution of Northern Ireland was in peril' he said. 'They are not representative of the decent Ulster women that I speak to' (in Fearon 1996: 14).

Remarks like these are part of the 'usual suspect' rhetoric of electoral politics. Politicians invariably claim to be singularly representative of those whose votes they are soliciting, although as Mallon's statement indicates, in this context such solicitation typically occurs either side of a broad division between unionist and nationalist voters. Yet Mallon's views are largely reflected in social scientific representations. Here, too, division – between unionist and nationalist, Protestant and Catholic, British and Irish – is taken to be the defining characteristic of Northern Ireland politics, society and culture (Curtin *et al.* 1993, Nic Craith 2002).

In contrast, the heart of this chapter is a series of stories for which the usual framework is inadequate. These focus on people who 'found themselves' in discursive situations that exposed them as unrepresentative, if not unrepresentable, political subjects (see Stewart 1991). On one level, these were situations of their own making, created by attempts to turn their 'felt desire' into political speech or action. Yet, as Lamont Lindstrom says: '[c]ontrol of the questions – even more than control of the answers – maintains social inequalities in that such control helps frame and make sense of felt desire' (in Wolf 1999: 55). Where Lindstrom's phrasing makes control sound like a deliberate tactic by manipulative elites, I want to suspend the conspiracy theory in favour of a more general concern with how too much agreement on which questions and which conflicts count restricts the prospects for politics. Only certain kinds of speech and action constitute appropriate answers to the dominant questions, other questions are marginalised as insignificant (cast as 'single issue', for example) and the frustrations of political *un*representatives become diagnostic of a wider situation in which some answers cannot make sense. In short, while much attention has been given to the question of putting Northern Ireland's government back in the hands of locally-elected politicians, I will argue that political frustrations such as those outlined in the following section point to a democratic deficit in the 'cultural conditions' of political representation (cf. Coombe 1998: 68-9).

The structures and conventions of elections, parliaments and parties are only part of the story here. A whole complex of institutions and practices make up what we might broadly call representative politics. Opinion polls, census categories and other mechanisms for mapping the population are obvious cases in which control of the questions makes sense of felt desire – and also works to produce mandates for authoritative political speech. The statistical sense of normality slides into the moral one, so that the numerical 'description' becomes a regulating standard (Hacking 1990: 161ff). Then these become inseparable from questions of authoritative representation in its multiple senses: speaking of, speaking for and speaking as or standing for particular positions or groups. Academic, media and commonsense perceptions of the key constituencies are also implicated in the construction of representative voices in any context. In the case of Northern Ireland, so are parades, murals, flags and other public displays; violence designed to send a message; politicised geographies and histories; and accounts of what 'the conflict' is about and what is required to secure peace. 'The conflict is primarily ethno-national and it is this dimension which must be addressed, and addressed fairly if the conflict is to be ended' (McGarry and O'Leary 1995b: 859). To the extent that McGarry and O'Leary's statement is representative of the message sent by all these practices, it conveys a situation where what matters, politically, is one's position either side of 'the ethno-national divide'.

Yet, in over two years of ethnographic fieldwork and several more years living as a non-native citizen in Northern Ireland, I seemed continually to be meeting people whose lives and perspectives complicated this dichotomy. In some cases, these *were* people who located themselves squarely on one 'side' or the other of constitutional debate.[3] Moreover, I was an active member of the Northern Ireland Women's Coalition. The Coalition was formed to contest the 1996 Forum election partly to ensure that Northern Ireland's future would not be negotiated solely by men. But 'women in the talks' was just a beginning. The Coalition's starting point was the position that women are divided by constitutional politics. Its founders included unionists and nationalists as well as 'others'. But it also argued that, even for unionists and nationalists, these are not the only differences that matter, and that the way they matter is not immutable.

Thus, my own situation in this 'field' has been multiple: ethnographer and partisan; citizen and foreigner. No doubt, the peculiarities of my fieldwork and my own position as an unrepresentative citizen in Northern Ireland are among the factors accounting for what I learned during research.[4] They also inform my sense that it might be fruitful to put the conundrums inherent in democracy *qua* 'representative politics' into conversation with questions raised by the late twentieth century 'crisis of representation' in the human sciences. Modern democracy and the modern human sciences share common roots in the Enlightenment and, as such, are 'related cultural practices' (Greenhouse and Greenwood 1998: 2; also Coombe 1998, Vincent 1991). Anthropology's 'crisis' is inseparable from a broad set of political and epistemological questions that extend beyond the academy. One particularly relevant expression of anthropology's link to its wider situation lies in the widespread concern with how we should understand difference – and what difference it should make in public life. Current debates around multiculturalism in liberal regimes are key here, as these confront the

---

[3] Recent statistical indicators suggest that this complexity is more widespread than my sample, which is surely unrepresentative by any statistician's reckoning (Doherty and Poole 2002, Wilson 2003).

[4] On their own, these labels are minimally informative. As with all stories, mine could be told in various ways to various ends. Reflexivity offers another angle on ethnography, not the last piece in the puzzle. Also see Haraway (1991).

limits of the liberal model of equality as sameness[5]. But such questions are not limited to established liberal democracies. I would suggest that it may be productive to explore how crises of *ethno*graphic representation particularly might help us think about the limits of democratic inclusion in contexts like Northern Ireland, where political representation has often amounted to claims on behalf of *a people*, imagined to exist in substantive terms (cf. Vincent 1991: 56). To the extent that the 'objects' of anthropological and political representation have been understood as such, it becomes critical to ask what we are to make of people and phenomena that are not, and perhaps cannot be, representative of some cultural system or community (see, e.g., Malkki 1995, Moore 1987). Finally, playing a little more with this connection, could the ethnography of political representation itself be considered 'an active form of democratic participation'? (Greenhouse and Greenwood 1998: 3). I will end up with a set of reflective speculations on these questions. But first, let me offer some examples of people who found themselves in situations that constituted what might be called a personal crisis of representation.

POLITICAL UNREPRESENTATIVES

I was sitting at home in Belfast one evening in the winter of 2000, waiting for my friend Maxine,[6] with whom I had plans for dinner, and reading a paper from a recent issue of *American Anthropologist* in which Jack Santino (1999) characterises Northern Ireland's major political constituencies in this way: 'Unionists identify with the superordinate, imperialist

---

[5] In this ideal, individuals are politically interchangeable inasmuch as they are held to 'share the same nature, the same rights and the same terms of regard by state institutions'. As such, the conceptual opposite of liberal equality has not been inequality but difference (Brown 1995: 153).

[6] All names are pseudonyms, with the exception of matters of public record.

elite, Nationalists with the subordinate, colonized people.' He
elaborates his taxonomy: 'Unionist and Loyalist organisations [are] politically "right" and Nationalist and Republican
groups [are] politically "left".' This shorthand 'may be prob-
lematized as simplistic,' since there is great social and political diversity within and among the groups. But Santino feels
justified in 'using the terms as applicable, in a way that I
have found them generally to be used among the populace of
Northern Ireland' (Santino 1999: 516).

> It is immediately apparent in Northern Ireland that there are
> 'two sides' that debate issues of national identity through these
> public displays. Whether there are *only* two sides is debatable,
> but that is certainly how the troubled political situation in
> Northern Ireland is characterised in the international media –
> and domestically as well. In Northern Ireland, one frequently
> encounters the term *the two traditions,* which refers broadly to
> British and Irish histories and heritages (Santino 1999: 517).

For Santino, the result of these divided loyalties, which he
maps onto religious affiliation in the usual way, is that 'there
exists in Northern Ireland a kind of national identity crisis'
(1999: 517)[7].

When Maxine arrived, I teasingly asked which description
applied to her. She laughed. 'Oh, the colonisers, of course!'
But, she added more seriously, for years she had felt guilty
about the political history she associated with Northern Ireland Protestantism. I had met Maxine in the Women's Coalition. During the 1996-98 multi-party talks, we worked together on several projects and I quickly came to admire her

---

[7] The conflation of political and religious labels is more widespread than
the mapping of a 'left-right' division onto the broadest distinctions of
national identification. It, too, is often justified on the basis of following
local convention (e.g. Aretxaga 1997: xii; cf. Whyte 1990: 18-22). It is
worth noting that, if he finds a shared 'national identity crisis', Santino
suggests that unionists have additional problems of their own: 'The
Nationalists want "Brits Out"; the Unionists, confused and conflicted
by their seeming abandonment by the government of Great Britain in
their opposition to the Nationalists, want leaders who will support
them and their position' (1999: 516).

skill in negotiating contending political perspectives and styles within the Coalition and beyond it. Her willingness to take positions that confounded assumptions about what a Protestant 'would' say made it more thinkable for others in the Coalition to follow suit. An example of the kind of issue I have in mind would be the Women's Coalition response to the arrest of Róisín McAliskey on foot of a German request for her extradition for questioning in relation to an IRA attack on a British army barracks in Osnabruck[8].

In the exhausted days after the delivery of the GFA, Maxine told me that one of the most important passages to her personally was the affirmation that it is 'the birthright of all the people of Northern Ireland to identify themselves and be accepted as Irish or British, or both ...'. It made her think she might reclaim an Irishness she had felt in the 1960s but that seemed increasingly off-limits after the troubles began. Later, in a political life story interview, she recalled a sense of affinity with the British Labour Party while growing up, something she attributed largely to her father and to 'reading the *Manchester Guardian* from ... whenever I could read. ... It wasn't based on any analysis, except the broadest response to socialism as opposed to conservatism.' Her father was English. He was unionist simply in the most general sense: 'that was how the state was and he wasn't anti-state'[9]. It was her mother who had a 'sense of Irishness

---

[8] What this example also shows is that self-construction is never a strictly personal matter: the frustrations presented in this paper are symptoms of the extent to which political speech, actions and intentions are read in ways that reassert the two communities framework, even when they hope to subvert it. Also see Finlay's (1999) reflexive account of a fieldwork encounter in which his sense of the possibilities offered by socialism is challenged when the woman he is interviewing refuses to meet him on that ground and instead constructs him as a Protestant.

[9] Maxine said that her father did not see himself as Irish, although he was happy to be living in Northern Ireland. Had he developed a more thoroughgoing sense of identification with the country, what might the GFA's reference to 'birthright' have meant to him?

... even though she was a unionist'[10]. Maxine had found the early SDLP with its links to civil rights and labour politics, appealing. That changed as it absorbed the old Nationalist Party and John Hume became leader. By then, she said, the party 'seemed to be for the oppressed as opposed to arguing ... for people who are oppressed, and therefore I didn't seem to belong.' It appeared, in other words, that the SDLP was for a particular kind of *person* as much as a type of politics that might be described as 'left'.

Sharon, another Coalition member, said something similar in relation to her political autobiography. Growing up a decade or so after Maxine, she was politicised by international debates, such as those around Apartheid in South Africa. At sixteen, she wrote to the British Labour Party, then soliciting new members through the UK-wide media.

> That was probably the start of my [she paused briefly], beginning to wonder where I belonged, if you like, because they wrote back saying: "[j]oin the SDLP." Which, for somebody who grew up in [a solidly unionist town] as a unionist, wasn't exactly a logical answer! Or it didn't seem to be. And it never became a logical answer ... Probably the reasons have changed over time, but [she ended with a laugh].

Her sense of 'wonder[ing] where I belonged' suggests a double displacement. She was informed that, unionist or not, she was not a citizen of the UK just like any other. The British Labour Party might treat the SDLP as a sister party. To someone 'like her', it was nationalist, first and foremost. As a unionist interested in 'progressive' politics, it seemed there

---

10 Following her father's lead, she had looked to Britain for her politics, 'in the sense of wider social policies, but not in the sense of politics in Northern Ireland'. She coninued: 'I mean, we lived partly in Britain – i.e., England – and we lived geographically in Northern Ireland, and the two strands were just part of the way it was for us. So we followed English football teams and post-war efforts, and that was very much part of, I suppose, our allegiance. But I felt Irish as well and that was a significant [pausing for thought] attachment.'

was nowhere for her to go, in party terms. Sharon later moved away from unionism as a political orientation. Her national orientation has also shifted, so that she now identifies herself as Irish. But still, no local party seemed a natural home:

> I didn't vote before the Coalition existed. I was somebody who … lived and breathed politics since before my adult life [laughing] and the first time I voted was for my-self, which is pretty weird … People complain about the politicians, and the response that comes back from politicians and the media is: "[w]ell, you get who you vote for." And my response to that is: "[w]ell, you can only vote for who's there, standing."

On one level, these women complicate Santino's image of mutually exclusive and immutable national identities (British *or* Irish) as well as any exclusive equation of 'left' and nationalist politics in the Northern Irish context. Yet, their political frustrations also seem to uphold the claim that this is the way the terms are 'generally used'. And of course, as Santino suggests, 'the populace' is not alone in using a dichotomous shorthand to discuss Northern Ireland politics and decide what kinds of voices and viewpoints make a good story.

In the wake of the 1996 'Drumcree crisis,' I went with a friend to a loyalist bar in Belfast. The place was packed, and we found ourselves sharing a table with a twenty-something man who I will call Paul. When the English reporters at the next table were forced to beat a hasty retreat after a UVF-tattooed Scotsman, in Belfast for the Orange Order celebrations on 12th July, discovered his conversation was being committed to tape, Paul turned to me and asked if *I* had a tape recorder. I assured him I did not[11]. Paul said that was too bad. He would like to have been interviewed. He seemed to feel he had a perspective that rarely got public represen-

---

[11] Presumably, my Canadian accent made him think I might be a journalist.

tation. He was a working class Protestant critic of Orange-ism[12].

A month or two after my conversation with Paul, I was in Derry drinking coffee with a woman who I had met at a couple of different events, exploring the possibility of an interview. I had told her I was interested in talking to Protestant social activists for my doctoral research. But where Paul had wanted to be interviewed, Laura was reluctant. In fact, she got quite agitated as we talked. She said she was often asked along to events in Derry, where the population is predominantly Catholic, because she was a Protestant and there was a desire or an official requirement for cross-community representation. But she felt she could not possibly 'represent Protestantism': because of how she had been brought up, the way she voted and the area in which she lived. I could almost say the dominant versions of what it means to 'be' Protestant left her feeling like 'bad data' in relation to the category. Certainly, she felt she could not speak compellingly as one, which may suggest something about the intimacy between local standards of authority and authenticity.

This woman's anxiety about public speaking can be linked to some advice I got in the early days of my doctoral fieldwork in Derry. I should focus on a working class estate I was told, for there I would find the more 'authentic' Protestant voice. I was warned that many of the activist women with whom I had made contact had distanced themselves from what was perceived as Protestantism in the city. This advice was meant to tip the gullible outsider off to local perceptions and categories of meaning. It was also informed by a democratising impulse, for I was being directed to voices that got little public hearing in Derry. Still, it showed how local and social scientific discourses can conspire to create a situation where one must speak *as* something or in the name of it, yet to speak in the wrong way is to risk finding oneself to be inauthentic, even an impostor.

---

[12] I heard community workers make similar complaints when the international media descended on Derry, anticipating photogenic trouble during the Apprentice Boys' August parade.

From a slightly different direction, here is how one partici-
pant reflected on conventions of peace-talk at a 'community
dialogue' workshop on the question 'do words matter?', held
in Derry's Waterside late in 1996:

> I am frustrated when I find myself in situations where I am seen
> to be representing 'my own kind', when I have difficulty enough
> speaking on my own behalf with integrity and without comp-
> romise. The notion of reaching across divides traps us in a
> ready-made language of peace which I find arid. What hope is
> there if we only communicate from a position of supposed
> difference, as defined for us, to someone else's supposed
> difference as defined for them?[13]

DEMOCRACY AND DIFFERENCE

I could continue piling up fieldwork stories like these, ac-
counts of people who found their desires for speech or action
frustrated by a sense that they fit awkwardly in relation to
recognised political registers, by their inability or unwillingness to inhabit their 'proper' category in an untroubled way.
Thinking of Santino, if there is an identity crisis common to
these stories, it is not the 'national identity crisis' that he
locates in the division of Northern Ireland's people into British-identified and Irish-identified blocs, it is a matter of how
identity itself has been made the privileged grounds for political speech or action, with identity posed as a quality of
being. What one says is taken as a symptom of what one 'is'
and so can be read back as evidence. In some discussions,
political identities in Northern Ireland come close to sound-
ing like Arjun Appadurai's (1988: 37) characterisation of
anthropological constructions of nativeness: '[t]hey are confined by what they know, feel, and believe. They are prison-
ers of their "mode of thought."' Or, in the words of a rejoin-

---

[13] Kate Newman (1997: 21). I quote from her written submission rather
than from my fieldnotes.

der familiar in Northern Ireland politics, 'well, they *would* say that'.

What connects these stories is a sense that the price of participation in Northern Ireland's public sphere has not been the erasure of specificity implicit in the liberal model of equality as sameness. Rather, the political subject is a marked subject, at least when it comes to national identity. Eilish Rooney (2000: 173) puts it this way:

> Historically, in the North of Ireland, "democracy" has worked and continues to "work" – theoretically and [in practice] ... on the basis of the "difference" the individual brings with her into the polling booth. The unattached, undifferentiated individual of liberal democracy is not the basic unit of "democratic" life in the North of Ireland. Here, democracy *admits* and, to use [Anne] Phillips's phrasing, is defined by "the pertinence of continuing difference and inequality" in the voter's allegiance to, and relationship with, the state. Either the "individual" supports the union of Northern Ireland with Great Britain, within the United Kingdom ... or the "individual" aspires to some form of Irish unitary state ... (Rooney 2000: 173).

For Rooney, this situation has clear implications for the demands of democracy:

> The Good Friday Agreement is founded on a recognition that "liberal democracy", within a context where the subordination of one group by another is historically and "democratically" sedimented into the socio-economic, cultural, political and gender structures, requires radical change. The language of the agreement admits and safe-guards *difference* in the operations of democracy in the new assembly (2000: 173).

Arguably in fact, much of the GFA does fall within some version of the liberal tradition. Charles Taylor (e.g. 1994) and Will Kymlicka (1995), among other well-known liberal theorists, have long argued for the recognition of group rights as a liberal principle in multicultural democracies (see Harvey 2003; cf. Finlay 2003 and Wilson 2003). At least technically, Northern Ireland's citizens are as 'free' under the terms of the Agreement to enter the polling booth and vote for the party or candidate of their choosing as those in the rest of the UK or Ireland. Yet, Rooney is surely right that voting practices in Northern Ireland strain any model of universal suffrage in which individuals are imagined as interchangeable units. Claude Lefort (1988: 18-19) has written that

> It is at the very moment ... when the people is assumed to actualize itself by expressing its will, that social interdependence breaks down and that the citizen subject is abstracted from all the networks in which his social life develops and becomes a mere statistic. Number replaces substance.

Lefort is talking at the level of logic. As Rooney points out, the grievous history of democracy in Northern Ireland means that particular individuals are frequently formed, and their 'free' choices informed, by membership in a 'community' defined by attachment to one national identification or another (cf. Lefort 1988: 19-20). True, in the language of Northern Ireland politics, appeals to 'community' are made as much to defend or create a situation as to describe one. True too, Stormont-era unionists were often as concerned to fend off the threat that labour-oriented Protestant or cross-community rivals posed to the solidity of the 'majority community' as they were to defend the state from Catholic-nationalist 'treachery' (Foster 1988: 585 and Mulholland 2000: 18ff, 44ff)[14]. Nevertheless, all these practices have contributed to the ethnicisation of Northern Ireland politics.

Against this backdrop, Séamus Mallon's 'single-issue' comment about the Women's Coalition in the run-up to the Forum election carries a meaning different than it might have in a context where 'special' interests stand in implied contrast with those of the 'general' good. If Mallon hoped to

---

[14] This is not to say that class politics are immune to ethnicisation. Religion, like 'race', can be a modality in which class is lived (Harris 1972: 195-197 and Mulholland 2000: 18 and 45; cf. Gilroy 1991: 30). Still, the sectarian basis of party politics was not completely secure, a threat that concerned nationalists as well as unionists (McCann 1993: 68).

tap into that transatlantic discourse, his subsequent comment about which parties comprise the weight of political
opinion suggests that there is no 'general public' here.
Similarly, Rooney's either/or phrasing and 'the language of
the Agreement' itself suggests that the Agreement's *difference* democracy' (Rooney 2000: 173) is a matter of difference
between 'the two communities'[15]. This location of difference
was reinforced in one of the earliest official rulings on the
meaning of Agreement 'safeguards' for the participation and
protection of 'all sections of the community' in the operation
of the Assembly: the stipulation that each Assembly Member
(MLA) must 'register a designation of identity – nationalist,
unionist or other – for the purposes of measuring cross-
community support in Assembly votes under the relevant
provisions'[16]. At the inaugural Assembly session the
Women's Coalition MLAs Monica McWilliams and Jane Morrice signed the roll as 'Nationalist/Unionist/Other Other'.
During recess, they were called back and instructed to
amend their designations on the basis that their identities
were ambiguous[17].

Whether they come 'within an inch of separate electoral
rolls for Catholics and Protestants' (McCann 2000) – within
an inch, that is, of giving substance to Lefort's numbers –
the designation rules are surely among the accord's most
obvious departures from the liberal prototype. They assume
that political representatives have a substantive identity: unionist or nationalist. Others are defined purely in negative

---

[15] *Agreement Reached in the Multi-Party Talks* (cited hereafter as *Agreement)*: Constitutional Issues 1 (v); Strand One 5 (e), 6, 11; Strand
Three, Rights, Safeguards and Equality of Opportunity 4; Rights, Safeguards and Equality of Opportunity: Economic and Social Issues: 2(iii).

[16] *Agreement* Strand One: 6.

[17] To be precise, McWilliams signed as 'Nationalist/Unionist/Other Other',
while Morrice signed as 'Unionist/Nationalist/Other Other.' Both replaced these initial designations with 'Inclusive Other.' See *The New
Northern Ireland Assembly Official Report of Debates* (1/7/98: 6) for a
brief recorded discussion. I explore the implications of the Coalition's
designation and reactions to it in greater detail in Whitaker 2001.

terms; all that matters is what they are not[18]. For its part, the Coalition had supported the principle that unionists and nationalists, as such, be granted due recognition under the GFA[19]. For many of its members however, what defined the Coalition was its refusal to be reduced to one thing or the other. After all, its membership included British-identified unionists and Irish-identified nationalists, as well as people who would not be described by either label. To disallow an attempt to combine an official designation of 'other' with an indication of this complexity seems to be at odds with the GFA's recognition of 'the birthright of all the people of Northern Ireland to identify themselves and be accepted as Irish or British or both'[20]. Critically for this chapter, it also points to the difficulties faced by political actors who are defined as much by the differences they incorporate as by the exclusions that mark their boundaries. For if the stories included here seem at first glance to be too heterogeneous, too unsystematically related or too unrepresentative to count in discussions of post-conflict democracy, this is the thread that connects them. The trouble for parties like the Women's Coalition and for people like Maxine, Sharon and Paul is that the differences that define their politics are multiple, contending and coexist *within* them as subjects. This is not only so in relation to the most obvious examples – Maxine's multinational orientation (British and Irish) or the Coalition's incorporation of nationalists, unionists and others – it also holds for the prospects for combining, say, socialism or anti-imperialism and unionism, Protestantism and anti-Orangeism (cf. de Lauretis 1986: 14).

---

[18] In contrast, in the terms of classic liberalism, otherness means being 'exiled into positivity' (Warner 1993: 252).

[19] However, the Coalition's 2003 Election Manifesto called for amending the Assembly voting system to give equal weight to the votes of 'cross-community' parties in key decisions, while maintaining the cross-community safeguards of the original arrangements (see NIWC 2003).

[20] *Agreement:* Constitutional Issues: 1 (vi).

DEMOCRATISING ETHNOGRAPHY

As Rooney's reflections on the GFA indicate, the problem of democracy in Northern Ireland has not been understood simply in terms of how to restore 'rule by the people', imagined as a collection of abstract individuals. Rather, attempts to resolve it have been absorbed with the question of how to secure the representation of particular peoples (also see McGarry and O'Leary 1995a, 1995b and O'Leary 2001). For its part, modern anthropology as a definitively '*ethno*graphic' endeavour has also been defined by its representation of '"peoples" rather than, for example, polities, places, or problems' (Vincent 1991: 56). In terms of the concerns of this particular chapter, it is worth recalling that the wider context for anthropology's ethnicisation was that of European nationalism and 'the expansionist, administrative, law-and-order phase of British and German Colonialism' (Vincent 1991: 56). That is, the discipline consolidated itself as the scientific arbiter of cultural difference at the same time that European governments were making it their business to administer such differences. But if colonialism was one of the material conditions for modern anthropology, the political arrangements that authorised some people to represent others *as peoples* were inseparable from historically specific ways of knowing the world: frameworks within which 'cultures' could appear as stable entities, susceptible to scientific representation. In recent decades, this reifying approach has been displaced in favour of arguments for 'putting culture in motion' (Rosaldo 1989). I suggested above that modern democracy and modern anthropology are related practices. In this final section, I explore whether conceptual and political problems associated with the one endeavour can usefully be considered in light of the other.

Writing about fieldwork among Hutu refugees in Tanzania, Liisa Malkki (1995: 87) asks: '[w]hat should be the status of the material that has conventionally been cleaned off a finished ethnography – the freak occurrence, the anomaly, the unrepresentative figure, the nonrepeating pattern, the impermanent and unremarked cultural form?' From a disciplinary perspective, as Malkki indicates, the backdrop to the 'problem' of anomalies is a tradition in which anthropology is the 'science of the ordinary', ethnographic phenomena and informants' consciousness are expressions of an underlying cultural grammar, and ethnographic data should be representative of 'the life of the culture and of the people' (1995: 89). That is, the casting of some as representative and others as aberrant presumes an underlying order. This assumption about social order also informs governmental administration insofar as the systematic plans of modern statecraft require populations to be legible: knowable in terms of standard categories (J.C. Scott 1999).

In Northern Ireland, the 'two communities' model underpinning many such endeavours takes it as given that the population is clearly divided into two main groups and that political and national identity map onto religion (Doherty and Poole 2001). Yet in the 1991 census, more than eleven per cent of respondents could not be classified as Protestant or Catholic, either because they did not state a religion or because they reported having none. In 2001, the proportion refusing religious identification was closer to fourteen per cent (CONI 2001: Table KS07a). These census results tell us nothing about political allegiance; people who reject confessional identification may still be strongly committed to unionism or nationalism. But they do complicate the 'sectarian headcount' approach to political reckoning. This did not stop a number of commentators from attempting to reassign people to one 'community' or the other, in just such an interested fashion (e.g., Gudgin 2002a, 2002b; cf. Friel 2002)[21].

The stories of political frustration discussed in earlier sections of this chapter are at once symptoms of the extent to

---

[21] Religion was partly decoupled from constitutional perspective in some commentaries. Not surprisingly, the manner of such decoupling was linked to the political perspective of the writer. Graham Gudgin, for example, while reassuring readers that Protestants were in no imminent danger of losing majority status, added that not all Catholics support a united Ireland, so that the unionist majority could be assumed to be larger still.

which the two communities model constitutes the grounds
for political engagement here and an argument that these
add up to a democratic deficit at the level of the cultural
conditions of political representation. The census adds a
numerical dimension to these narrative ones. Looking a little
more closely, it is possible to argue that most of those refusing identification by religion came from Protestant back-
grounds[22]. As it happens, so are the individual examples
presented above. Still, apart from the issue of a research
sample that is anything but representative in statisticians'
terms, I hesitate to present these stories as illustrations of
an emerging social phenomenon. For one thing, we know
very little about people's motivations for ticking off one census box or another. I have been party to enough conversa-
tions in which people debated form-filling strategies to suspect that census data are a complex social product. Then, if
fewer 'Catholics' have such explicit category trouble, that
does not mean that they all fit seamlessly into some imagined solidary community. That is, I am reluctant about de-
stabilising one set of categories at the risk of restabilising
another by implication. More fundamentally, I think it would
be a mistake to treat the stories presented above as 'representative cases', whether of Protestant dissidents or of some
'third force', to be slotted into an expanded political taxonomy (cf. Doherty and Poole 2001: 86). The impulse behind
this chapter was an uneasiness with the tendency to make
'representativeness' the price of admission to political
speech. Adding new identity categories while leaving intact

---

[22] Compare Table KS07a, 'Religion' with KS07b, 'Community
Background: Religion or Religion Brought Up In.' In relation to the
latter, 53.13 per cent are placed in the 'Protestant and Other Christian'
category compared with 45.47 per cent among those currently
reporting a religion. The comparable figures for Catholics are 43.76 per
cent 'brought up' and 40.26 per cent currently identifying as Catholic.
A potentially complicating factor, of course, is conversions, but it
seems unlikely to skew the numbers too badly.

the assumption that such categories stand for stable and coherent constituencies only defers the problem[23].

None of this is an argument for returning to a model of political representation built around the abstract individual, however. As Sharon, the would-be Labour party member, remarked in an interview conducted five years after the signing of the GFA, individuals are generally discriminated against as a result of their membership in groups. For her, the primary issue is not her Protestant background but a sense that the promise that 'being Irish in this place would be legitimate and would have reality' remains unfulfilled. The question, then, is how to redress the wrongs done to people by virtue of their membership in particular groups without foreclosing on the multiple and changing nature of anyone's belonging. In this regard, Wendy Brown's (1995) caution that (group) rights can work both as an emancipatory force and as a site of regulation, is apposite. While it would be at best naive, at worst disingenuous, for those in a position of privilege to counsel others to abandon the effort to acquire and use rights, Brown nevertheless wants us to attend to the political risks entailed. In particular, she notes that rights tend to operate through an intensely bureaucratic juridical apparatus. Well aware of the part the mythical 'individual' has played in relations of domination, Brown suggests that the democratic value of rights may yet lie not in their concreteness but in their abstract 'idealism, in their ideal configuration of an egalitarian social, an ideal that is contradicted by substantive social inequalities' (1995: 134). In short, the commitment to contesting 'exclusionary closures whether practiced by others *on* minority communities or *within* those communities' (Finlay 2003), must be an open-ended one.

To return to the question that opened this chapter, what difference should unrepresentative political subjects make to

---

[23] The diversity in the interviews presented in Hyndman (1996) offers another argument against reducing Protestants with category trouble to a single group. This diversity extends to differences within, as well as between, the stories featured in the collection.

our thinking about democratic inclusion? Not simply to ex-
pand our writings to include them, but to remind us to ask
how certain figures come to count as typical or authentic
and how such representativeness becomes the price of political speech. The point, in other words, is not to 'give voice
to the voiceless'. On the one hand, that formulation reprises
troubling privileges of scholarly authority. On the other, it
runs the risk of assuming authentic speakers whose voices
the ethnographer, political spokesperson or policy-maker
can simply re-present, asserting the authority-without-
responsibility implied when representation is reduced to description. And it skips over the way the voices and insights
that constitute ethnographic, demographic and political ac-
counts are themselves produced in a wide range of power-
laden intersubjective engagements, including those between
anthropologists and 'informants'. In this spirit, ethnography
might engage in democratising discourse through Joan Vincent's (1991: 48) idea of empowering texts: 'rich, multi-vocal
texts, giving the reader an alternative analysis to fight back
with'. Such texts refuse to resolve into just-so stories. They
might also challenge the premise that people must be one
thing or the other: not only Irish or British (for example) but
also victim or oppressor, hero or villain. And alongside people, democracy itself might be pluralised (Honig 2001: 120-
21).

The GFA is one response to the obvious inadequacy for
Northern Ireland of a liberal model premised on the idea of
the abstract citizen subject. As with Brown's reflections on
rights, I think we must refuse any anti-democratic impulse
to limit debate to the narrow question of whether one is 'for
or against the Agreement'24. Both supporters and critics
have noted that the GFA's consociationalist framework is
less about transforming division than about finding a way to
manage or administer it by creating mechanisms for unionists and nationalists *as such* to work together (Harvey 2003

---

24 For the record, I not only voted for the Agreement but publicly
    supported it, though not without expressing doubts on certain issues
    (see Whitaker 1998).

and Taylor 2001). The arguments for this strategy should not stop us from considering the costs attached to particular interpretations of it. These include the danger of replacing the unmarked abstract citizen with a subject still imagined as self-identical but this time fully at home in its proper category, whatever that category is. For if the Agreement recognises the differences *between* citizens, I have argued that the dilemmas facing people like Maxine and Paul and parties like the Women's Coalition might be better understood to stem from differences *within* subjects. Rather than seeing such people as troublesome exceptions, we might look for political arrangements that are open to the political potential of a concatenation of differences that refuses to resolve into a settled 'identity-authenticity', making a 'critical difference from [one]self' that *'undermines the very idea of identity'* (Trinh T Minh-ha, in Haraway 1992: 93). This multiplicity is not just evanescent 'postmodern play.' As Judith Butler (1993: 4) puts it, 'it may be that the persistence of *dis*identification is equally crucial to the rearticulation of democratic contestation'. Such difference is a necessary condition for the creation of new solidarities, forged not through already-settled identities but through political effort. To deny the promise of such multiple subjects might well mean replacing democratic politics – ongoing struggle about which differences matter, in what ways – with the institutionalised administration of certain differences.

REFERENCES

The Agreement (1998) (Command Paper 3883), Belfast: Her Majesty's Stationary Office (April).

Appadurai, A. (1988), 'Putting Hierarchy in Its Place', *Cultural Anthropology* 3, 1, 36-49.

Aretxaga, B. (1997), *Shattering Silence: Women, Nationalism and Political Subjectivity in Northern Ireland*. New Jersey: Princeton University Press.

Brown, W. (1995), *States of Injury: Power and Freedom in Late Modernity*. Princeton: Princeton University Press.

Butler, J. (1993), *Bodies That Matter*. New York: Routledge.

CONI (Census Office of Northern Ireland), *Northern Ireland Census of Population 2001*: http://www.nisra.gov.uk/census/pdf/Key%20Statistics%20ReportTables.pdf

Coombe, R. (1998), *The Cultural Life of Intellectual Properties: Authorship, Appropriation and the Law*. Durham: Duke University Press.

Curtin, C., Hastings, D. and Wilson, T.M. (1993), 'Anthropology and Irish Urban Settings', in C. Curtin, D. Hastings and T.M. Wilson, eds, *Irish Urban Cultures*. Belfast: Institute of Irish Studies.

de Lauretis, T. (1986), 'Feminist Studies/Critical Studies: Issues, Terms and Contexts', in T. de Lauretis ed., *Feminist Studies/Critical Studies*. Bloomington: Indiana University Press.

Doherty, P. and Poole, M.A. (2002), 'Religion as an Indicator of Ethnicity in Northern Ireland – An Alternative Perspective', *Irish Geography*, 35, 2, 75-89.

Fearon, K. (1996), 'Painting the Picture', in *Power, Politics, Positionings: Women in Northern Ireland*. Democratic Dialogue Report 4. Belfast: Democratic Dialogue.

Finlay, A. (1999), '"Whatever You Say, Say Nothing": An Ethnographic Encounter in Northern Ireland and its Sequel', *Sociological Research Online* 4 3. http://www.socresonline.org.uk/socresonline/4/3/finlay.html.

Finlay, A. (2003), 'Beware of Communal Rights', *Fortnight* 419:9 (November).

Foster, R. (1988), *Modern Ireland 1600-1972*. London: Penguin.

Foucault, M. (1980), *Power/Knowledge: Selected Interviews and Other Writings 1972-1977*, C. Gordon ed., New York: Vintage Books.

Foucault, M. (1984), 'Polemics, Politics, and Problematizations' (interview with Paul Rabinow), in P. Rabinow ed., *The Foucault Reader*. New York: Pantheon.

Friel, L. (2002), 'Now You See it, Now You Don't: The Unionist Majority, the Census and the Electoral Register', *An Phoblacht/Republican News*, 16/1/02.

Gilroy, P. (1991), *There Ain't No Black in the Union Jack: The Culture and Politics of Race and Nation*, Chicago: University of Chicago Press.

Greenhouse, C.J. and Greenwood, D.J. (1998), 'Introduction: The Ethnography of Democracy and Difference', in C.J. Greenhouse, ed., (with K. Roshanak), *Democracy and Ethnography: Constructing Identities in Multicultural Liberal States*. Albany: SUNY Press.

Gudgin, G. (2002a), 'Making Sense of the Census', *Belfast Telegraph* 20/12/02.

Gudgin, G. (2002b), 'Reports of End of Protestant Domination Exaggerated', *The Irish Times*, 15/2/02.

Hacking, I. (1990), *The Taming of Chance*. Cambridge: Cambridge University Press.

Haraway, D. (1991), *Simians, Cyborgs and Women: The Reinvention of Nature*. New York: Routledge.

Haraway, D. (1992), 'Ecce Homo, Ain't (Ar'n't) I a Woman and Inappropriate/d Others: The Human in a Post-Humanist Landscape', in J. Butler and J. Scott eds, *Feminists Theorize the Political*. New York: Routledge.

Harris, R. (1972) [1986], *Prejudice and Tolerance in Ulster – A Study of Neighbours and 'Strangers' in a Border Community*. Manchester: Manchester University Press.

Harvey, C. (2003), 'Sticking to the Terms of the Agreement', *Fortnight* 416, 9 (July/August).

Honig, B. (1996), 'Difference, Dilemmas, and the Politics of Home', in S. Benhabib ed., *Democracy and Difference: Contesting the Boundaries of the Political*. Princeton: Princeton University Press.

Honig, B. (2001), *Democracy and the Foreigner*. Princeton: Princeton University Press.

Hyndman, M. (1996), *Further Afield: Journeys from a Protestant Past*. Belfast: Beyond the Pale Press.

Kymlicka, W. (1995), *Multicultural Citizenship*. Oxford: Oxford University Press.

Lefort, C. (1988), *Democracy and Political Theory* (D. Macey, trans.). Minneapolis: University of Minnesota Press.

Malkki, L.H. (1995), 'News and Culture: Transitory Phenomena and the Fieldwork Tradition', in A. Gupta and J. Ferguson, eds, *Anthropological Locations: Boundaries and Grounds of a Field Science*. Berkeley: University of California Press.

McCann, E. (2000), 'The Way it is, was and always will be', review of S. McKay, (2000) *Northern Protestants: An Unsettled People*, in *Sunday Tribune* 21/5/00.

McCann, E. (1993), *War and an Irish Town*, Third Revised Edition. London: Pluto Press.

McGarry, J. and O'Leary, B. (1995a), *Explaining Northern Ireland: Broken Images*. Oxford: Blackwell.

McGarry, J. and O'Leary, B. (1995b), 'Five Fallacies: Northern Ireland and the Liabilities of Liberalism' in *Ethnic and Racial Studies* 18, 4, 837-861.

McKay, S. (2000), *Northern Protestants: An Unsettled People*. Belfast: Blackstaff Press.

Moore, S.F. (1987), 'Explaining the Present: Theoretical Dilemmas in Processual Anthropology', *American Ethnologist* 14, 4: 727-751.

Mulholland, M. (2000), *Northern Ireland at the Crossroads: Ulster Unionism in the O'Neill Years, 1960-9*. Basingstoke and London: Macmillan Press.

Newman, K. (1997), untitled submission, in D. Duggan ed., *River and Hills: Texts from the 'Time to Listen' and 'Languaging Peace' Seminars 1996*. Derry/Londonderry: Fingerpost and Waterside Voices, joint publication.

Nic Craith, M. (2002), *Plural Identities, Singular Narratives: The Case of Northern Ireland*. New York: Berghahn Books.

NIWC (2003), *Change the Face of Politics: Women's Coalition Manifesto 2003*. Belfast: Northern Ireland Women's Coalition (Election Communication).

O'Leary, B. (2001), 'Comparative Social Science and the British-Irish Agreement' in J. McGarry ed., *Northern Ireland and the Divided World: Post-Agreement Northern Ire-*

land in Comparative Perspective. Oxford: Oxford University Press.

Rooney, E. (2000), 'Women in Northern Irish Politics: Difference Matters', in C. Roulston and C. Davies eds, *Gender, Democracy and Inclusion in Northern Ireland.* Houndsmills: Palgrave.

Rosaldo, R. (1989), *Culture and Truth: The Remaking of Social Analysis.* Boston: Beacon Press.

Santino, J. (1999), 'Public Protest and Popular Style: Resistance from the Right in Northern Ireland and South Boston', *American Anthropologist,* 101, 3, 515-528.

Scott, D. (1992), 'Criticism and Culture: Theory and Post-Colonial Claims on Anthropological Disciplinarity', *Critique of Anthropology,* 12, 4, 371-394.

Scott, D. (1999), *Refashioning Futures: Criticism After Postcoloniality.* Princeton: Princeton University Press.

Scott, J.C. (1999), *Seeing Like a State: How Certain Schemes to Improve the Human Condition Have Failed.* New Haven: Yale University Press.

Stewart, K. (1991), 'On the Politics of Cultural Theory: A Case for "Contaminated" Cultural Critique', *Social Research,* 58, 2, 395-412.

Taylor, C. (1994), 'The Politics of Recognition', in A. Gutmann ed., *Multiculturalism: Examining the Politics of Recognition.* Princeton: Princeton University Press.

Taylor, R. (2001), 'Northern Ireland: Consociation or Transformation?', in J. McGarry ed., *Northern Ireland and the Divided World: Post-Agreement Northern Ireland in Comparative Perspective.* Oxford: Oxford University Press.

Vincent, J. (1991), 'Engaging Historicism', in R.G. Fox ed., *Recapturing Anthropology: Working in the Present.* Santa Fe: School of American Research Press.

Warner, M. (1993), 'The Mass Public and the Mass Subject', in B. Robbins ed., *The Phantom Public Sphere.* Minneapolis: University of Minnesota Press.

Whitaker, R. (1998), 'The Agreement: What's in it for Women?', *Fortnight,* 370 (May).

Whitaker, R. (2001), *Talking Politics: Gender and Political Culture in the Northern Ireland Peace Process*, PhD dissertation, University of California (Santa Cruz).

Whyte, J. (1990), *Interpreting Northern Ireland*, Oxford: Clarendon Press.

Wilson, R. (2003), 'Am I Me Or Am I One of Them? Who Has Rights: Groups or People?', *Fortnight*, 414, 11 (May).

Wolf, E. (1999), *Envisioning Power: Ideologies of Dominance and Crisis*. Berkeley: University of California Press.

9. From Nationality to Citizenship: Cultural Identity and Cosmopolitan Challenges in Ireland

GERARD DELANTY

The assumption that citizenship is defined by nationality has been widely questioned over the past two decades. The separation of citizenship from the condition of membership of a specific state has been one of the major themes in recent social and political theory (Isin and Turner 2002). Yet the implications of these debates and developments in the theory and practice of citizenship as a post-national condition for Ireland have rarely been discussed. New conceptions and practices of citizenship point to something considerably more differentiated and multifaceted than nationality. If in the most general sense citizenship entails membership of the political community, it is apparent that many of the legal and cultural assumptions inherited from the previous two centuries are questionable. The very status of membership has become highly contested as a result of new conceptions of rights and new expressions of belonging. Where citizenship was once confined to a passive condition as a legal status based on rights and duties, today in the view of many it has become a condition of empowerment.

In addition to the conventional rights of citizenship – civic, political and social – as described by T.H. Marshall in his classic essay, there is a now a growing emphasis on cultural rights and questions of participation (Marshall 1992 [1950]). This has led to two major changes in citizenship. First, it has led to the recognition that some degree of group rights is necessary in order to extend citizenship to minorities, especially ethnic minorities, migrant groups or disadvantaged groups, and that consequently citizenship cannot entirely be reduced to the rights of birth. In this respect, citizenship must be capable of a certain flexibility, for example in reconciling individual and group interests. Secondly, partly as a result of the need for the legal recognition of minorities but

183

also because of the growing sense that citizenship entails the right to express one's identity, culture has entered more and more into the politics of citizenship and democracy, as in for example debates about forms of commemoration, heritage, minority languages, religion, special rights or dispensations from certain duties etc. In sum, citizenship as membership of a political community now extends into a much broader notion of participation than was previously the case.

However, the implications of these new conceptions of citizenship extend beyond issues of rights and the identity of minority groups to the very self-understanding of national identities (Povenilli 2002). It is a fact of great significance that the debate on rights is occurring at a time when the national polity is itself being challenged as the primary location of citizenship and of national self-understanding. No account of citizenship today can neglect the wider transformation in the very nature of political community understood in terms of a sovereign and territorially defined polity based on an underlying cultural identity (Castells 1996). As a result of the growing impact of global processes and world cultural concepts, political community itself has become open to new definitions, some of which point to the contemporary salience of cosmopolitan community. There are enough empirical indications to make the claim that political community cannot be codified as a national community in which political identity is based on a prior cultural identity. The nation-state is no longer the primary reference for loyalties, identities and democracy. This does not mean that the nation is an exhausted category or that the state has ceased to be an effective agent of justice and democracy; what it means is that the nation has become pluralised and open to new imaginaries about belonging, community and identity. The nation is now a fragile, liquid and contested category. Nowhere is this more evident than in responses to multiple cultural identities and cosmopolitan self-understanding.

One of the most important developments in recent times as far as citizenship is concerned is the cultural transformation of national identity as a result of what may be broadly subsumed under the category of globalisation. National identities are not immune to the growing sense of the inter-connectivity of the world, the emergence of global civil soci-ety, world ethics, planetary problems and, within its member states, the EU and the emergence of a European public sphere. These expressions of political community have had an undeniable impact on the capacity of national identity to define political community exclusively in particularistic terms. It is widely agreed that globalisation is not simply bringing about a new global and homogenised order as such, or that the universal is replacing the particular; on the con-trary, the global and the local complement each other (Robertson 1992). Nations are perfectly capable of appropri-ating and adapting to globalisation, producing new national imaginaries such that something like 'nations without na-tionalism' are possible (Kristeva 1993). The imagined community of the nation now extends far beyond the bor-ders of the nation-state. In sum, cosmopolitan political com-munity has become a reality and no national polity can de-fine itself in exclusively particularistic terms (Delanty and O'Mahony 2002).

The aim of this chapter is to consider the implications of these two developments – the emergence of new discourses of the rights of citizenship and new expressions of nation-hood – for Ireland. Having become a country of immigration over the last decade, the cultural self-understanding of the Republic of Ireland as a country of emigration is being chal-lenged by the social realities of the twenty-first century. It is significant that this is occurring at a time when the older debate about political community as a conflict between two national traditions has reached a decisive threshold, as marked by the GFA. Precarious though this is, it does ap-pear – as the editor and several contributors to this volume argue – that a degree of polynational pluralism has been reached as far as the legacy of history is concerned. How-ever, despite other positive developments indicative of a post-national consciousness, there is much to suggest that what has been attained is more an accommodation of nationalities than a recognition of the limits of nationality as a framework for citizenship and political community.

In the first section, I discuss some of the main debates on post-national citizenship, focussing in particular on the question of culture and rights. In the second section I look at the cultural transformation of national identity, assessing the impact of globalisation and the significance of cosmopolitan community. In the third section I will explore with some application to the case of Ireland the implications of these developments. Here the argument will be that the republican conception of citizenship as nationality has not abated and what is needed, I shall argue by way of conclusion, is a rethinking of the cultural assumptions of membership of political community.

THE IDEA OF POST-NATIONAL CITIZENSHIP: CULTURE AND RIGHTS

The idea of post-national citizenship is a departure from the older traditions. In civic republican theory citizenship has largely been associated with the idea of the participation of the public in the political life of the community. This has given rise to a strong association of citizenship with civil society and in general with a definition of citizenship as an active condition. In liberal theory, which has tended to stress the passive dimension of citizenship, what is important is that it is a legal status, based on rights and duties. In these conceptions, despite their differences, citizenship is something that presupposes a strict definition of insiders from outsiders and, moreover, has a strongly territorial basis to it: citizenship defines the rights and duties of the members of the polity. In general, most modern nation-states have determined a legally codified citizenship as a set of rights incurred by virtue of birth in the territory of the state. Citizenship, enshrined in the passport, thus served as an instrument of state control over its population and as a means of cultural homogenisation (Mann 1987, Hindess 1998 and Torpey 2000). For several reasons citizenship and nationality have become blurred today. The following brief list will suffice to indicate the degree of bifurcation.

Firstly, as is the case in the countries of the EU, residence rather than birth is increasingly coming to be an important factor in determining citizenship rights. Although still based on a prior national citizenship, a legally codified European citizenship now exists as a post-national citizenship (Eder and Giesen 2001). Most civic and social rights are determined by residence rather than by birth. In this respect nationality is not the decisive feature of rights.

Secondly, in addition to the blurring of citizenship and nationality, the older distinction between the rights of citizenship and human rights is also becoming more and more hazy. In many countries minorities, migrant groups, refugees etc. can claim various kinds of rights on the basis of appeals to human rights, which are now part of the legal framework of most European nation-states (Soysal, 1994). In general, legal pluralism is becoming more and more important. Legal systems are increasingly overlapping, as in the recognition of indigenous law in Canada, New Zealand and Australia. European integration is itself an example of legal pluralism, whereby national and European legal systems are interpenetrating.

Thirdly, new kinds of rights arising from technology are becoming more important (Frankenfeld 1992, Zimmerman 1995). As a result of new technologies such as communication and information technologies, new reproductive technologies, the new genetics, biotechnologies, surveillance technologies, and new military technologies aimed at populations rather than states, technology has transformed the very meaning of citizenship, which can no longer be defined as a relation to the state. The new technologies differ from the old ones in that they have major implications for citizenship, given their capacity to redefine the very nature of society, and in many case personhood.

Fourthly, one of the traditional assumptions of citizenship, namely the separation of the private from the public, has been undermined. Feminist theorists have shown how citizenship must be seen as something that extends into the private (Lister 1997 and 1998). In this respect, the politics of citizenship cannot be separated from identity politics. The focus on production and social class, which informed Marshall's account of citizenship, has given way to greater interest in subcultures based around leisure pursuits and consumption. Citizenship is increasingly about the right to express one's identity, as in for example gay marriages, rights for disabled people (Lurry 1993, Stevenson 2000).

Lastly, as mentioned earlier, the rise of group or cultural rights is replacing the previous concern with individual rights and more generally is displacing the older aspiration for equality as the primary aim of citizenship. It is now generally agreed that citizenship is also about the preservation of group differences (Parekh 2000, Touraine 2000). Multiculturalism cannot be reduced to policies designed to manage incoming migrant groups (Hesse 2000). Migrant groups have become increasingly part of the mainstream population and cannot be so easily contained by multicultural policies and, on the other side, the 'native' population itself has become increasingly culturally plural, due in part to the impact of some four decades of ethnic mixing, but also due to the general pluralisation brought about by post-industrial and postmodern culture (Delanty 2003a).

In view of these developments we can say citizenship has entered the domain of culture which has become both a sphere in which legal rights are mapped out and at the same time a realm in which major shifts in identity are occurring (Isin and Wood 1999, Turner 1990 and 1993). There have been several theoretical responses to this trend towards post-national citizenship within political philosophy. Charles Taylor's essay, 'The Politics of Recognition', is one key work in this direction (Taylor 1994). Taylor's essay established the argument that citizenship must take account of the need for cultural recognition. In this respect his work has been a major statement of what has become known as liberal communitarianism, that is a liberalism that is modified by the desirability of granting official recognition to cultural identities, or in more general terms the need to modify a politics of citizenship based on individualism with one based on community (Mulhall and Swift 1996). Taylor argued that an essential feature of democracy must be the right to protect a cultural way of life. However, Taylor's position has generally been seen as a limited one and confined to the recognition of large-scale national minorities.

In this respect the work of Will Kymlicka offers an alternative, but also from a broadly liberal position (Kymlicka 1995). His contribution to the communitarian debate has been to argue for the recognition not just of the cultural claims of large-scale sub-national groups, but for the recognition of the claims of minorities. According to Kymlicka, the recognition of cultural differences does not endanger democracy. He argues that group rights can be defended for some kinds of national minorities such as indigenous minorities (who at the time of their incorporation into the state possessed a distinct cultural way of life and territory). However, he does extend this to groups created by migration (who voluntarily gave up their cultural way of life and entered a new society). In fact, Kymlicka's arguments make only very limited concessions to diversity and, like Taylor, are heavily influenced by factors specific to Canada.

Departing radically from Taylor and Kymlicka's adherence to liberal communitarism, Iris Marion Young has made the case for a differentiated concept of citizenship (Young 1990 and 2000). Her position – in effect an argument for radical pluralism – is one that defends the necessity for group rights in order for minority groups to maintain their autonomy against the mainstream society. Of principal importance in her view is the practical necessity that the rights of citizenship be differentiated in order to make justice possible. Universal citizenship rights fail to secure the practical efficacy of justice, she argues. While her concern is not merely with ethnic groups or large-scale national minorities but with all socially disadvantaged groups, radical pluralism ultimately leads to the implication that citizenship is entirely a matter of justice as such. Although it is not Young's aim, radical pluralism has given legitimation to a politics of cultural difference in which equality is now firmly challenged by difference. Here the aspiration is not simply equality but the right to remain or be different.

The implications of radical pluralism, when taken to the extreme, would undermine the possibility of a shared political culture. However, although largely rejecting the universalistic premises of liberal communitarianism, Young's concerns are mainly confined to specific issues of justice and democratic multiculturalism. Nevertheless, the problem of how to balance universalism with particularism remains a central challenge for post-national citizenship. Jürgen Habermas and Alain Touraine can be mentioned as two leading social theorists who have tried to do precisely this (Habermas 1998, Touraine 2000). In their work the universalistic idea of citizenship must be able to accommodate the recognition of particular cultural claims. But this does not entail a compromise as much as a creation of a common civic culture. In Habermas's formulation, the only universalistic normative framework possible in culturally diverse societies is one that is grounded in the constitution and the norms of democratic deliberation. He rejects as unviable the idea of a common ethos underlying the demos and, moreover, rejects the relativistic scenario of extreme pluralism.

The idea of constitutional patriotism advocated by Habermas is not without problems. It has often been criticised for being too minimal in its demands and for making the assumption that all cultural obstacles to citizenship can easily be overcome. As a response to these limits within Habermas's position several critics, such as Gutmann and Benhabib have argued for a stronger cultural dimension to democratic citizenship (Gutmann 2002, Benhabib 2002). In these approaches culture is itself a site of democratic explorations, translations and dialogue suspended between particularism and universalism. Where Habermas thinks culture can be transcended and a culturally neutral civic citizenship created, these critics suggest that democratic citizenship is constituted in deeper levels of cultural dialogue.

The dialogic model has gained increased support in much of recent writing. Several studies show that there are costs and benefits in granting minority rights and it is important not to overstate the dangers (Kymlicka and Norman 2000, Cowan *et al.* 2001) There are some convincing arguments that minority rights do not involve a zero-sum game between citizenship and minority rights and that a balance can be achieved between conflicting conceptions of the common good. The view of culture in these studies is far from the culture wars of the 1980s and early 1990s. Culture is not divisive and can be a basis for citizenship. It is unlikely to be a basis of common citizenship in the classic liberal sense, but it is essential to the working of a democratic order and the costs of not granting minority rights will be greater as there is likely to be increased resentment and hostility stemming from exclusion. Insofar as democracy rests on citizenship, along with representation and constitutionalism, and to the extent that citizenship entails participation in political community, then minority rights are essential. With some 5000 to 8000 ethno-cultural groups in the world and only 200 states to accommodate them, clearly democracy must find a way of dealing with the reality of ethno-culturalism, as very few states are, or can be, monocultural. The problem is not the validity of special minority rights but establishing their limits. If one group's rights are accepted, we will be pushed more and more into conceding other rights to a point that may make the political unit non-viable. There are also problems of reconciling the rights of different groups – even of defining what constitutes a group in the first instance – and problems in reconciling the autonomy of the individual with the rights of the ethno-cultural group. Yet, there is common ground between cultures and moreover there are few ethnic cultures that are untouched by the critical and reflexive values of modernity (Ong 1999, Povinelli 2002, Smelser and Alexander 1999).

This short discussion has highlighted some of the current debates on post-national citizenship. A general conclusion that can be drawn from these debates is that citizenship has been inextricably drawn into cultural issues over identity and belonging. As a result of these developments the form of citizenship is no longer reducible to nationality.

GLOBALISATION AND THE NATION: COSMOPOLITAN IMAGINARIES

It was not the aim of the preceding discussion to suggest that the category of the nation has been overcome by a post-national order, or that national identities have been rendered obsolete. The de-coupling of citizenship and nationality has been reflected in another decoupling process, namely the de-coupling of state and nation. While there is no evidence that nations and states are disappearing from the allegedly global age, it is arguably the case that the nation-state as such is undergoing major reshaping, not least as a result of globalisation. But globality can be understood only in relation to locality and what is decisive is the way the local appropriates the global. Globalisation, itself a multi-faceted process, in fact offers national cultures many opportunities for new expressions of nationality to be codified, ranging from extreme right-wing to cosmopolitan projects. The upshot of this is that the local-global nexus will not necessarily result in the continuation of state-codified conceptions of the nation. Few states today can claim to rest securely on the shoulders of a unitary nation. Exactly what constitutes the nation, where its borders lie and who belongs to it have become major issues in recent years. This means that states cannot simply attempt to secure the political identity of the polity in an underlying cultural identity. National identities are constituted in multi-centric ways and cannot be reduced to unitary or homogenous projects (Westwood and Phizacklea 2000). It is important to recognise that national identities are themselves open to new codifications.

Cosmopolitan currents are evident both within and beyond the nation and can be related to various processes of globalisation (Breckenridge *et al.* 2002, Cheah and Robbins

1998, Vertovec and Cohen 2002). For the purpose of illustration, globalisation can be analysed under four headings – economic, legal, political and cultural – all of which can be related to processes of differentiation. Political globalisation refers to the new politics of governance on a global scale, that is the growing importance of non-state actors in politics, such as NGOs and global civil society. Legal globalisation refers to the growing importance of international law and changes in the nature of sovereignty. Economic globalisation refers to global capitalism, markets, information and communication technology etc. Cultural globalisation refers to the growing role of transnational culture, societal interpenetration, hybridity and multiculturalism. Taking each of these in turn we can see how the cosmopolitan influences have reshaped the imaginary of the nation and are thus presenting new challenges for national identity.

Political globalisation has marked a significant turn in politics from the nation and the state to civil society. This is the domain of politics that is distinct from the institutions of the state, such as parties and government, and which is also distinct from the idea of the nation insofar as this is conceived of in terms of an undifferentiated notion of the people or an ethnos. With the growing consolidation of global civil society, national civil societies are increasingly forced to address global concerns. This has clear implications for national identities and for the established conceptions of the nation and prevailing forms of political legitimation. New loyalties challenge older ones, and the outcome of the ensuing shift in identities and values can be reactionary nationalism rather than a cosmopolitan reorientation of the nation.

Legal globalisation is frequently a product of political globalisation and is most evident in the growing importance of international law. As discussed in the previous section, international laws, tribunals and treaties are now increasingly embedded in national legal systems. The result of this legal pluralism is a blurring of human rights and citizenship rights. In a wider sense, too, globalisation has led to new regulatory regimes in a wide variety of areas – environment, markets, crime, health – resulting in what is often called a crisis of national sovereignty. However, this alleged crisis can also be viewed as the expression of a cosmopolitan sovereignty whereby sovereignty is shared rather than residing exclusively in the state.

Economic globalisation is generally seen as the most extreme kind of globalisation, often equated with global Americanisation. Where the political and legal forms of globalisation are multi-faceted, economic globalisation is 'top-down' and driven by the pursuits of global markets. In the extreme, as in 'McDonaldisation', it is a process of standardisation and rationalisation in which all parts of the world are subject to homogenisation determined by capitalism, but a homogenisation that does not produce social integration or even system integration. The information revolution is often seen as consolidating this process which leaves little room for the heterogeneity of national cultures.

Cultural globalisation in contrast to economic globalisation, is a process by which globality is appropriated by the local and given new and more heterogeneous meanings. Such processes can be described in terms of hybridity or indigenisation. Theorists who stress the cultural dimensions of globalisation stress the role of agency and tend to see globalisation in terms of global-local links. In this view, information and communication technologies and other processes of globalisation offer opportunities for national cultures to reinvent themselves.

From the perspective of globalisation, nations and nationalism are far from being erased, although they are certainly on the defensive. The nation has indeed lost its capacity to create social integration based upon cultural cohesion. This is possibly one of the greatest changes occurring in the role of national culture. As many authors have argued, most notably Gellner, nationalism and national identity since the mid-nineteenth century have served to provide modern societies with a uniform system of communication to offset the differentiation – and with it the dislocations – brought about by modernisation, such as urbanisation, industrialisation and migration (Gellner, 1983). The creation of a national culture, achieved through national education, capital cities and architecture, forms of commemoration, state churches, a legally defined citizenship in the form of passports etc., provided modern societies with a common system of communication and identity. By creating a cohesive cultural order, a degree of social integration was possible. What is different today is that national culture no longer fulfils this function of social integration. Globalisation has unleashed numerous processes of differentiation, as well as of de-differentiation, which cannot easily be resisted by recourse to nation-building or nationalism. The nation has ceased to perform an integrative function not just because of the changing role of the nation-state but also because culture in general has lost its integrative function.

Rather than being integrative and based on an underlying consensus, culture must be seen as fluid and negotiable; it is not fixed or rooted in immutable principles, and is not defined by reference to territory, the state, an elite, a church or a party. Culture consists of different forms of classification, cognitive models, narratives, forms of evaluation, collective identities, values and norms, aesthetic forms. Some of these will be shared, others will not. Culture is primarily a system of communication rather than a form of integration and is always open to different interpretations and to new codifications. We have only to consider the role of the internet to see that culture cannot be separated from its modes of communication. As noted in the previous section, culture is also a medium in which citizenship is articulated. In addition to the classic social, civic and political rights, cultural rights relating to language, information, heritage, memories, and what in general concerns symbolic expression, is increasingly becoming a focus for citizenship.

Today more than ever, integration is sustained by forms of communication rather than by a stable system of cultural values and norms. The cultural form of modern society is responding to globality by becoming more and more discursive. Societies must evolve the cognitive capacity to cope with the increasing volume of communication. According to Jürgen Habermas, no society can simply opt out of the critical and reflexive forces at work in modern culture which have 'rationalised' societies' modes of legitimation to a point where communication is now the cultural form of societal reproduction. The result is that a 'post-national' polity can only be based on cultural forms of commonality that can accept certain basic principles, such as procedural rules for the resolution of conflicts, the need for communicative solutions, and the limited patriotism of an identification with the constitution – a 'constitutional patriotism' – rather than with territory, cultural heritage or the state. It shows how cultural forms of identification and loyalty are still possible and that therefore culture is reconcilable with diversity and is not threatened by conflict but is in fact sustained by the constant negotiation of conflict.

Finally, it can be argued that national culture can no longer be identified with the state: the nation has become too entangled in wider cultural processes to be easily tied to the project of the state. The globalising world has brought about a new situation for the nation, especially in relation to authority and loyalty, conceptions of territory and sovereignty, national narratives and symbolic structures. The traditional forms of authority have been undermined and new loyalties are emerging. Loyalty today is becoming increasingly conditional and can no longer be regarded as a durable resource to be tapped by political elites. Loyalties can be recalcitrant and unpredictable and this is especially the case where political elites are perceived as having betrayed democracy. Today more than ever loyalties are refracted through democracy and cannot be simply derived from the uncritical values of duty, patriotism or obedience (Delanty, 2003b). Territory and sovereignty, too, cannot be exclusive foundations for national identities. Especially within the EU, territorial borders are becoming more fluid and with new levels of governance, sovereignty is becoming more multifaceted.

The crisis of representation in all of culture has had its impact on the symbolic practices of commemoration. These have become more contested and open to new interpretations in recent times. As a result of more expansive modes of democratisation, multiculturalism, inter-cultural encounters, authoritative forms of cultural representation are giving way to more reflexive, ambivalent and critical expressions of cultural belonging. The crisis of representation has not led to the decline of commemoration, but to new forms and new discourses about it (Spillane 1997). Inescapably such discourses are centrally about the changing form of the state and the political community of the nation. Commemoration is now inseparable from the wider question of cultural citizenship, for to commemorate is to make a symbolic statement about belonging. Who and what is commemorated is also a performative act in which the commemorating subject symbolically constitutes itself in an act of commemoration. Public debates today about commemoration are about the meaning such events have for particular groups, rather than just for the state; and for this reason they are related to different subject positions: the subject as a victim, a spectator, or a perpetrator (Gray and Oliver 2001). Commemoration is now more about the remembrance of the living than of the dead.

To sum up, national identities are increasingly taking on a post-national form; they are compatible with multiple identities and require identification only with the limited values of the demos. Habermas has argued that as a result of the diversity of the cultural forms of modern societies and the accelerated rate of change, cultures will survive only if they adapt themselves to the principles of discursivity and critique. If he is correct then national cultures and cosmopolitan values are not entirely antithetical.

CITIZENSHIP AND THE NATION IN IRELAND

In the foregoing analysis it was argued that on the one hand, the tie between citizenship and nationality has been broken and on the other that the nation and state have been decoupled. Processes of differentiation that can be related to globalisation have created new scenarios for citizenship poli-

tics, nations and the state. The result of this is that citizenship and national culture have ceased to perform functions
of social and system integration for states and can be indicative of cosmopolitanism, conceived of in terms of a civic
conception of the nation. In this section of the chapter the
implications of these developments will be considered with
respect to Ireland.

It must firstly be noted that Irish political modernity has
been strongly influenced by the republican conception of the
polity as derived from the Jacobin tradition that emerged
with the French Revolution. The central feature of this is a
belief in the absolute superiority of a political leadership
which establishes political goals for society; it is a view of
polity as shaped by political elites who represent the popular
will, which the elites codify in new political institutions. In
this way, some of the defining tenets of Jacobin republicanism – the idea of self-determination, secularism, security of
the nation, a purely state-centred conception of society –
tended towards authoritarianism and towards a nation-*state*
and state patriotism rather than a civic nation. This was the
central animus of Irish republicanism from the late eighteenth century and gave to it a radical impetus, the legacy of
which was that political institutions were continuously
fraught with the spectre of violence. As in other countries,
this Jacobin tradition had a strong secular thrust, but in
Ireland as in other European countries this secular thrust
waned by the late nineteenth century; moreover, in the Irish
case an accommodation with the rising tide of political Catholicism was evident by the 1890s and from 1922 Catholic
doctrines were finally institutionalised by a national state
that had, in the aftermath of Civil War, renounced many of
the aspirations of republicanism (O'Mahony and Delanty
1998). From 1922 political and cultural nationalism combined to produce a political culture in which ethnos and
demos were effectively equated; political liberty tended towards cultural authoritarianism; and the idea of self-
determination, the nation's right to autonomy, mutated into
the right of the nation to decide who should belong to it and

under what terms. The civic nation with its cosmopolitan elements was entirely eroded by a centralising ideology that put the rights of the nation above the rights of citizens.

The problem with political modernity in Ireland was not a weak democratic or constitutional tradition. Unlike many European countries, the constitutional tradition and most democratic liberties, which since 1801 had been heavily institutionalised in the political culture, were not destroyed during the bleaker moments of the twentieth century. The problem was that unlike, for example the Scottish tradition of nationhood, political modernity in Ireland was, like that in England, characterised by a weak civic tradition. The civic nation – as opposed to the state nation or the cultural nation – does not define the nation in the image of the state or in purely cultural terms. The nation is the political community of citizens and signals an inclusive conception of the polity rather than one defined in purely exclusionary or power terms. With its origins in eighteenth-century Enlightenment cosmopolitanism, the civic nation was neither particularist nor universalist. It has been one of the chief rivals of the dominant traditions of the nation-state (or state nation) and the cultural nation. One of its notable characteristics is the relative absence of a strong nationalist current to it. Where the state nation and the cultural nation have fostered violent forms of nationalism, the civic nation has not nurtured nationalism.

There is much to suggest that the state nation and the cultural nation as major projects of modernity are now in decline in Ireland as elsewhere. Although in many countries the extreme right attempt to resuscitate such forms of state patriotism, they are still marginal forces. The cosmopolitan currents immanent in certain tendencies resulting from globalisation provide opportunities for the nation to be redefined in civic terms, thus allowing us to speak of nations without nationalism. Trends towards a civic nation are in evidence in Ireland. There are four major markers of such trends.

The first is the creation of a politics of recognition, in the sense of the liberal communitarian political philosophy of

Charles Taylor, which, as discussed earlier in this chapter, offers a normative interpretation of an official kind of multi-culturalism. The key event in this politics of recognition is the GFA, which has led to a certain reconciliation of the older confessional and territorial politics inherited from the earlier days of the foundation of the state. While the peace process has a long way to go before significant progress will be evident, the fact that such a process is underway is an indication of the institutionalisation of pluralism and the need to move beyond forms of identity based on identifica-tion with statehood and territory such as republicanism and its rivals, unionism and loyalism, which have been some of the more extreme forms of state patriotism that endured into the late twentieth century. It is however evident that the emerging pluralism is highly limited, confined as it is to the reconciliation of the dominant confessional groups and there has been no attempt to extend the politics of recognition to other groups. Although what is at issue here is not the rec-ognition of minorities but the accommodation of dominant national groups, nevertheless a significant dissolution of hegemonic identities has occurred.

The second indication of an emerging cosmopolitanism is less developed and relates to the emerging new pluralist agenda. Where the old pluralism concerns the accommoda-tion of the confessional/territorial identities – and is mostly pertinent to Northern Ireland – the new pluralism concerns the accommodation of immigrants, minorities of various kinds and indigenous groups such as Travellers. It may be the case that the new pluralism will have nothing to learn from the old pluralism, which was never conceived of in terms of accepting difference. If this is correct, the impulse for a new politics will have to come from other ideas.

A third example of a loosening of the older forms of nation is the fact of Europeanisation. There can be little doubt that there is a high degree of identification with the EU in Ireland and less resistance to Europeanisation than in Britain and many other countries. Undoubtedly some of this can be ex-plained by the need to move beyond the antagonism to Britain and the Civil War legacy in order to find new reference points for national identity. Coupled with this there is also the simple fact that many of the older national myths are no longer credible. Like many other countries Ireland has now become for the first time a country of immigration. In this context the older myth of Ireland as a poor country of emigration has to be reconsidered.

Finally, one of the most significant factors in shaping a potential cosmopolitanism is a major shift in identity and values amongst young people. Throughout Ireland the collapse of the moral standing of the Catholic Church and the financial scandals surrounding the political elites have undoubtedly contributed to a climate that is conducive to a move to a new national self-understanding. The growing importance of non-national politics, such as environmentalism, gender politics and quality of life issues, has also played a significant role in redefining the terms of debate of nationhood.

It might be suggested that the problem is not merely in separating the demos from ethnos, but in transforming the ethnos. So long as there is an undifferentiated cultural self-understanding, it is unlikely that progress will be made in creating a civic nation.

CONCLUSION

Migration has changed the field of citizenship in European societies today. Where citizenship was once confined to issues of civic, political and social rights within national societies, it now extends more and more into the domain of culture and identities and is increasingly taking 'post-national' forms. As a result of migration, changes in the relation of nationality to citizenship, new human rights regimes, intersocietal cross-fertilisation, globalisation and other major social transformations, citizenship has become an issue that cannot be addressed without consideration of its cultural dimensions, especially in the context of migration and ethnic mixing. As a result of these developments, multiculturalism is now in a very different situation today: not only are ethnic identities in a state of flux, but so too are national and regional identities.

One of the greatest challenges for the emerging post-national Irish society is to articulate core cross-national values that will give citizenship substance in an age of flux, uncertainty and flows. Different national and regional identities are redefining themselves in their relation to each other and to national ethnic minorities, which are now more likely to include new and possibly transient groups. Indeed the very category of what constitutes a group can no longer take for granted some of the older assumptions (Brubaker, 2002). It may be suggested that Irishness refers less to an identity as such (whether personal or collective) than to a category within which different collective identities exist. The notion of an Irish identity needs to be deconstructed of essentialism. Collective identities do not exist on the level of such generalised categories. There are different kinds of Irish identities (Catholic Irish identity, an Irish left identity, a Protestant Irish identity) as there are different kinds of European identities, but there is no single Irish identity any more than there is a single European identity. One of the major problems for late liberal societies is in articulating forms of collective identity that do not reduce the nation to an essentialist identity. Instead what is needed is a conception of the nation as an inclusionary category in which different kinds of collective identities co-exist and interpenetrate.

In Ireland as in many European countries citizenship and nationality, until recently closely linked, are becoming increasingly loose. The de-coupling processes discussed in this chapter are present in Ireland, but like other comparable countries, for example Denmark, Ireland has difficulty in moving beyond the notion that there is only one cultural conception of nation. Although this is clearly a problem for all European countries, most of which have been formed on the basis of one cultural group whose values either directly or indirectly formed the basis of polity, it is particularly a problem for Ireland. As noted in this chapter and in several contributions to this volume, the GFA does reflect an accommodation of another national tradition. But it remains to be seen whether the politics of recognition will go beyond this conventional level of poly-national coexistence to a more extensive multiculturalism. Essential to this task is the creation of a civic sense of the nation rather than a national identity defined by reference to the nation-state or to a particular cultural conception of the society. It is a question of new national imaginaries for defining people-hood rather than the idea of 'the people'. The republican model of politics is poorly placed to generate such critical and reflexive forms of self-understanding since the very basis of the republican ethos has been the pursuit of a state-centred conception of the polity to house an undifferentiated conception of the national community.

REFERENCES

Benhabib, S. (2002), *The Claims of Culture: Equality and Diversity in the Global Era*. Princeton: Princeton University Press.
Breckenridge, C.A., Pollock, S. Bhabha, H.K. and Chakrabarty D. eds (2002), *Cosmopolitanism*. Durham: Duke University Press.
Brubaker, R. (2002), 'Ethnicity Without Groups', *Archives Européennes de Sociologie*, XLII, 2, 163-89.
Castells, M. (1996), *The Rise of the Network Society, Vol. 1 The Information Age*. Oxford: Blackwell.
Cheah, P. and Robbins, B. eds (1998), *Cosmopolitics: Thinking and Feeling Beyond the Nation*. Minneapolis: Minnesota University Press.
Cowan, J.K., Dembour M-B. and Wilson R.A. eds (2001), *Culture and Rights: Anthropological Perspectives*. Cambridge: Cambridge University Press.
Delanty, G., (2000), *Citizenship in a Global Age*. Buckingham: Open University Press.
Delanty, G. (2003a), *Community*. London: Routledge.

Delanty, G. (2003b), 'Loyalty and the European Union', in M. Waller, A. Linklater and P. Thornberry eds, *Loyalty and the Post-National State*. London: Routledge.

Delanty, G. and O'Mahony, P. (2002), *Nationalism and Social Theory*. London: Sage.

Eder, K. and Giesen, B. eds (2001), *European Citizenship: National Legacies and Transnational Projects*. Oxford: Oxford University Press.

Frankenfeld, P. (1992), 'Technological Citizenship: A Normative Framework for Risk Studies', *Science and Technology and Human Values* 17, 4.

Gellner, E. (1983), *Nations and Nationalism*. Oxford: Blackwell.

Gray, P. and Oliver, K. (2001), 'The Memory of Catastrophe. Views on Commemoration of Historical Disaster', *History Today* (February).

Gutmann, A. (2003), *Identity in Democracy*. Princeton: Princeton University Press.

Habermas, J. (1998), *The Inclusion of the Other: Studies in Political Theory*. Cambridge, Mass.: MIT Press.

Hesse, B. ed. (2000), *Un/Settled Multiculturalism: Disaporas, Entanglements, Transruptions*. London: Zed Books.

Hindess, B. (1998), 'Divide and Rule: The International Character of Modern Citizenship', *European Journal of Social Theory* 1, 1, 57-70.

Isin, E. and Wood, P. (1999), *Citizenship and Identity*. London: Sage.

Isin, E. and Turner, B. eds (2002), *Handbook of Citizenship Studies*. London: Sage.

Kristeva, J. (1993), *Nations Without Nationalism*. New York: Columbia University Press.

Kymlicka, W. (1995), *Multicultural Citizenship: A Liberal Theory of Minority Rights*. Oxford: Clarendon Press.

Kymlicka, W. and Norman, W. eds (2000), *Citizenship in Diverse Societies*. Oxford: Oxford University Press.

Lister, R. (1997), *Citizenship: Feminist Perspectives*. London: Macmillan.

Lister, R. (1998), 'Citizenship and Difference: Towards a Differentiated Universalism', *European Journal of Social Theory* 1, 1, 71-90.

Lurry, C. (1993), *Cultural Rights*. London: Routledge.

Mann, M. (1987), 'Ruling Class Strategies and Citizenship', *Sociology* 21, 3, 339-54.

Marshall, T.H. (1992), *Citizenship and Social Class*. London: Pluto Press.

Mulhall, S. and Swift, A. (1996) [2nd edition], *Liberalism and Communitarianism*. Oxford: Blackwell.

O'Mahony, P. and Delanty, G. (2001) [1998], *Rethinking Irish History: Nationalism, Identity and Ideology*. London: Palgrave.

Ong, A. (1999), *Flexible Citizenship: The Cultural Logics of Transnationality*. Durham: Duke University Press.

Parekh, B. (2000), *Rethinking Multiculturalism: Cultural Diversity and Political Theory*. London: Macmillan.

Povinelli, E. (2002), *The Cunning of Recognition: Indigenous Alterities and the Making of Australian Multiculturalism*. Durham: Duke University Press.

Robertson, R. (1992), *Globalisation: Social Theory and Global Culture*. London: Sage.

Smelser, N. and Alexander, N. eds (1999), *Diversity and Its Discontents: Cultural Conflict and Common Ground in Contemporary American Society*. New Haven: Princeton University Press.

Somers, M. (1995), 'Narrating and Naturalizing Civil Society and Citizenship Theory: The Place of Political Culture and the Public Sphere', *Sociological Theory*. 13, 3, 229-74.

Soysal, Y. (1994), *The Limits of Citizenship*. Chicago: University of Chicago Press.

Spillane, L. (1997), *Nation and Commemoration: Creating National Identities in the United States and Australia*. Cambridge: Cambridge University Press.

Stevenson, N. ed. (2000), *Culture and Citizenship*. London: Sage.

Taylor, C. (1994), 'The Politics of Recognition', in A. Gutman ed., *Multiculturalism: Examining the Politics of Recognition.* Princeton: Princeton University Press.

Torpey, J. (2000), *The Invention of the Passport: Surveillance, Citizenship and the State.* Cambridge: Cambridge University Press.

Touraine, A. (2000), *Can We Live Together? Equal and Different.* Cambridge: Polity Press.

Turner, B.S. (1990) 'Outline of a Theory of Citizenship', *Sociology* 24, 2, 189-217.

Turner, B.S. ed. (1993), *Citizenship and Social Theory.* London: Sage.

Urry, J. (2000), *Sociology Beyond Societies: Mobilities for the Twenty-First Century.* London: Routledge.

Vertovec, S. and Cohen, R. eds (2002), *Conceiving Cosmopolitanism.* Oxford: Oxford University Press.

Walzer, M. (1983), *Thick and Thin: The Moral Argument at Home and Abroad.* New York: Basic Books.

Westwood S. and Phizacklea, A. (2000), *Transnationalism and the Politics of Belonging.* London: Routledge.

Young, I.M. (1990), *Justice and the Politics of Difference.* New Haven: Princeton University Press.

Young, I.M. (2000), *Inclusion and Democracy.* Oxford: Oxford University Press.

Zimmerman, A. (1995), 'Toward a More Democratic Ethics of Technological Governance', *Science, Technology and Human Values*, 20, 1, 86-107.

10. The Unbidden Ireland: Materialism, Knowledge and Inter-culturality

MICHAEL CRONIN

In November 1963 the world's mind was on other things. And one of these was certainly not the then current issue of *Ireland of the Welcomes*, the showcase publication of the Irish Tourist Board established in 1952. In the November-December issue we find an article by the English writer Kenneth Alsop entitled simply, 'Ireland.' After lamenting the disappearance of the corncrake from the English countryside and celebrating its longevity in Ireland, Alsop describes a visit to the Kerry coast where he naively asks some local people near Ballybunion about the existence of smuggling in the area. The response from a local fisherman is suitably oblique: '[w]e never held customs officers very popular in these parts – they have a bit of a rigid idea about how you earn a living' (Alsop 1963: 6). Alsop is not deterred by enigmas and he claims that even if the visitor has no great curiosity about history and legend in Ireland, they are not to be avoided:

> You submerge without a struggle in the stream of a tumultuous and violent past, for on every side are the relics and the memories, physically there or part of the talk and conversation of the villagers and town-dwellers you meet (Alsop 1963: 6).

A tumultuous and violent past and present seemed to place Ireland for many years in the class of slow learners of European modernity. For those who had a bit of a rigid idea about what constituted the Enlightenment, Ireland seemed to be a reminder of the nightmare from which the young modernist sought to awake. Religious hatreds, ethnic rivalries, the apparent absence of a Left/Right divide (with ritual denunciations of cross-class support for Fianna Fáil and the Ulster Unionist Party) represented an anomaly in the bipolar worldview of Cold War thinking. The end of what Philip Bobbitt calls the Long War with the signing of the Charter of

207

Paris allowing for parliamentary institutions in all the participating member-states of the Conference on Security and Cooperation in Europe also signalled a decisive shift in the categories that would now be used to interpret the world (Bobbitt 2002: 61). If previously ideology had been the principal way of structuring political communication, identity now took over. This is not to say, of course, that the issues raised by ideological critiques somehow disappeared or were no longer important but issues such as marginalisation, dispossession and powerlessness were increasingly mediated through discourses of identity.

In the words of Gerard Delanty, '[t]he older ideologies of modernity – capitalist liberal democracy and state socialism – and their geopolitical foundations in east versus west appear to have dissolved into new kinds of binary opposites, such as those of *self* and *other*' (2000: 130). So now Irish preoccupations with identity no longer seem so retrograde. The attempts to think through the theoretical and practical implications of a notion of citizenship that acknowledge both individual and collective rights and that conceive of politics as as much a striving after equality as a safeguarding of difference now makes the fate of villagers and town-dwellers on the island of Ireland of marked global significance in a post-Cold War world. How these selfsame villagers and town-dwellers view identity is, of course, in part determined by local place and local histories, even if one of the central insights of Renaissance humanism is that we need not always be bound by the circumstances of our origin. So what this chapter would like to ask is: what is happening in contemporary Irish society and what might this tell us about the kinds of identity that are likely to be offered to us in the future? In this context, I would like to explore the concept of welfare materialism, the ideal of the knowledge society, and the notion of interculturality in the context of an Ireland that is often not so much hidden as unbidden.

Nationalisms have traditionally defined themselves in opposition to other nationalisms. German nationalism versus French nationalism, Norwegian nationalism versus

Swedish nationalism, Irish nationalism versus British nationalism and so on. The enemy was a clearly defined territorial other with real or imaginary national characteristics. However, if we look at new extreme nationalisms from France and Holland to Austria and Russia, what defines them is not so much jingoism as xenophobia. In other words, the problem is not now perceived to be another competing nation state but mobile immigrant populations from a plethora of different (often distant) nation states. To cite Delanty once more, '[e]xtreme nationalist movements in the developed world define national identity by reference to immigrants and not by reference to other western nationalities; the other is increasingly becoming the internal other' (2000: 97). Of course, this movement is not confined to individual nation-states. At the level of a supra-national body like the EU, a European nationalism of a kind may emerge not through a consensus on cultural commonality but through a united stand on what is deemed to be desirable or undesirable immigration. So rather than national identity becoming less of an issue in the years ahead, it is likely to become more of an issue but not in the terms that have hitherto been used to frame debates on national questions. In particular, the driving force is likely to be a form of welfare materialism, by which I mean both the welfare entitlements of the citizens or residents of a state and the material self-interest of the inhabitants of a specific country. As in the post-Cold War world we all more or less subscribe to majoritarian politics; if sufficiently large numbers of people feel their material interests threatened, then the electoral consequences of mobilising extreme nationalism around welfare materialism should be a cause for alarm, but not surprise.

In Ireland, over the last three decades, we have understandably devoted a great deal of our political and intellectual energies to understanding the different traditions on the island. This has had tangible benefits in the peace agreement, and no matter how endangered it may appear at various stages, our understanding of Ireland is very different from what it was thirty or forty years ago. However, the way in which people represent themselves to each other and to themselves is not just a function of different histories, it is also bound up with the way they are invited, encouraged or obliged to participate in the economy and society in the contemporary world. A much-repeated observation on Irish society is that with the exception of the North East, the island as a whole largely bypassed the Industrial Revolution to go from agriculture to the post-industrial economy. Though this type of observation often minimises the importance of the manufacturing sector of the Irish economy, it nonetheless has validity in pointing to the strong performance of the services sector and the involvement of Ireland in high-tech economic activities (Ó Gráda 2000: 263-82). What about identity then in a post-industrial economy and the society it produces? If three-quarters of foreign direct investment in Ireland has come from the US and American corporations are significant employers in any number of areas from software to pharmaceuticals, what has been the impact of the shift to a post-industrial economy in the US? Richard Sennett argues there that the answer at one level is relatively simple, there is no such thing as the long term, '[i]n work, the traditional career progressing step by step through the institutions is withering; so is the deployment of a single set of skills throughout the course of a working life' (1998: 22). Nowadays, young Americans with at least two years of university education can expect to change jobs at least eleven times in the course of their working lives and radically change their skill base at least three times during forty years of labour. Subcontracting is the order of the day, temping agencies are everywhere and what governs managerial policy is less the long-term interests of its workforce than the short-term interests of its shareholders. The shareholding class has indeed grown exponentially in the Western world, as we witnessed in the Republic during the highly symbolic and much publicised privatisation of Eircom.

For proponents of the new economy the watchwords are flexibility, opportunity, lifelong learning and mobility. These are indeed attractive concepts, particularly when contrasted with what is presented as the disabling fatalism of the grey

years of Irish austerity. However, these new economic arrangements have real consequences for people's lives and
these include vastly increased uncertainty over long-term
employment futures, harmful relational and familial consequences of 24/7 working practices and changing attitudes to
trust and commitment due to the fickleness of equity-driven
corporate policies (making a profit is no guarantee of keeping
your job if even more profit can be made out of doing the
same job elsewhere). In short, as Sennett asks:

> How do we decide what is of lasting value in ourselves in a
> society which is impatient, which focuses on the immediate
> moment? How can long-term goals be pursued in an economy
> devoted to the short term? How can mutual loyalties and
> commitments be sustained in institutions which are constantly
> breaking apart or continually being redesigned? (1998: 10).

These developments in business, the economy and society
obviously make the working out of any kind of identity –
which implies a sense of continuity over time – problematic.
In a sense, the difficulty may be not so much in deciding
whether you are Irish or British or English or European but
in retaining the possibility of working out any kind of identity at all. The danger is that as a sense of uncertainty or
risk becomes more and more prevalent, the temptation is to
reach for a notion of identity which is wholly concerned with
economic entitlement and detaches identity from any idea of
collective, social transformation which goes beyond the
needs of the market. Once we have individuals as consum-
ers rather than as citizens, who are defined by what they
have and will have, rather than by what they are, and more
importantly, might be, then we run the paradoxical risk of
increasingly virulent forms of nationalism in a globalised
world with its much-vaunted decline of the nation-state.
Identity in this scenario is the bleak, defensive interface
between a global economy and infinitely malleable human
material.

If we have concentrated on the economic dimension to
identity so far, it is partly because as we saw in the 2002

general elections in the Republic and as we read every day in the newspapers, questions of budgets, deficits, spending, employment and tax returns occupy public commentary to the exclusion of almost everything else, except, perhaps, the Tribunals[1]. The focus on the economic is understandable in view of the catastrophic social consequences of certain economic policies in the past but we run the risk, in the words of the founding editor of *Le Monde* newspaper, Hubert Beuve-Méry, of letting our means of existence compromise our reasons for existence. So what we would like to do now is to indicate very briefly areas where the scope for work on identity on this island of Ireland is both exciting and daunting.

KNOWLEDGE SOCIETY

One area is that of the knowledge society. In 1957, J.V. Kelleher, a well-known Irish-American, argued in a famous article in the journal *Foreign Affairs* that a hatred of intellectual and psychological freedom was poisoning the body politic in the Republic of Ireland (1957: 48-95). Since then, the Irish body politic has done much to rid itself of these particular toxins and is eager to be integrated into the global informational economy as the intelligent island, the island of online saints and cyber-scholars. In the agricultural mode of development, increasing surplus comes from increases in the amount of labour or natural resources (such as land) available for the production process. New energy sources (steam, electricity) are the principal basis for productivity in the industrial mode of development alongside the ability to distribute energy through appropriate circulation and production processes. In the post-industrial economy, it is the change from a technology based primarily on cheap inputs of energy to one predominantly based on cheap inputs of information that generates growth. Much has rightly been

---

[1]. Established to investigate corruption in public life.

made, in this context, of a young educated workforce in Ireland in sustaining Irish competitive adventage.

However, the question must be asked as to why more is not done to promote intellectual debate and the dissemination of ideas in contemporary Ireland. Why, as the country's population is becoming more and more educated, are there fewer rather than more programmes in the mainstream media devoted to books and ideas? Why has TG4[2], with the exception of the odd documentary and the excellent series of personal interviews conducted by Liam Ó Muirthile, failed to offer a genuine '*súil eile*' (another perspective) on Irish culture through offering viewers access to hundreds of years of political, aesthetic and linguistic thought in Irish? Why has Lyric FM become an almost exclusively music-playing radio station despite initial claims that it would air a similar range of programmes to that aired by BBC Radio 3, offering both music and in-depth arts/culture programming? Why do we have fewer general journals of ideas than at any other time in our recent history? The questions are not meant to be a litany, a well-rehearsed broadside from a culture of complaint, but rather, are intended to point to the perils for any meaningful exploration of identity in the context of a radically impoverished public sphere. The budget for Science Foundation Ireland (SFI), the government body established to promote science research in Ireland, is almost fifty times greater than the budget for the Irish Research Council in the Humanities and Social Sciences. Only a tiny fraction of the sociologists, psychologists, anthropologists, ethnographers, geographers and linguists who work in Irish universities and are paid for by the state, are ever afforded the opportunity to address an audience beyond their own discipline or their academy. And yet the perspectives of these different disciplines are crucial if we are to arrive at any comprehensive sense of who we are and who we might be.

To give an example of how we are failing to exploit our intellectual potential to examine crucial aspects of Irish iden-

---

[2]   The Irish language television channel.

tities, let us take the referendum on the Nice Treaty. Most
analysts agreed after the defeat of the first referendum that
one of the reasons for the defeat was deep uncertainty about
the impact of further European integration on Irish identity.
Yet, what we saw in the second campaign by all sides was an
almost exclusive concentration on a narrowly-focused, mate-
rially self-interested version of Irish-European identity. This
is not to belittle the importance of jobs or the economic future of the children who featured so prominently in the
campaigns, but it is to ask if cultural concerns were prominent in the minds of many who voted both for and against
the first time around, why they were wholly absent from the
second campaign? Why did we not hear one single contribution from experts in five universities in the Republic who
have spent all their working lives engaged with the different
cultures of the EU, namely the teaching staff of modern language departments? Is there not a sense in which too utili-
tarian a conception of Irish identity is finally beginning to
backfire on those who seek to promote Ireland's economic
interests? Too often when the 'knowledge society' is invoked
in public policy, it is in the narrow, instrumental sense of
scientific and technological deliverables, again derived from
the restricted sense of identity that was referred to earlier.
The challenge for us is to make the knowledge society a reality in the fullest and broadest sense of the term so that all
knowledges are equally valued and brought to bear on the
understanding and elaboration of new Irish identities. A
great deal still remains to be done in terms of giving the citizens of the island greater public access to the intellectual
resources of our communities. A rich, diverse and stimulat-
ing public sphere is particularly important in offering models
of belonging that go beyond an identity politics rooted in welfare materialism.

The relative weakness of the public sphere in Ireland does
indeed beg the question as to why this is so. A tentative answer which may also paradoxically be a sign of hope is that
for over three decades intellectual life on the island of Ireland was strongly over-determined by violent political con-

flict. Conor McCarthy's account in *Modernisation: Crisis and Culture in Ireland 1969-1992* of a number of the debates that came to prominence in the period from the late 1960s to the early 1990s clearly illustrates the extent to which debate on just about everything from poetic diction to Irish musical history was shadowed by suspicions over allegiance (McCarthy 2000). In other words, where a writer or thinker stood on the National Question became an overriding concern in analysis of argument, nature of reception and virulence of engagement. Even when the conflict dared not speak its name, which was a great deal of the time, particularly in the Republic of Ireland, there was no gainsaying its massive, mute presence. Hence, the explosive bitterness of debates around Roy Foster's Oxford history of *Modern Ireland 1600-1972* (1998) or *The Field Day Anthology of Irish Writing* (Deane 1991) as if there was a genuine belief that careless talk could indeed cost lives. Given the fact that people did die, over three thousand of them, and often in the most appalling circumstances, the tense combativeness of the public sphere was understandable but the result was to severely restrict the vocabulary of political debate and to marginalise whole areas of intellectual enquiry. Furthermore, the ready pigeonholing of participants in debates as British or Irish nationalists meant that many engagements were seen to be reduced to a binary zero-sum game between competing essentialisms. In these conditions, the public sphere often found it difficult to be anything other than a combat zone, a fact borne out by the difficult and often controversial history of small journals such as *The Crane Bag*, *Graph* and *The Irish Review*. The all-pervasive culture of self-censorship in the South and the daily reality of the conflict in the North led to a further splitting of the public sphere across the border, with suspicion and resentment on both sides making debate not so much an opportunity for collective enquiry as one more reason for not enquiring in the first place.

One step towards the reconstruction of a vibrant public sphere would be a frank acknowledgement (particularly in the South) of the extent to which military conflict compro-

mised the viability of public debate. A second step would be
the acceptance of the centrality of an informed public sphere
to what might be termed the transmissive survival of a society. In the last ten years, there has been a remarkable shift
in Ireland from what we might describe as a society primarily concerned with *transmission* to a society preoccupied by
communication. Though the two activities are often confused,
they are in fact crucially different. Communication is primarily about conveying information across space in the
same historical period whereas transmission is about trans-
porting information through time between different spatio-
temporal spheres. The horizon of transmission is historical
and it needs a medium of transmission (stone, paper, mag-
netic disk) to make its action effective. Transmission also requires a social vector or a body such as a school, university,
church, state or family which provides the context for the
transmission of ideas, beliefs or values across time (Debray
2000: 15). In one version of Irish modernisation, the society
was presented as a sacrificial victim of transmission. A nation-state committed to passing on a closed, nationalist or-
thodoxy and a majority church committed to the inculcation
of its values and dogmas through the educational system
were seen as ample proof of the damaging effects of a rigid,
hierarchical system of transmission. So the last decade has
seen Ireland link up with the rest of the world in communicative euphoria and position itself through education,
training and investment on a map of global connectedness.
Transmission is Myles na gCopaleen's Old Grey Man mut-
tering to himself about a world gone to the bad and the Irish
who no longer have any claim to Save Civilisation.

   The question must be asked, however, about whether any
society can cohere or endure in the absence of an ethics of
transmission. If a transmissive society is one obsessed with
ends (Ireland's freedom, the integrity of the Union, the fate of
our soul) and a communicative society is one bewitched by
means (national competitiveness, broadband coverage, the
extent of government borrowing) does that imply we now live
in a post-revolutionary Ireland that knows no end other than

the vaguely formulated one of self-enrichment? Does this explain why, while we move towards a more deregulated economy, we now live in an ever more regulated society, with an unprecedented extension of police powers and a significant rise in the volume of litigation over the decade? In the absence of shared values and common ends, are external coercion and the ministrations of the courts the only grounds for social cohesion? The society and economy of both parts of Ireland have lived through a revolution over the last three decades, a revolution animated by a mixture of market fundamentalism and social liberalism, a revolution that is confusing because it is both reactionary and progressive all at once. It has been the most startling example of how change is possible in a society. The challenge now is to change that change, to make Ireland an island that serves the ends of the many, not the means of the few. To this end, a vigorous public sphere is essential to any meaningful debate about transmission, whether it is in deciding what we want to pass on to future inhabitants of the island or what we want to take from past inhabitants; what we want to do about our media of transmission (do we build participative democracy around broadband networks?) and what we should be doing to ensure the survival and well-being of different social vectors of transmission whether they be single-parent families in areas of social deprivation or universities subject to the instrumental short-termism of commercialisation strategies. A 'knowledge society' is a term containing two words and if there is no such thing as society, and no public sphere where that society can speak to itself, then knowledge itself is worse than useless, condemned to the solipsistic autism of the communication fix.

THE POSTHUMAN

In talking about identities, we can make assumptions, not only in the classic ethnocentric sense of assuming our way of doing things is the right way. We can also take for granted that we as humans will always remain human, that is, un-

changed in our finite physicality. But Jean-Claude Guillebaud in *Le principe d'humanité* (2001) and Francis Fukayama in *Our Posthuman Future: Consequences of the Biotechnology Revolution* (2002), among others, have begun to
question precisely that assumption. Hervé Kempf has described what he calls the *biolithic* revolution. He bases his
analogy on the Neolithic revolution which 12,000 years ago
caused humanity to move from a way of life largely based on
hunting and gathering to one centred around livestock
farming and tillage. In the present era, in his view, we are
witnessing a new revolution which marries the living (*bio*) to
the mineral (*litho*) (Kempf 1998). Central elements in this
biolithic revolution are biotechnology and genetic engineering. Implicit in this revolution is a fundamental alteration of
how we conceive of human beings whether in terms of their
origins (cloning possibilities), the understanding of human
intentionality (the body as the unwitting receptacle for the
cynical survivalism of selfish genes), or the integrity of the
human subject (whether or not a different genetic make-up
affects entitlements or rights in a society). In other words,
previous assumptions about corporeal unity and the existence of a dimension to the human experience which is not
reducible to the biological or the neuro-scientific in the case
of the cognitive sciences are being called into question by the
scientific vanguard of the biolithic revolution. This brings us
to another area of the knowledge society in Ireland which
rarely gets the attention it fully deserves. In an age of genetic
engineering, robotics, biotechnology and advances in cognitive psychology, we may ask what the constants in our debates around identity will be and whether debates around
identity in Ireland centre not so much on the postnational as
the posthuman? Although it is common now to speak of the
inter-cultural in the context of contacts with different ethnic
groups in Irish society, in particular newly-arrived immigrants, there is arguably an equally profound inter-cultural
shock in Ireland with consequences for identity that is not
often spoken of in these terms.

In speaking of inter-culturality here, we mean the burgeoning of the science sector and the relationship between science and the other humanities-based disciplines of enquiry in Ireland. The particular historical status of Irish science in the development of competing national identities has been well documented in John Wilson Foster's edited collection *Nature in Ireland* (1997) and Nicholas Whyte's monograph *Science, Colonialism and Ireland* (1999). However, little has been said or written about how the research in biotechnology (a target area for state funding) or genetics in Ireland will change our identities not as Irish or British, Catholic or Protestant, native or newcomer but as humans. The Royal Irish Academy has, of course, a Biotechnology Ethics Committee, and the main churches have kept a watching brief on a number of the ethical implications of scientific research but we arguably need a much wider public debate on the inter-cultural implications of the dramatic expansion of Irish science and on how in our universities, institutes of technology and research laboratories, new paradigms are evolving that will challenge our traditional ways of conceiving of identity at a very fundamental level.

In February 2002 the Irish Council for Science and Technology described biotechnology as a key area to 'sustain Ireland's economic growth and to enhance Ireland's capacity to become a knowledge based economy' (in Ahlstrom 2002a). The link is made explicit here between the activity of biotechnology and the new informational economy which seeks productivity gains through access to innovative and preferably inexpensive sources of information. Science Foundation Ireland is very explicit in its commitment to promoting biotechnology and information technology as the future mainstays of economic growth in Ireland (Ahlstrom 2002b). As Ireland can no longer offer the advantages of a low-cost manufacturing economy, and with its fiscal attractiveness coming under pressure from EU partners, the country is committed to the 'knowledge economy' as a way of moving up the value-added chain and avoiding unnecessary exposure when firms de-localise to cheaper manufacturing bases

(Clinch, Convery and Walsh 2002: 43-52). So the unfettered doer and maker of neo-liberalism, the dominant economic paradigm of contemporary Ireland, is now allied to the biolithic revolutionary who has the possibility of altering the physical basis of humanity itself – but only with help from the venture capitalist. The recent debate around stem cell research in Ireland showed a growing awareness of the ethical implications around research in biotechnology and genetics (McConnell 2003; Smyth 2003). However, the tendency of the debates to be endless re-enactments of Pro-Life/Pro-Choice arguments condemn them to the predictable dualism of the progressive Left embracing the emancipatory promise of modernising science versus the theologico-political right committed to the conventional pieties of obscurantism. The real debate, in a sense, lies elsewhere and does not allow itself to be reduced to the tidy binarism of vulgar forms of Enlightenment reason. Francis Fukayama points out that the signatories to the American Declaration of Independence believed in the existence of natural rights, that is, rights which were conferred on human beings by their human natures. Fukayama agrees with them and claims that '[h]uman nature is what gives us a moral sense, provides us with the social skills to live in society, and serves as a ground for more sophisticated philosophical discussions of rights, justice, and morality' (2002: 101-102). If it becomes possible to determine in an instrumental fashion the physical and mental composition of future human beings, to prolong life expectancy greatly beyond present 'natural' limits or to control behaviour deemed socially unacceptable through intensive neuro-pharmacology, then our debates around identity are going to change radically. They are going to change particularly on an island that has very much placed itself at the forefront of neo-liberal experiment and biotechnological enquiry. One of the questions that will have to be asked is: do we now have processes without subjects or events without agency? By this we mean that if human intentionality is displaced by genetic or neuro-chemical essentialism, where humans are the unwitting playthings of the sub-cutaneous, just as society and politics are rigidly subject to the 'invisible hand' of the market, can it still be meaningful to talk of identity as the great self-fashioning project of modernity coming to us from the Renaissance and the Enlightenment? Future answers to future debates cannot, by definition, be predicted but it is possible to see the very debate around identity itself in the Irish present not simply as the centrifugal response to the centrifugal forces of globalisation (Castells 1997). Rather, questions relating to identity must, by their very nature, challenge the agentless process of market fundamentalism and the materialist essentialism of sociobiology. Seeing identity as being defined by something other than biological specificity, as being shaped interactively through our human participation in a world of signs and symbols that has an inescapable historical dimension, offers access both to an Irish past, as a collection of shaping forces, and to an Irish future, as a realistic setting for transformative agency. If the only certainty now is uncertainty, then the last thing we want is for any of us to have too rigid an idea about what constitutes Irish identity or even about what it means as humans to have an identity. By extension, it is paradoxically through examining what it might mean to be Irish that leads us inevitably to ask what it means and will mean to be human.

REFERENCES

Ahlstrom, D. (2002a), 'Science Council Dismisses GMO Concerns' *The Irish Times*, 5/2/02.
Ahlstrom, D. (2002b), 'A Nation of Show-offs?', *The Irish Times* 12/2/02.
Alsop, K. (1963), 'Ireland', in *Ireland of the Welcomes*, 12, 4, 5-8.
Bobbitt, P. (2002), *The Shield of Achilles: War, Peace and the Course of History*. London: Allen Lane/Penguin.
Castells, M. (1997), *The Power of Identity*. Oxford: Blackwell.

Clinch, P., Convery, F. and Walsh, B. eds (2002), *After the Celtic Tiger: Challenges Ahead*. Dublin: O'Brien Press.

Deane, S. ed. (1991), *The Field Day Anthology of Irish Writing*. Derry: Field Day Publications.

Debray, R. (2000), *Introduction à la médiologie*. Paris: Presses Universitaires de France.

Delanty, G. (2000), *Citizenship in a Global Age: Society, Culture, Politics*, Buckingham: Open University Press.

Foster, J. W. ed. (1997), *Nature in Ireland: A Scientific and Cultural History*. Dublin: Lilliput Press.

Foster, R. (1988), *Modern Ireland 1600-1972*. London: Penguin.

Fukayama, F. (2002), *Our Posthuman Future: Consequences of the Biotechnology Revolution*. London: Profile.

Guillebaud, J-C. (2001), *Le principe d'humanité*. Paris: Seuil.

Kelleher, J.V. (1957), 'Ireland ... And Where Does She Stand?', *Foreign Affairs*, 48-95.

Kempf, H. (1998), *La Révolution biolithique: humains artificiels et machines animées*. Paris: Albin Michel.

McCarthy, C. (2000), *Modernisation, Crisis and Culture 1969-1992*. Dublin: Four Courts Press.

McConnell, D. (2003), '14-day Embryo Should Not Be Seen as a Person With Full Adult Rights', *The Irish Times*, 25/11/03.

Ó Gráda, C. (2000), 'From "Frugal Comfort" to Ten Thousand a Year: Trade and Growth in the Irish Economy', in R. Ryan ed., *Writing in the Irish Republic: Literature, Culture, Politics 1949-1999*. London: Macmillan, 263-82.

Sennett, R. (1998), *The Corrosion of Character: the Personal Consequences of Work in the New Capitalism*. New York/London: W.W. Norton.

Smyth, P. (2003), 'Stem Cells and Echoes of X Case', *The Irish Times* 24/11/03.

Whyte, N. (1999), *Science, Colonialism and Ireland*. Cork: Cork University Press.

11. Conclusion

ANDREW FINLAY

Identity has replaced ideology as the idiom for politics in the late modern world. The ideological projects that emerged from the European Enlightenment, whatever their differences, shared in the notion of Progress. The promise of Progress remained compelling through the nineteenth and the early twentieth centuries, but those who had been marginalised or trampled in the drive for Progress began to find a voice, and identity provided the idiom through which they articulated their predicament. They asserted themselves by asserting their collective, cultural difference. In doing so they presented a twofold challenge to conventional understandings of citizenship. On the one hand, they challenged the liberal idea of citizenship as a relationship between the individual and the state. On the other hand, they have contributed to a loosening of the relationship between citizenship and nationality that is explicit in cultural nationalism and implicit in liberal and republican regimes.

Notwithstanding its emancipatory promise, the rise of identity as the idiom for politics has ambiguous consequences. In the proliferation of cultural claims that it seems to encourage, the idiom of identity provides a vocabulary that can be used not only by those seeking redress for wrongs inflicted on them by virtue of their membership of a particular category, but also by those who would resist such changes claiming that change would threaten their way of life. Cultural claims of the latter sort are not merely reactive and opportunist. With its origins in the critique of Eurocentric dreams of Progress, the idiom of identity is one that encourages a reorientation from the present and future to the past. It thus has an inherent conservatism. Another ambiguous consequence of the rise of identity is that, while it provides the basis for a challenge to the nation state and to conventional understandings of citizenship, it also provides the state with an idiom through which it can administer and regulate difference.

These same ambiguities are immanent in the peace process in Ireland and make it difficult enough to assess the local situation let alone its status as an exemplar of conflict resolution for other parts of the world. The most direct approach to such an assessment is to ask whether or not the GFA facilitates or inhibits the negotiation of increasing cultural diversity in both parts of Ireland. Some of the contributions to this book are more optimistic than others, and there is no consensus on the GFA or on identity as an idiom for politics more generally. But something happened as I was preparing the manuscript for the publishers, which might help to clarify matters: In March 2004 the Irish government announced a referendum on citizenship.

In the referendum, held on 11 June 2004, nearly eighty per cent of people who voted – up to sixty per cent of the electorate – supported the government's proposal to qualify the right of anyone born on the island to Irish nationality and citizenship, which had been written into the constitution when Article 2 was redrafted as part of the GFA. Seeking to justify its proposed change to the constitution, the government described the granting citizenship rights to anyone born on the island as being an unintended consequence of the GFA: a 'loophole' that had been created in the process of securing an historic peace settlement, which was now being exploited by immigrants from outside the EU who were coming to Ireland with the intention of giving birth on Irish soil (*The Sunday Times* 11/4/04, *The Sunday Tribune* 25/4/04)

Originally, in the Constitution adopted in 1937, Article 2 defined the nation as being coequal with the territory of the island; something which unionists in Northern Ireland had long resented. As I pointed out in the introductory chapter, change to Article 2 was first seriously mooted in 1981 by Garret FitzGerald who, as Taoiseach, embarked on a shortlived constitutional crusade that aimed to make the Republic more attractive to Northern unionists. Nearly twenty year on, those unionists who signed-up to the GFA demanded change to Article 2, but it was rewritten so as to allay the fears of Northern nationalists that their entitlement to Irish citizenship and nationality was being diluted.

Initially, the main thrust of the opposition to the referendum in June 2004 was to dispute the evidence for the government's claim that the constitutional amendment ratified in the referendum in 1998 was being abused by 'citizenship tourists' (*The Irish Times* 22/4/04) – the implication being that the government was motivated by racism. But, it was also argued that the proposal to remove the automatic right of anyone born on the island to Irish citizenship was a breach of the GFA. Nationalist parties with a base in the North, Sinn Féin and the Social Democratic and Labour Party, complained that as co-signatories to the Agreement they should have been consulted on changes that affected its provision's, and expressed concern that that the government's actions had played into the hands of those Northern unionists who want to renegotiate other aspects of the GFA (*The Irish Times* 16/4/04 and 9/6/04). In response to these arguments, the Irish and British governments published a joint declaration that the changes proposed in the referendum did not breach the British-Irish Agreement that was completed at the same time as the GFA. The former Agreement dealt with the commitments of the two governments arising from the GFA, while the GFA only covered the commitments of the North's political parties (*The Irish Times* 20/4/04). The editor of *The Irish Times* concluded that the proposal contained in the referendum held in June 2004 would be 'a clear breach of the spirit, if not the letter, of the referendum [on the GFA] in 1998' (*The Irish Times* 17/4/04).

The referendum on citizenship and the debate that it generated was thus a defining moment when what I have called the old pluralist agenda, concerned with reconciling two indigenous communities, and the new agenda, concerned with immigrants, clashed. It is a moment when those working to each agenda, and, even more, those who thought they working to both, were confronted with the ambiguities within each agenda and the contradictions between them. In this conclusion, I will attempt to tease out some of these ambiguities and contradictions by drawing on the analyses offered by the contributors to this book. Some of these are more optimistic than others, and there is no consensus among them. While I draw on various chapters, I am not claiming to represent the authors' views; rather I am using them to develop my own. I will start with the implications of the citizenship referendum for an assessment of the old pluralist agenda and its enduring achievement, the GFA.

Declan Kiberd (2000) and Paddy Logue (2000) celebrated the GFA precisely because it seemed to inscribe a view of identity as multiple and fluid. For the reasons outlined in the introductory chapter, I never believed the Agreement was as open and generous as these commentators claimed, but I would have conceded that by allowing for the possibility that people born in Northern Ireland could choose to be Irish or British or both, and affirming that, in any case, they were entitled to Irish citizenship, the Agreement suggests a loosening of the relationship between citizenship, political community and nationality. The Irish government's assertion that the open, 'liberal' definition of citizenship contained in the draft of Article 2 ratified as part of the GFA was an unintended consequence of the search for peace settles the matter, and confirms Delanty's suspicion that the GFA was less a recognition 'of the limits of nationality as a framework for citizenship and political community' and 'more an accommodation of nationalities' (see Chapter Nine).

The extent to which the Agreement reached in 1998 was driven by the interests of two nation-states is made more apparent in the fact that, of all the parties to the GFA, the Irish government consulted only the British government about its proposed referendum. It is also apparent in the fact that, as Mary Hickman has pointed out (2004), since the Agreement was signed in 1998 what used to be referred to as Anglo-Irish relations are increasingly referred to as 'British-Irish' relations. Alluding to Irish immigrants in Britain, few of whom would ever choose to describe themselves as British-Irish, Hickman suggests that so concerned were the two government to ensure that the two nation-states were recognised as equal that they failed to deal with the messiness of identity.

If the GFA seemed to suggest a loosening of the connection between citizenship, political community and national identity, the referendum can be seen as part of an attempt to reassert the connection. According to *The Sunday Business Post* (25/4/04), Michael McDowell, who as Minister for Justice headed the government's referendum campaign,

> takes the view that citizenship is inextricably bound up with nationality. Article 9 of the constitution – which [presently] states that "loyalty to the nation and fidelity to the State are fundamental political duties of all citizens"[1]– encapsulated "the essence of the intertwined concepts of citizenship and nationality", he told the Dáil.

The referendum did not seek to amend Article 2, but rather Article 9 of the Constitution

> so as to provide that a person born in the island of Ireland, which includes its islands and seas, who does not have, at the time of his or her birth, at least one parent who is an Irish citizen or is entitled to be an Irish citizen, is not entitled to Irish citizenship or nationality, unless otherwise prescribed by law (*The Irish Times* 20/4/04).

Far from being a breach of the spirit of the GFA, as the editor of *The Irish Times* (17/4/04), amongst others, argued, it would seem to me that the referendum is confirmation of its reductive logic. The old pluralist agenda, concerned as it was with the interests of two communities or traditions, conceived in essentialist terms, is inadequate as a basis for those who would wish to make Ireland more hospitable to immigrants, Traveller and others. But, as the referendum shows, this does not mean that exponents of the new pluralist agenda can ignore the old.

---

[1] Article 9 actually states: 'Fidelity to the nation and loyalty to the State are fundamental political duties of all citizens'.

Exponents of the new pluralist agenda need to be familiar with the old for at least three reasons. Firstly, to avoid repeating its mistakes. Secondly, to better understand the response of exponents of the old agenda to the new. Thirdly, to further the new agenda by exploiting the ambiguities of the GFA. I will consider each of these points in turn.

Until the proposal for a referendum on citizenship, those who have sought to champion the interests of immigrants and Travellers – exponents of the new agenda – have stayed clear of the old pluralist agenda. This is unfortunate. Occasionally, when seeking to explain the negative reaction of some Irish people to immigrants, they have unwittingly rehearsed older themes. Lentin (2001), suggests that anti-immigrant sentiment can be traced to a disavowal of the past: a failure on the part of the Irish people to interrogate their own painful history as a people who once themselves suffered, and fled, colonial oppression. But was this not what the 'revisionist controversy' was about? It might be said that revisionists are guilty of such disavowal, but hardly the traditional nationalists they criticised or the postcolonial theorists who responded to this critique. And this is to say nothing of the evidence that suggests that a preoccupation with the suffering of one's ancestors is no guarantee that one will be sympathetic to those who are suffering today (see Chapters Five and Seven of this volume). As the 'revisionist controversy' made clear, the trouble with the theory that Ireland's political problems are caused by underlying conflicts and confusions of cultural identity is that the same theory can produce diametrically opposed conclusions. Thus Steve Loyal (2003) seems to reiterate the old revisionist critique of traditional nationalism, when he suggests that the roots of anti-immigrant sentiment lie in the hegemonic, exclusive narrative of national identity developed by the Irish state after independence. In other words, racism is a product of a communal identity that is too homogenous, too cohesive. Against this, Declan Kiberd (2001) seems to suggest that it is the deracinated person who is prone to prejudice; i.e. that racism is the product, not of an identity that is too strong, but of an identity that is weak and precarious. Instead of rehearsing tired old theoretical themes, we need some concrete empirical research focussing not only on racism, including state racism (see Mac Éinrí in Chapter Five), but also on anti-racism and instances of solidarity (see de Paor in Chapter Three; see also Lentin and McVeigh 2002 and Gibbons 2002).

So Cronin (Chapter Ten) is correct when he argues that the debates about Irish identity that informed the old pluralist agenda remain relevant. Those who wish to build an Ireland that is open and more hospitable to immigrants and to Travellers – exponents of the new agenda – need to be aware of the older debates not only so that they can avoid repeating its mistakes, but also to better understand the responses of exponents of the old agenda, and those whose interests it serves, to the new one.

The appropriation of the language of multiculturalism by racists is not peculiar to Ireland, but the justification for the intimidation of Chinese people living and working in a part of South Belfast in terms suggesting that they posed a threat to the heritage, way of life and Britishness of local Protestant residents (*The Irish Times* 13/3/04, *The Scotsman* 16/3/04) has a specific resonance in the context of the peace process. More insidious is the way that advocates of each of the two hegemonic political forces in Ireland – Irish Nationalism and Ulster Unionism – attempt to appropriate the more visible presence of racialised minorities in Ireland to their own hegemonic ends, or to silence each other.

In Chapter Six we saw an example of how immigrants were invoked by both sets of protagonist to the controversy surrounding the proposed Orange Order parade in Dublin. In Northern Ireland, some nationalists fear that talk of increasing cultural diversification is a unionist ploy to dilute what they achieved in the GFA: '[w]hen Irish nationalists hear reference to multi-ethnic integration they naturally are concerned that their gains will be lost' (Harvey 2003: 9). Such fears are severely limiting, but they are perhaps understandable given the attitude of unionist politicians – past and present – to expressions of Irish culture. For example, shortly after the appointment of Ministers to the new Northern Ireland Executive established under the terms of the Agreement, the Minister of Culture, Arts and Leisure, Michael McGimpsey, a liberal member of the Unionist Party, was asked how he felt about his new responsibility to promote the Irish language. He replied to the effect that, though his own medium was English, he had no problem promoting minority languages such as Scots-Irish and Gaelic, but added that 'Cantonese was the second language of Northern Ireland' (BBC Northern Ireland, 2/12/99). McGimpsey's tongue was in his cheek, but his statement and the anxieties that it might arouse, particularly among nationalists, are indicative of the subtleties of cultural politics in Ireland after the Agreement.

Its not all bad. Exponents of the new pluralist agenda might be able to exploit some of the ambiguities of the GFA. As Nic Craith points out in Chapter Six, the Agreement makes provision for a Northern Ireland Human Rights Commission (NIHRC) to advise the Secretary of State on the development of a Bill of Rights that would supplement the provisions of the European Convention for Human Rights and to work with the Human Rights Commission in the South towards a joint charter of rights for the island as a whole. The rhetoric of equality and human rights is potentially at odds with the bicultural logic of the GFA because human rights are usually based around individual, not group, rights (O'Cinniede 2004: 15). This contradiction might offer possibilities for those who would wish to go beyond biculturalism, but it will not be easy.

According to Robin Wilson (2003: 11) there have already been tensions within the NIHRC between commissioners who thought that the Bill of Rights should stick with 'the international norm in attaching rights to individuals', which implies a 'recognition of those who choose "not to be treated as a member of what might be perceived to be their national, ethnic, religious or linguistic community"' and commissioners who thought it should more strongly reflect the principle of parity of esteem, which 'would involve deleting the right-of-exit clause'. Under the terms of the GFA, the Bill of Rights was supposed to 'reflect the particular circumstances of Northern Ireland and the principles of mutual respect for the identity and ethos of both communities and parity of esteem' (NIHRC, 2000), and the government of the Irish Republic weighed into the debate, 'putting very heavy pressure on the NIHRC ... to endorse what might be described as Dublin's "two tribes" view of the North' (Wilson, 2003: 11). Drawing attention to the kinds of 'unrepresentative subjects' discussed by Whitaker in Chapter Eight, Wilson pointed to data from a Northern Ireland Life and Times Survey that 'suggest that around 30 per cent of both Catholics and Protestants – never mind members of ethnic minorities – would prefer not to be labelled as "nationalist" or "unionist"'. Wilson feared that the NIHRC was succumbing to pressure to endorse group rights 'at the expense of individual's rights not have their ethnic affiliations assumed'.

Some of those who have been left out of the bicultural or 'two communities' model institutionalised by the Agreement, notably the Alliance Party[2], have responded by arguing (*The Belfast Telegraph* 5/4/04) for a return to something like the classical liberal notion of the abstract individual. This is understandable, but wrong-headed: individuals are never free-floating, but are formed and develop in and through culture. It is also true that as Crozier notes in Chapter Two, 'in times of despair or celebration ... people ... repair to the places of their fundamental allegiance'. There are times and circumstances, usually of crisis, when the distance between indi-

---

[2] Like the members of the Women's Coalition who were elected to the local Assembly set up under the terms of the GFA (see Chapter Eight), elected members of the Alliance Party fell foul of the requirement that, for the purposes of measuring cross-community support for proposals, members must designate themselves as nationalist, unionist or other. To designate oneself as 'other' meant that one's vote was of less worth, and in crucial votes in the election of First and Deputy First Ministers, members of the these parties came under pressure 'to sacrifice their principles' and change their designation to unionist or nationalist to ensure the 'right result' (Hadden 2001/2002: 8).

vidual and collective identities collapses and the latter 'crystallise' such as to exhibit the emotionally-laden sense of belonging to a bounded group with a distinct culture that an essentialist concept of identity would suggest (Brubaker and Cooper, 2000). This was the case for many in Northern Ireland during the Troubles. But it is the exception rather than the rule in the late modern world. Culture can no longer be understood simply as the way of life of a group or a people; rather it is better understood as symbolic practice, a contested process through which we attach meaning to our lives and our world (Wright 1998).

The great achievement of the GFA was that it removed or lessened the crises that precipitated two communal identities which sometimes exhibited the features that essentialist theory would predict. Its great weakness is that by making identity the name of the political game, it not only ensures the perpetuation of these two communal identities but tends to promote their further reification.

Ireland, like the rest of the late-modern world is no longer divided up into discrete, hermetically sealed, internally coherent cultures, one to each community. Nor is it proven that the individual needs a single, coherent communal culture to give shape and meaning to his or her life. As Stuart Hall says, this is not to deny the role that culture plays in enabling individuals to exercise autonomy and to make meaningful choices, rather it is to insist that in doing so we all, deliberately and inadvertently, 'draw on the fragmented traces and broken repertoires of several cultural and ethical languages' (2000: 233).

Recognising that identities crystallise in forms that approximate to the essentialist concept of cultural identity only in particular circumstances means that we should be very wary of attempts to enfranchise the claims of communal cultures and values over individuals without at the same time allowing individuals to dissent or exit from their communities of origin. It is not only wrong-headed but dangerous. It is wrong-headed because valorising the distinctive values of particular 'communities' at one moment in time

Conclusion 233

denies the reality that they are always in a moving relationship to all the other competing values around them. It is
dangerous because it licences those who would wish to
freeze or fix communal boundaries such that their 'traditional' authority is enhanced and that they can more effectively police internal differences. But none of this is to suggest a return to a notion of the abstract individual, rather it
is to argue that we are all grounded in multiple identities,
and with this in mind, to resist the privileging of any one or,
thinking of the GFA, any two.

Notwithstanding the reluctance of the Irish and British
governments, there are signs that the Human Rights Com-
missions are beginning to endorse such perspectives on the
relationship between individual and collective identities. The
most recent draft of the Bill of Rights prepared by the NIHRC
has taken into account the rights of members of ethnic minorities, though significantly not by reference to the GFA,
which takes care of the rights of only two communities, but
by incorporating international conventions (Dickson 2004,
The News Letter 21/4/04). Beyond this there is the work of
the Joint Equality and Human Rights Forum, which 'was
established to provide an opportunity for members to share
ideas and expertise, to engage in joint work and to contribute to wider equality and human rights discussions at British-Irish and European Union level' (Zappone 2003: 2).

I highlight the work of this forum for two reasons. Firstly,
because it has sponsored research (Zappone 2003) which
seeks to go beyond the familiar preoccupation with Irish
identity and the familiar opposition between the Catholic
and Protestant communities to focus on understanding how
individuals holding multiple identities perceive and articulate their sense of belonging to different social groupings,
and how their various identifications influence their experiences of the health services and employment. The research
included, amongst others, disabled people, women, lesbians,
gay and bisexual men, and members of various ethnic
groups. Secondly, because the Forum includes members of
statutory bodies in Ireland, Northern Ireland, and Britain;

this together with the fact that its work was facilitated from Ireland is suggestive of a broadening of the public sphere, discussed by Cronin in Chapter Ten, on North/South and East/West axes.

Chapter Seven started with Joppke and Lukes's (1999) observation that the institutionalisation of multicultural principles seems to beget a proliferation of identity categories and claims. They point out that original multicultural claimants came from two kinds of minority: those created by slavery in the New World and those who lost out in nation building, especially in Europe. The 'crucial moment in the proliferation of minority status was the piracy of minority discourse by immigrants ... and by life-style groups, such as gays and lesbians' (1999: 13). Exponents of multiculturalism are resistant to cultural claims of the latter sort. Parekh (2000), for example, distinguishes between multicultural diversity proper and other kinds of diversity based on lifestyle or on an alternative perspective such as feminism. Ultimately, as McLennan (2001: 986) notes, the distinction that Parekh makes between lifestyle identities and 'perspectival' identities on the one hand and, on the other, the 'communal or ethnicist cultures' he wishes to privilege are that the latter are based on 'traditional, long-inherited practices'; in other words the distinction is based in an essentialist theory, which I hope his book has problematised.

Joppke and Lukes (1999) are concerned about the tendency for identity categories and claims to proliferate in a social order based in multiculturalism, principally because of the problem of arbitrating such claims. Their concern is warranted, but the difficulties are greatest in forms of pluralism or multiculturalism that accept, or are based on, a normative essentialism. If we recognise that individual or personal identity is multiple in the sense that we are all grounded in a variety of different social positions and as Hall says, 'draw on the fragmented traces and broken repertoires of several cultural and ethical languages' (2000: 233), a truly emancipatory vista is opened up. For, as Whitaker suggests in Chapter Eight, difference exists not only between groups but within individual subjects, and 'such difference is a necessary condition for the creation of new solidarities, forged not through already-settled identities but through political effort'. But she also alerts us to a danger: 'to deny the promise of such multiple subjects might well mean replacing democratic politics – ongoing struggle about which differences matter, in what ways – with the institutionalised administration of certain differences'. As the consequences, intended and unintended, of what was agreed on Good Friday 1998 ramify throughout Ireland, the task for intellectuals is not to construct, invent, reinvent or reimagine an Irish identity for the people, but to work towards the conditions in which the people – natives and newcomers alike – are permitted to work it out for themselves. The emerging story of Ireland is no longer monocultural or even bicultural; it is, as Francis Mulhern argues (1998: 157), 'an unprogrammed hybrid'.

References

BBC Northern Ireland, 2/12/99.
The Belfast Telegraph, 5/4/04.
Brubaker, R. and Cooper, F. (2000), 'Beyond "Identity"', *Theory and Society,* 29, 1-47.
Dickson, B. (2004), "Human Rights in Ireland North and South", *Irish Association Seminar.* Dublin (8/5/04).
Gibbons, L. (2002), 'The Global Cure? History, Therapy and the Celtic Tiger', in P. Kirby, L. Gibbons, and M. Cronin, eds, *Reinventing Ireland: Culture, Society and the Global Economy.* London: Pluto.
Hadden, T. (2001/2002), Counting the Other Votes, *Fortnight* 402, 8 (December 2001/January 2002).
Hall, S. (2000), 'Conclusion: the Multicultural Question' in B. Hesse, ed., *Un/Settled Muliculturalisms: Diasporas, Entanglements, "Transruptions".* London: Zed Books.
Hickman, M. (2004), 'Multiple Identities', *Through Irish Eyes.* Seminar organised by the British Council, the Institute for

British Irish Studies at University College Dublin and the Irish Association, Dublin (11/02/04).

Harvey, C. (2003), 'Sticking to the Terms of the Agreement', *Fortnight* 416, 9 (July/August).

The Irish Times, 16/4/4, 17/4/04, 20/4/04.

Joppke, C. and Lukes, S. eds, (1999), *Multicultural Questions*. Oxford: Oxford University Press.

Kiberd, D. (2000), *Irish Classics*. London: Granta Books.

Kiberd, D. (2001), Strangers in Their Own Country: Multi-Culturalism in Ireland, in E. Longley, and D. Kiberd, *Multi-Culturalism: The View From The Two Irelands*. Cork: Cork University Press and the Centre for Cross-Border Studies.

Lentin, R. (2001), 'Responding to the Racialisation of Irishness: Disavowed Multiculturalism and its Discontents', *Sociological Research Online*, 5, 4, http://www. Socresonli ne.org.uk/5/4/lentin.html

Lentin, R. and McVeigh, R. eds (2002), *Racism and Anti-Racism in Ireland*. Belfast: Beyond the Pale.

Logue, P ed. (2000), Introduction, *Being Irish*. Dublin. Oak Tree Press.

Loyal, S. (2003), 'Welcome to the Celtic Tiger: Racism, Immigration and the State', in C. Coulter and S. Coleman eds, *The End of History? Critical Reflections on the Celtic Tiger*. Liverpool: Liverpool University Press.

McLennan, G. (2001), 'Problematic Multiculturalism', *Sociology* 35, 4, 985-989.

Mulhern, F. (1998), *The Present Lasts a Long Time, Essays in Cultural Politics*. Cork: Cork University Press in Association with Field Day.

The News Letter 21/4/04.

NIHRC, (2000) *The Bill of Rights Culture and Identity*. Belfast. http://www.nihrc.org.

O'Cinneide, C. (2004), *Equivalence of Rights? The Belfast Agreement, Institutional Rights and Citizenship*, MPhil in Ethnic and Racial Studies Seminar, Department of Sociology, Trinity College Dublin, 20/2/04.

Parekh, B. (2000), *Rethinking Multiculturalism Cultural Diversity and Political Theory.* London: Macmillan.

The Scotsman, 16/3/04

The Sunday Business Post, 25/4/04.

The Sunday Times 11/4/04.

The Sunday Tribune 25/4/04.

Wright, S. (1998), 'The Politicisation of "Culture"', *Anthropology Today* 14, 1, 7-15.

Zappone, K.E. (2003), *Re-Thinking Identity – The Challenge of Diversity.* Dublin: The Joint Equality and Human Rights Forum.

Index

African-American, 39, 132
Alliance Party, 231
Anglo-Irish Agreement, 4, 9, 10, 118, 127
anthropology, 17, 18, 23, 112, 161, 167, 172, 173, 176, 213
anti-racism, 229
Arnold, M., 17, 18
Article 2 (Irish Constitution), 8, 9, 224, 226, 227
Australia, 44, 45, 52, 55, 56, 98, 105, 149, 187
bicultural model (two tribes/traditions/communities), 1, 5, 6, 10, 23, 24, 27, 49, 117, 118, 122, 131, 140, 151, 152, 162, 170, 173, 227, 230, 231, 235
Bill of Rights (Northern Ireland), 230, 231, 233
biotechnology, 187
Black Power, 132
Boas, F., 17, 23
Brubaker, R., 5, 21, 202, 232
Canada, 96, 98, 105, 126, 187, 189
Catholic, 1, 8, 9, 10, 14, 34, 36, 86, 91, 93, 97, 98, 100, 132, 147, 152, 157, 158, 166, 169, 173, 198, 201, 202, 219, 233
Celtic Tiger, 51, 60, 66, 68, 69, 71, 72, 73, 86, 98
citizenship, 1, 3, 4, 5, 26, 27, 28, 35, 92, 98, 103, 111, 112, 113, 114, 115, 116, 120, 122, 125, 126, 127, 144, 183, 184, 185, 186,

187, 188, 189, 190, 191, 192, 193, 195, 197, 201, 202, 208, 223, 224, 225, 226, 227, 228
civil society, 85, 102, 185, 186, 193
class, 16, 94, 102, 107, 132, 142, 166, 188, 207
colonialism, 8, 24, 25, 47, 48, 132
commemoration, 12, 95, 184, 195, 196
community, 35, 56, 89, 112, 115, 169
constitutional crusade, 9, 10, 11, 224
cosmopolitan, 184, 185, 192, 193, 194, 197, 199
Cultural Traditions Group, 10, 14, 36, 37
culture, 19, 23, 111, 112, 113, 114, 115, 127, 142, 172, 184, 188, 191, 195, 232
  as contested process, 232
  as way of life, 17, 18, 20, 112, 189, 223, 229, 232
  British, 125
  civic, 190
  Irish, 48, 49, 50, 51, 55, 60, 61, 63, 64, 66, 68, 69, 70, 78, 79, 81, 117, 125, 230
  national, 192, 194, 195, 196, 198
  societal, 21
Deane, S., viii, 12, 13, 14, 19, 22, 23, 26, 90, 215

democracy, 2, 86, 107, 142, 160, 168, 170, 171, 172, 176, 184, 189, 191, 196, 217

Democratic Unionist Party, 158

Diaspora, 89, 98

disability, 99, 188, 233

discrimination, 5, 52, 64, 106, 121

diversity, vii, viii, 2, 5, 7, 16, 23, 24, 36, 37, 38, 39, 43, 44, 49, 52, 86, 91, 99, 100, 105, 107, 134, 135, 136, 146, 162, 189, 196, 197, 224, 234

Drumcree, 165

Enlightenment, 15, 16, 17, 19, 149, 160, 199, 207, 220, 223

equality, 24, 26, 28, 35, 39, 100, 116, 119, 120, 121, 122, 123, 124, 141, 161, 168, 188, 189, 208, 230

Erikson, E., 19, 20, 21, 23

essentialism, 14, 21, 23, 24, 140, 141, 142, 145, 146, 202, 220, 227, 232, 234

ethnography, 161, 172, 176

European Union (EU), 3, 34, 46, 61, 66, 67, 68, 69, 74, 75, 76, 77, 185, 187, 196, 200, 209, 214, 219, 224, 233

feminism, 5, 24, 234

Fianna Fáil, 12, 74, 92, 207

Fine Gael, 9, 12

Finkielkraut, A., 16, 17, 23, 148

FitzGerald, G., 7, 8, 9, 10, 11, 12, 19, 22, 26, 224

Foster, R., 10, 11, 145, 148, 151, 169, 215

France, 16, 85, 112, 113, 114, 115, 209

Gaelic League (Conradh na Gaeilge), 10, 52

gay, 24, 188, 233, 234

Germany, 17, 90, 93, 114, 115, 123

Gibbons, L., 10, 12, 15, 16, 17, 18, 19, 145, 146, 149, 229

Glazer, N. and Moynihan, D.P., 38

Gleason, P., 20, 21, 142

globalisation, 2, 62, 76, 81, 185, 186, 192, 193, 194, 197, 199, 201, 221

Good Friday Agreement (GFA), 1, 4, 21, 49, 55, 81, 103, 119, 131, 134, 163, 168, 185, 224

Habermas, J., 27, 28, 190, 195, 197

Herder, J., 16, 17, 23, 114

Human Rights Commission, 127, 230, 233

Hume, J., 6, 164

hybridity, 47, 64, 87, 193, 194, 235

identity, vii, 11, 15, 16, 17, 20, 21, 22, 23, 26, 28, 36, 48, 61, 63, 69, 120, 121, 124, 140, 152, 174, 177, 184, 188, 192, 200, 208, 210, 211, 213, 218, 219, 220, 223, 224, 232, 233, 234

and the Good Friday Agreement, 3, 4, 5, 24, 81, 119, 141, 167, 170, 226, 227, 232

British, 119, 125
crisis, 7, 8, 9, 19, 20, 162, 167
cultural/ethnic/communal , 1, 2, 3, 6, 11, 19, 20, 21, 24, 37, 39, 41, 43, 44, 53, 54, 99, 112, 113, 123, 141, 150, 184, 192, 228, 231, 232
Irish, viii, 1, 3, 7, 12, 14, 15, 25, 48, 62, 63, 64, 65, 68, 72, 73, 78, 80, 85, 91, 93, 98, 99, 101, 103, 123, 124, 145, 201, 202, 214, 221, 228, 229, 235
multiple, 4, 21, 64, 81, 171, 175, 177, 184, 197, 226, 233, 234
national, 27, 28, 45, 47, 107, 148, 162, 168, 173, 184, 185, 186, 193, 194, 203, 209, 227
personal/individual, 20, 21, 28, 142, 145, 202, 232, 233, 234
politics, 5, 21, 26, 138, 214
Protestant, 140, 141
lack of, 8, 27, 125
immigrants, 1, 24, 25, 27, 28, 49, 51, 52, 53, 54, 89, 96, 105, 115, 131, 135, 144, 151, 200, 209, 218, 224, 225, 226, 227, 228, 229, 234
immigration, 27, 45, 52, 89, 95, 97, 105, 142, 144, 185, 201, 209
inequality, 35, 106, 168
inter-cultural, 197, 218, 219
Iraq, 3, 99

Irish Association, vii
Irish language (Gaelic), 8, 12, 14, 47, 48, 50, 52, 53, 54, 93, 117, 125, 230
jingoism, 28, 209
Joppke, C. and Lukes, S., 19, 131, 144, 151, 234
Kiberd, D., 4, 5, 6, 14, 28, 145, 226, 228
knowledge society, 208, 212, 214, 217, 218
Kymlicka, 19, 21, 122, 168, 189, 191
lesbian, 99, 233, 234
Levi-Strauss, C., 23
liberalism, 16, 20, 63, 188, 217
loyalism, 40, 152, 162, 165, 166, 200
Lyons, F.S.L., 6, 7, 10, 11, 17, 18, 19
memory, 87, 145, 146, 148, 149, 150
minorities, 102, 123
minority, 21, 123, 132, 138, 142, 144, 152, 234
group, 122, 124, 132, 137, 138, 142, 151, 175, 184
groups, 20, 123, 151, 231
languages, 34, 51, 52, 184, 230
rights, 122, 137, 183, 187, 189, 191, 233
monocultural, 25, 101, 191, 235
Mulhern, F., 15, 26, 235
multicultural, 2, 35, 39, 52, 131, 132, 138, 147, 149, 152, 168
multiculturalism, 16, 20, 27, 34, 41, 49, 101, 106, 133, 151, 160, 188, 190, 193,

197, 200, 201, 203, 229, 234
critical, 131, 137, 140, 144
liberal, 21, 23, 24, 131, 140
nationalism, 2, 8, 9, 13, 15, 17, 22, 23, 25, 27, 47, 49, 61, 62, 64, 65, 73, 76, 78, 80, 81, 96, 107, 112, 114, 116, 138, 144, 172, 173, 185, 193, 194, 198, 199, 208, 211, 223, 228
neo-liberalism, 28, 220
New Ireland Forum, 9, 22
New Social Movements, 16
Nice Treaty, 25, 61, 65, 66, 72, 73, 74, 77, 78, 79, 81, 214
Northern Ireland, 1, 2, 5, 6, 8, 9, 10, 14, 22, 24, 25, 27, 33, 35, 36, 37, 38, 39, 41, 64, 79, 100, 111, 115, 117, 118, 119, 120, 122, 123, 124, 126, 127, 131, 132, 133, 134, 138, 143, 147, 150, 151, 152, 153, 157, 158, 159, 160, 161, 162, 165, 167, 168, 169, 171, 172, 173, 176, 200, 224, 226, 229, 230, 231, 232, 233
O'Brien C.C., 11, 12, 13
oppression, 6, 96, 132, 142, 143, 144, 145, 228
Orange Order, 133, 165
    proposed parade in Dublin, 133, 134, 135, 139, 147, 229
Parekh, B., 188, 234
parity of esteem, 5, 20, 21, 23, 24, 119, 120, 122, 124,

131, 134, 140, 141, 151, 231
particularism, 190
Partition, 7, 93
peace process, 2, 21, 24, 64, 77, 81, 118, 124, 147, 200, 224
Pearse, P.H., 13, 47, 48, 50
pluralism, viii, 1, 3, 7, 11, 12, 14, 15, 16, 19, 20, 21, 22, 23, 24, 27, 34, 106, 131, 133, 137, 140, 144, 185, 187, 189, 190, 193, 200, 234
postcolonial theory, 4, 6, 14, 15, 16, 19, 21, 143, 145, 228
postmodern, 92, 98, 177, 188
postmodernism, 91
Presbyterian, 7, 26
Progress, 149
Protestant, 1, 8, 15, 34, 36, 62, 86, 94, 100, 111, 126, 133, 137, 138, 141, 142, 147, 151, 152, 157, 158, 163, 166, 169, 173, 174, 175, 202, 219, 229, 233
psychology, 14, 28, 218
public sphere, 121, 149, 150, 168, 185, 213, 214, 215, 216, 217, 234
racism, 2, 6, 25, 40, 100, 103, 105, 225, 228
recognition, 20, 27, 34, 118, 119, 120, 121, 122, 123, 125, 127, 138, 151, 168, 171, 188, 189, 190
    (politics of), 138, 199, 200, 203
refugees, 25, 33, 54, 102, 106, 134, 135, 137, 139, 172, 187

Chilean, 97
Hungarian, 25, 96
Jewish, 25, 97
Vietnamese, 25, 97
reification, 6, 172, 232
relativism, 131, 142
Republic of Ireland, 2, 26, 46,
    49, 60, 61, 81, 82, 116,
    131, 132, 142, 143, 185,
    212, 215
republicanism, 27, 85, 107,
    198, 200
revisionism, 6, 10, 11, 12,
    14, 15, 16, 19, 21, 22, 23,
    96, 144, 145, 147, 228
rights, 35, 53, 86, 101, 107,
    113, 116, 127, 136, 137,
    140, 141, 176, 183, 195,
    199, 201, 208, 220, 230
    civil, 118, 122, 132, 164
    group, 35, 118, 121, 137,
        168, 175, 183, 184, 189,
        191
    human, 34, 35, 39, 187,
        193, 233
    individual, 35, 188, 230,
        231
    of citizens, 111, 112, 115,
        120, 183, 185, 186, 189,
        224
    residence, 102, 187
    women's, 95
Sinn Féin, 9, 10, 85, 135,
    136, 137, 138, 143, 144,
    146, 157, 225
Social   Democratic   and
    Labour Party (SDLP), 157,
    164
socialism, 5, 16, 24, 163,
    171, 208
Taylor C., 120, 168, 177,
    188, 189, 200

territory, 9, 28, 114, 116,
    124, 145, 186, 189, 195,
    196, 200, 224
tradition, 8, 9, 10, 11, 17, 22,
    23, 24, 37, 50, 55, 60, 63,
    69, 95, 111, 116, 120, 124,
    131, 132, 134, 136, 138,
    141, 198, 233, 234
trauma, 8, 143, 144, 146,
    147, 148
Travellers, 5, 24, 25, 97, 139,
    146, 200, 228, 229
Troubles, 1, 9, 11, 24, 151,
    152, 232
Ulster-Scots, 126, 127
unionism, 8, 22, 26, 111,
    115, 116, 117, 119, 120,
    122, 124, 125, 152, 164,
    165, 171, 173, 200, 224,
    225, 229
Unionist Party, 157, 207, 230
United States of America, 20,
    69, 98
universal, 121, 190
universalism, 15, 16, 86,
    112, 120, 121, 169, 190,
    199, See
UVF (Ulster Volunteer Force,
    165
values, 2, 16, 22, 33, 34, 44,
    89, 113, 142, 191, 193,
    195, 196, 197, 201, 202,
    216, 217, 232
victimhood, 41, 138, 139,
    143, 145, 147, 148, 151
Women's Coalition, 27, 157,
    160, 162, 169, 170, 171,
    177
women's movement, 98, 132
xenophobia, 2, 28, 209

European Studies in Culture and Policy
edited by Prof. Máiréad Nic Craith
(University of Ulster)

Ullrich Kockel; Máiréad Nic Craith (Eds.)
Communicating Culture

Communicating Cultures explores contemporary and historical issues. The title may be read in various ways, including cultures as communicative systems; cultures communicating with one another; or, communication about cultures. The contributors to this volume represent different fields within or related to European ethnology, such as anthropology, geography, folklore, linguistics, or area studies. "The editors have assembled a rich collection of papers. The questions that they address – migration and diasporas; the invention of traditions; education and language; media and representation – are at the very heart of today's agenda in cultural analysis." *Philip Schlesinger, from the Foreword*

Bd. 1, 2004, 320 S., 30,90 €, br., ISBN 3-8258-6643-2

LIT Verlag Münster – Berlin – Hamburg – London – Wien
Grevener Str./Fresnostr. 2 48159 Münster
Tel.: 0251 – 62 032 22 – Fax: 0251 – 23 19 72
e-Mail: vertrieb@lit-verlag.de – http://www.lit-verlag.de